WITHDRAWN

IBSEN'S DRAMA
Author to Audience

Einar Haugen is a scholar, writer, and educator in the field of Scandinavian languages and literature. He was Victor S. Thomas Professor of Scandinavian and Linguistics at Harvard University from 1964 until his retirement in 1975, and before that Torger Thompson and Vilas Professor at the University of Wisconsin, where he taught from 1931 to 1964. At both universities he taught courses in Ibsen and wrote articles on the reception of Ibsen in America. He also translated Halvdan Koht's biography of Ibsen as well as Harald Beyer's *History of Norwegian Literature*. He has also published textbooks for the teaching of Norwegian, including a *Norwegian-English Dictionary*. He is best known for his studies of bilingualism and the history of the Scandinavian languages, fields in which he has published numerous books and articles. Born in Sioux City, Iowa, in 1906 of Norwegian parents, he received his Ph.D. in English and Scandinavian from the University of Illinois-Urbana in 1931. He has traveled widely and has lectured in Europe, Japan, Canada, and the United States.

⌐IBSEN'S DRAMA⌐

Author to Audience

by Einar Haugen

Victor S. Thomas Professor of
Scandinavian and Linguistics
Harvard University

UNIVERSITY OF MINNESOTA PRESS □ MINNEAPOLIS

Published by the University of Minnesota Press,
2037 University Avenue Southeast, Minneapolis, Minnesota 55455.
Printed in the United States of America.

Library of Congress Cataloging in Publication Data

Haugen, Einar Ingvald, 1906-
  Ibsen's drama.

  Bibliography: p.
  Includes index.
    1. Ibsen, Henrik, 1828-1906—Criticism and
interpretation. I. Title.
PT8895.H37   839.8'2'26   79-9106
ISBN 0-8166-0893-8
ISBN 0-8166-0896-2 pbk.

The University of Minnesota
is an equal opportunity
educator and employer.

Art is a lie that makes us realize the truth.
Picasso (1923)

Given as you were to revelation, a timeless tragic
poet, you had to translate this fine-spun activity
at one stroke into the most convincing gestures,
into the most present things. . . . There was a
rabbit, a garret, a room where someone paced
to and fro; there was the clatter of glass in a
neighboring apartment, a fire outside the
windows; there was the sun. There was a church
and a rock-strewn valley that was like a church.
But that did not suffice; towers had ultimately
to be brought in; and whole mountain ranges;
and the avalanches that bury landscapes
destroyed the stage, overladen with things
tangible used for the sake of expressing the
intangible.
Rainer Maria Rilke (1910)

Ibsen was a true agonist, struggling with very
real problems. "Life is a combat with the
phantoms of the mind"—he was always in
combat for himself and for the rest of mankind.
More than any one man, it is he who has made
us "our world," that is to say, "our modernity."
Ezra Pound (1916)

Prologue

This book is based on a series of lectures given in 1978 at Concordia College, Moorhead, Minnesota. They were conceived as an attempt to answer a question that had puzzled me in the years I taught courses in Ibsen to university and college students. This went back to my first years of teaching in the 1930s at the University of Wisconsin. On the one hand, I encountered academic scorn for Ibsen's "lack of poetic vision" (after all, he wasn't Shakespeare) and Marxist contempt for his "bourgeois individualism" (Plekhanov had spoken). On the other hand, to my students (and me) he seemed ever exciting and relevant. Even though most of them had to read his works in the same (often inadequate) translations as the critics, these young people flocked into Ibsen classes and were exhilarated by the readings, and by the discussions that followed. Clearly Ibsen was communicating to them. What, exactly, was he communicating?

It can hardly have been the simple reformist ideas that are attributed to him because of his "social" plays. His Nora is not just a woman arguing for female liberation; she is much more. She embodies the comedy as well as the tragedy of modern life. Traditionally, tragedy went only with poetic grandeur. But what can be more bitterly tragic than the fate of a Mrs. Alving or poetically grander than the fall from his tower of Masterbuilder Solness? Whatever Ibsen is communicating, there is a quality here that in the opinion of many places him in a class with the greatest creators of drama. He is not just the "father of the modern drama"—he *is* the modern drama, the most representative dramatist of our age.

Strong words, some will say. They are increasingly being justified by his frequent reappearance on the stages of the world. We have recently been given two major (and many minor) retranslations into English. For the British, an eight-volume collection of all his dramas, the so-called *Oxford Ibsen* edited by James W. MacFarlane, was completed two years ago. For Americans, a one-volume collection of *The Complete Major Prose Plays* by Rolf Fjelde appeared last year. These (and others mentioned below or listed in the Bibliography) can now replace the classic, for us rather Victorian, versions in the *Collected Works* edited by William Archer (originally in eleven volumes in 1906–8, expanded to twelve in 1912). No other Norwegian author, and few other Scandinavian ones, have been the objects of so much loving attention. Collected works in German, French, Dutch, and Russian testify to his continuing European, and we may say his worldwide, appeal.

Biographers, critics, and literary scholars have probed his works and the man behind them, ever since Paul Botten Hansen in Norway wrote the first biographical sketch in 1863 and Georg Brandes in Denmark the first critical study in 1867. In Norway he now has his shrines, from two "Ibsen houses" and an Ibsen theater in Skien, his birthplace, to the apothecary-shop-turned-museum in Grimstad, where he wrote his first drama. An Ibsen society called *Ibsenforbundet*, founded in 1948, has cherished his memory and promoted an ever-increasing literature about him. (See the volume commemorating its first twenty-five years, *Ibsenforbundet gjennom 25 år*, published in 1973 in Skien by Einar Østvedt, one of its founders.)

When writing this book, I drew freely on the published literature, without attempting to be exhaustive. At the end of each chapter, further readings and references are listed, especially those available in English. It is assumed that readers of this volume either are reading or have read Ibsen's plays. It is to be hoped that they will also have the pleasure of seeing some of his plays performed, as I have, in Norway, Sweden, England, and the United States.

As professor of Scandinavian languages I have taught Ibsen more times than I care to count. Even before that I had him in my bones, for I was barely adolescent when I began picking his works off the bookshelf in the home of my Norwegian-born parents. Reading these through in the original shaped my thinking, though his "claim of the ideal" was forever beyond my reach. The many-splendored humor of *Peer Gynt*, the tragicomedy of *Ghosts* and *The Wild Duck*, the profound insights of *A Doll's House* and *Hedda Gabler*, the psychological riddles of *Rosmersholm* and *The Master Builder*,—all these left an indelible impression.

This book is the first to consider Ibsen's skill as a communicator and his methods of communication. It reflects at least part of what I have taught and what I have learned (in great measure from my students) about Ibsen. I hope that it may stimulate readers who are not yet aware of this aspect of Ibsen to search him out and learn even more than I can tell them.

Ibsen has been interpreted as well as misinterpreted; that is a privilege of the artist's communication. The misinterpretation may well have been foreseen by the poet and be part of his intention. As William Empson taught us (in his *Seven Types of Ambiguity*), ambiguity can be built into a poet's work. Ibsen may not be all things to all men, but he has been a great many things to many men (not to speak of women). By entitling my book *Ibsen's Drama: Author to Audience*, I have committed myself to an analysis that asks the reader to listen to Ibsen's voice in his work and to accept it as a message from his undying spirit.

This book is gratefully dedicated to the professors and students of Concordia College, the "Cobbers" but for whom I might never have been enticed back into the labyrinth of Ibsenism. I wish also to record my deep gratitude and personal fondness for Roman Jakobson, whose harmonization of linguistics and poetics inspired the framework on which these essays are constructed.

Belmont, Massachusetts
March 1979

Table of Contents

IBSEN'S DRAMA
Author to Audience

Introduction

A Dramatist for All Seasons

All these fading and decrepit figures who have pounced on my play [Ghosts] will one day receive their crushing judgment in the literary histories of the future. . . . My book belongs to the future.

Ibsen to his publisher, 16 March 1882[1]

THERE ARE few if any theatrical seasons in which one or another play by Ibsen is not being performed somewhere around the world. Dramatists come and go; they strut their little hour on the stage and vanish. But Ibsen bids fair to go on, at least for as long as the theater we know continues to exist. His position as an enduring piece of theatrical property seems secure.

Let us carry the metaphor of the seasons a step farther. Ibsen had his own seasons of varying creativity. The spring of his life was chilly, but bracing, coinciding with the spring of his country and its budding culture. His summer was spent in the hothouse of Italian sunshine, where he blossomed out with his masterpieces of dramatic poetry, *Brand* and *Peer Gynt*. His autumn bore the air of a fruitful German harvest, the "Knackwurst and Bier" atmosphere (as he termed it in 1870) of *The League of Youth* (and by extension, of its more famous successors).[2] His winter began when he returned to Norway in 1891, after which his dramas of old age were written, poetic perspectives on life and art, beginning with *The Master Builder*.

Ibsen's plays, too, have had their seasons, fluctuating fortunes of popularity and neglect.[3] As the world has changed, new issues have

3

sprung up to engage the attention of the political, cultural, and theatrical world. Yet time and again someone finds that Ibsen has said something that is relevant to these issues and revives him, either on the stage or in new translations and adaptations.

We can measure the distance Ibsen has come by comparing quotations from two leading American theater critics of their times, William Winter and Edmund Wilson.

Winter (1836–1917) was drama critic of the *New York Tribune* from 1865 to 1909, according to one source respected as "the Great Cham of the New York theater" (a Cham being some kind of oriental dictator).[4] In 1892 he wrote:

> Mr. Ibsen, as the writer of a number of insipid, and sometimes tainted compositions, purporting to be plays, could be borne, although, even in that aspect, he is an offence to taste and a burden upon patience. But Mr. Ibsen obtruded as a sound leader of thought or an artist in drama is a grotesque absurdity.[5]

Wilson (1895–1972) was born three years after this diatribe was written. He, too, became an eminent critic of the New York theater, described (in the 1974 *Britannica*) as "the leading man of letters in the United States."[6] Reviewing performances of *Hedda Gabler* and *Little Eyolf* for *The New Republic* in 1926, he wrote:

> As the theatrical seasons come and go and he maintains his popularity, we begin to realize that he is perhaps really to be reckoned among the few great tragic dramatists. In his combined mastery of human character, he deserves a place beside them, Sophocles and Shakespeare; we cannot doubt that many generations will continue to be stirred by the intensity and astonished by the intellect which has disentangled a highly complex and a poetic vision of life into the perfect lucidity and logic of Ibsen's plays—which has achieved actor-proof masterpieces of the theatre without ever sacrificing for a moment the seriousness and the significance of the severest art.[7]

The reversal of opinion could hardly be more complete, from condemnation to praise, not only of Ibsen's dramatic craftsmanship, but also of his artistic quality and power of intellect.

Ibsen's way to fame was marked by a series of shock treatments to the audiences of his time. He provoked potential readers and viewers by deliberately scandalizing them. He challenged accepted and conventional views and broke taboos on what could be printed in books and spoken on the stage. A litany of abuse followed him throughout life and well into posterity; in the theater he was a notorious gadfly. But it is a long step from notoriety to fame, and even longer from being famous to becoming a classic. Like many another iconoclast, he has been accepted by the very establishment he attacked.

Catiline—Spokesman of Discontent

Ibsen's first artistic and critical shocks were administered to the small-town society in Grimstad on the south Norwegian coast, where he was first employed. In his 1875 preface to the second edition of *Catiline* (1850), he tells of his years as an apprentice in the apothecary's shop:

> Those were turbulent times. The February Revolution, the uprisings in Hungary and elsewhere, the war over Schleswig . . . I wrote resounding poems to the Magyars encouraging them, in the cause of freedom and humanity, to hold out in their just struggle with the "tyrants." . . . On more elevated occasions I could not refrain from expressing myself along the same passionate lines as in my poetry—from which, however, I derived only dubious benefit, both from those who were and those who were not my friends. . . . To tell the truth, I must add that on a number of occasions my behavior did not justify any great hopes that society in me would have someone in whom the solid middle-class virtues could be expected to flourish. Through my epigrams and caricatures I also quarreled with many who had deserved better of me, and whose friendship I in fact prized.[8]

This period of being at war with his community climaxed in the writing of *Catiline*, his first play. It concerned a famous Roman rebel, the patrician Catiline, fulminated against by Cicero, whom Ibsen in the same preface called "the indefatigable spokesman of the majority." Cicero's orations have been the bane of many a schoolchild's Latin lessons, no doubt of Ibsen's as well. He combined Cicero's account with the historian Sallust's less biased one to produce a spokesman for his own discontent. Alas, the only ones to be shocked by it were the classicists, who found its treatment of historical facts misleading and its "pathetic effects" overdone. Ibsen's first attack on the establishment was almost wholly smothered in indifference.

But at least it was in print in the capital, Christiania (now Oslo), when Ibsen himself arrived there, intent on a university education. The play won him a perceptive review by philosophy professor M. J. Monrad, who discerned in it "the individual's obscure longing for freedom," one of Ibsen's lifelong motifs.[9] It also caught the eye of world-renowned Norwegian violinist Ole Bull (1810–80), who was about to start a theater in his native town of Bergen. An ardent patriot, Bull was promoting a Norwegian stage to replace the prevalent

Danish plays and actors. He needed a house dramatist and in 1851 imported Ibsen for six crucial *Lehrjahre*. During these years he wrote plays and instructed actors as stage manager. We shall look at the plays later, but note here that his work aroused so little attention that in a newspaper controversy one critic could write: "Mr. Ibsen is a gigantic nonentity, around whom the nation cannot with any enthusiasm plant a protective hedge."[10]

The Scandalous Comedy of Love

In this desperate situation Ibsen again resorted to the shock technique. After returning to Christiania to manage the Norwegian Theater there in 1857—a period of low productivity—he wrote *Love's Comedy* (1862), which implied that getting engaged and married would kill love! He most decidedly won the attention of his public, especially the gossips, who found such sentiments scandalous coming from a newly-married man. As he later wrote, "My wife was the only one who approved."[11] She was strong and intelligent enough to suspect what all the world would one day realize: that in this play Ibsen had for the first time developed the fusion of dramatic skill and challenging ideas that we know as "Ibsenian." It marked the end of his apprenticeship and his emergence as the "angry young man" in Norwegian literature. "I can assure you," he wrote to a Danish critic who had taken notice of it, "that if ever an author had to get a mood and a subject off his chest, it was the case when I sat down to write that."[12]

The critics were so hostile that Christiania Theater did not dare put it on the stage. Here was a play in the best romantic style of rhymed verse, but in theme so antiromantic that it shook critics to the bottom of their conventional souls. The same philosophical Monrad who had welcomed *Catiline* called this play "an offense against human decency." Ibsen, he asserted, was making himself "a mouthpiece for the distraught tendencies of the age and its spiritually enfeebling atheism." He found the underlying theme untrue, immoral, and unpoetic. Ditmar Meidell, a leading newspaper critic, called it "a wretched specimen of literary dilettantism," and he asserted that Ibsen did not possess genius, merely talent, and one could only regret that he was wasting it.[13]

Only Ibsen's friend and protector, the literary critic Paul Botten Hansen, defended it. And it won him the friendship of his more popular younger contemporary and lifelong rival, the writer Bjørnstjerne Bjørnson (1832–1910), who assisted him in getting the means to go abroad in 1864. In his preface to the second edition, which appeared in

Denmark in 1866, Ibsen sardonically remarked that the play "aroused a tempest of ill will, more violent and more widespread than most books can boast of in a society where the overwhelming majority otherwise regard literary matters as of no concern to them."[14] He observed that his countrymen evidently lacked the philosophical training needed to distinguish "loves and marriages," which he satirized, from "love and marriage" (in the abstract), which he did not reject. But no one could doubt that Ibsen had won the attention of his countrymen.

Rebellious Pretenders

At the same time he felt their criticism as a kind of excommunication. This is evident in *The Pretenders* (1863), his next work, a Shakespearean history play from Norway's period of medieval glory. Amid all its pageantry, it reveals touches of personal bitterness. One of its protagonists is another rebel drawn from history, Earl Skule, who failed in his thirteenth-century revolt against King Haakon. Another figure is a poet, the *skald* Jatgejr, who seems to be speaking for the author when he says that he won his gift of poetry through sorrow. A scheming bishop, Nikolas, prophesies (and seeks to ensure) that Norwegians will always be at war among themselves, uniting only on stoning and destroying their geniuses. The play challenged his countrymen to awaken in the present and look to the future. Only through the noble Bjørnson-like figure of King Haakon did he make of it a play that could also be read as a patriotic spectacle.

Having directed its opening in Christiania, Ibsen set sail for Copenhagen on his way to Italy, to an exile that would last twenty-seven years. Angry and disillusioned with his countrymen, he was at the same time jubilant at the new freedom that beckoned from the sunny hills of Rome. Within two years he dropped another bombshell, producing shock waves that were felt throughout Scandinavia. This was the play *Brand*, which at one blow made him the most talked-of writer in these countries.

The *Brand* of Success

The story is familiar: Ibsen's new publisher, Frederik Hegel of the Danish house of Gyldendal, did not at once realize what a goldmine he had acquired. On getting the manuscript, he wrote to ask Ibsen's permission to cut the edition of 1,250 copies in half. Ibsen's agreeable reply was lost, so the full edition was printed. Within the year three new printings were called for. *Brand* became one of the great publishing successes of the century, and by also winning him a government stipend for life, it laid a secure financial foundation for his entire literary career. He could now devote himself entirely to the writing of plays, and he could live wherever he pleased.

Yet this *Brand* was a chastisement, not only of his countrymen but of all humankind. He pictured the lonely, tragic life of a consistent idealist, willing to sacrifice career, mother, wife, child, and, in the end, himself for an ideal (if nebulous) cause. The light thrown on Brand's fellow men is unflattering: the country folk, so much admired by romantics, prove to be earth-bound and penurious, the artists frivolous, the officials petty and corrupt, the clergy self-seeking and grasping. Everyone in general turns coward under the pressure of opinion.

Again the reviewers were hostile. Even the perceptive poet Aasmund Vinje, Ibsen's friend, wrote that the play was "too raving mad to be serious," and so he mockingly chose to treat it as a comedy. Bjørnson felt ill after the reading and hated it, holding that it put an end to all sincere religion; he predicted that it would be dead in two months. Professor Monrad severely criticized Brand's extremism, calling it "a misjudgment of the pure nature of the ideal" and maintaining that true self-sacrifice consisted in the ability to make compromises. One minister warned against the "unchristian" spirit of the play and defended the very characters whom Ibsen had derided.[15]

The controversy about *Brand* established a new epoch in Ibsen's dramatic development. One young philosopher, G. V. Lyng, declared that "the poem has made a powerful and inspiring impression on hundreds of our countrymen."[16] It took Bjørnson twelve years before he was prepared to recant his earlier opinion: "Now at last I am grateful to Ibsen for it."[17] Ibsen's biographer, historian Halvdan Koht, reports: "There is scarcely another literary work, by Ibsen or anyone else, that has given the Norwegian language so many pungent epigrams. The generation of 1866 took it as its gospel, and for twenty years and more it became for them a stimulus to thought and to action. . . ."[18] Its effect in Denmark and Sweden was no less than in Norway. The Swedish writer Gustaf af Geijerstam declared that for his generation "Ibsen became the bond between friends and between loving couples; no more sacred gift could be given than *Brand*—it was considered a tribute to one's intelligence and one's character."[19]

Brand was received as a breviary of youthful idealism, a bodying forth in living characters on the stage of the "either-or" philosophy that Kierkegaard had proclaimed. It was the first Ibsen play to be translated into German (1869); before the end of the century five other attempts would be made to render his powerful verse into German. More than ever before, Ibsen had demonstrated his mastery of the verse drama, and he put his skill to the test again in *Peer Gynt* (1867), as well as in his collection of verse (1871).

Shaking the Pillars

It was therefore a new shock when Ibsen turned away from verse and began writing prose dramas in a realistic mode. The poetic-philosophical allegories *Brand* and *Peer Gynt* gave way to *The League of Youth* (1869), which brought to the stage highly recognizable types of modern people, speaking in everyday language. In this play he portrayed a politician and orator, a would-be reformer with liberal views who was dishonestly ready to use any means to gain office and influence. The conservatives cheered, while the liberals hissed. Ibsen was prepared: "I expected resistance, and I would have been disappointed had it not come."[20] A few plays later he righted the balance by lashing out at conservative politicians as well. He just did not like politicians, of whatever variety.

From now on, the shocks kept coming, more and more skillfully administered. We note a rising curve from *Pillars of Society* (1877) to *A Doll's House* (1879) to *Ghosts* (1881). *An Enemy of the People* (1882) was little more than a mild epilogue to these three. In five years these four plays transformed Ibsen from a Scandinavian to a European celebrity. He had created the block of dramas on which his world reputation was going to rest, and to which it would, at least in some circles, remain confined.

Like Samson in the temple, he had dared to shake the pillars on which society's sacred structure was presumed to rest, namely the capitalistic entrepreneurs. Their homes and families were pilloried as institutions that stifled the freedom, not only of women but of children and fathers as well. Society stood accused of branding its true benefactors "enemies of the people."

The response was swift and, in part, vicious. Theaters in Scandinavia and Germany received the first of the four with innocent enthusiasm. Its social criticism was tempered by a "happy" ending, offering at least some hope for the future. Within four months it was running simultaneously in five Berlin theaters in at least three different translations. In England it remained undiscovered for a decade, and when it was performed in 1889, one critic could write that "every one of the characters . . . is phenomenally disagreeable."[21] *Pillars* touched on the topic of woman's restricted place in society (the central theme in *A Doll's House*). What could people make of the final bit of dialogue in *Pillars* between repentant capitalist Bernick and liberated Lona Hessel:

> CONSUL BERNICK: That's another thing I've learned in the last days: it's you women who are the pillars of society.
>
> LONA HESSEL: Then it's a pretty flimsy wisdom you've gained, Karsten. No, my dear, the spirit of truth and the spirit of freedom—*those* are the pillars of society.[22]

In *A Doll's House* Nora refuses, in the name of freedom and truth, to remain a pillar of society, i.e., a slave of her husband's social status. She walks out, slamming the door behind her, a slam that echoed around the world. Nora was discussed, not as a fictional personality, but as a real person, a tribute to Ibsen's stagecraft. He had given a social problem flesh and blood in a female part that actresses have stood in line to play ever since.

The play was an immediate success in the theater and on the book stands. Coming as it did in the midst of a period when woman's position was being much debated, Nora's dramatic exit upset both readers and spectators. A leading German actress, Frau Hedwig Niemann-Raabe, refused to perform it unless the ending were changed: "*I* would never leave *my* children."[23] The play swept not only Scandinavia and Germany but also Finland, England, Poland, Russia, and Italy. It made Ibsen a world author, and it is no doubt the play most frequently connected with his name.

Although the play made Ibsen a hero to some, it made him anathema to most. In Germany, and later in America and England, watered-down versions tried to evade the fact of Nora's desertion of her children. Others tried to write a "fourth act" that would bring Nora back, so that her "miracle of miracles" (*det vidunderligste*) could occur. Discussion raged on its plausibility (could Nora be serious?), its juridical issues (would Nora have been punished?), but above all on its morality (is it right for a woman to put her own freedom above her obligations to her family?).

The Gibbering of Ghosts

Meanwhile Ibsen was preparing the greatest shock of his authorship, the play that alienated even many of those who had approved of his liberation of Nora. This was *Gengangere*, which has come to be known as *Ghosts* in English but which might as well have been rendered "Phantoms." For the ghosts are phantoms of the past returning to plague the living: "Old dead opinions and all kinds of old dead beliefs," in Mrs. Alving's words.[24] But this was the least of it. The shock came with the treatment of Osvald's illness, the presumed syphilis inherited or caught from his father. Likewise in Mrs. Alving's open rejection of conventional religion and morality, in opposition to the Reverend Manders. Finally, there was Osvald's gruesome degeneration in the light of the rising sun, with his mother hovering irresolutely over him, not knowing whether she could make herself provide the euthanasia she had promised.

This time the shock did not benefit Ibsen's purse. Booksellers returned unsold copies, and theaters refused to stage what was universally regarded as an obscenity. Ibsen had characteristically not used a single immodest word, but the theme was only too perceptible in "the eyes of the beholders." In good society one simply did not speak of such things. The day of the freely spoken obscenity was far in the future (and Ibsen might very well not have approved).

Again he became the shock troop of a new vanguard, the Naturalistic theater. Only small and radical groups could afford to play this daring piece. In 1889 it marked the opening of the Freie Bühne in Berlin, a landmark in German theatrical history. In 1890 it was mounted by André Antoine at his avant-garde Théâtre libre in Paris. In England it was daringly performed at the Royalty Theatre in 1891.

Scandinavian and German commentary was pungent enough. But the English Press, still in the thrall of Victorian prudery, was the most outspoken. Its comments were lovingly collected and anthologized by Ibsen's leading advocate and translator, William Archer, in a classic article appropriately entitled "Ghosts and Gibberings."[25] This chorus of loathing seems hilarious today, but in those days it took a man like George Bernard Shaw to see the humor. He selected some of the more bloodthirsty epithets applied to *Ghosts* in the English press: "Ibsen's positively abominable play . . . disgusting . . . an open drain; a loathsome sore unbandaged; a dirty act done publicly; absolutely loathsome and fetid . . . dismal and repulsive . . . revoltingly suggestive and blasphemous . . . a wicked nightmare . . . garbage and offal." It could be a section in a dictionary of synonyms for obscenity. Those who favored the play, the "Ibsenites," were described as "lovers of prurience and dabblers in impropriety who are eager to gratify their illicit tastes under the pretence of art . . . nasty-minded people . . . unsexed females . . . educated and muck-ferreting dogs." A magazine called *Truth* uttered this palpable untruth: "Outside a silly clique, there is not the slightest interest in the Scandinavian humbug or all his works." It is clear, as Shaw pointed out, that "here Ibsen struck at something much deeper than the fancies of critics as to the proper way to write plays."[26] This "frantic and indecent vituperation" showed that Ibsen had hit the very nerve of Victorian moralism.

But when Shaw espoused Ibsen against this flood of abuse, it was not only because he judged him a great playwright, being himself a distinguished critic and a famous playwright-to-be. He also saw Ibsen as an ally of his Fabian Society, which advocated a mild form of socialism. Shaw is one of the exhibits I am here offering to show that Ibsen was indeed a dramatist for all seasons. Shaw could claim him as an opponent of "idealism," meaning conventional morality, which Shaw regarded as insincere. But we shall see later that Ibsen was, in fact, an idealist in anyone else's definition of the word.

The Riddle of *The Wild Duck*

Even with *Ghosts* Ibsen had not exhausted his possibilities for the shock technique. Having established himself as an advocate of uncompromising honesty in social relations, he wrote *The Wild Duck* (1883) to show the tragic consequences of applying this philosophy literally and unimaginatively. In the person of Gregers Werle, Ibsen portrayed a man who tries to reorder life in harmony with the concept of the moral imperative. He clearly belongs to the same tribe as Brand, Lona Hessel, or Dr. Stockmann, and yet he is anything but admirable; he is a neurotic, unthinking, insensitive man. His influence leads to the unpremeditated and surprising suicide of young Hedvig. One English critic called *The Wild Duck* "a *reductio ad absurdum* of the views with which he has been credited by his disciples."[27]

Ibsen warned his publisher that in this play he was consciously seeking "new paths." He expected that "critics will no doubt find something to squabble about."[28] The result was general bewilderment, and for some even disillusionment. A reviewer wrote, "One can puzzle and puzzle over what Ibsen means and still not find it out."[29] Those who had expected "some truth or other that the author wanted to impress on his age, or some kind of problem that was to be discussed," were hardly happy.[30] An English critic declared that "its meaning and significance are so obscure as to baffle even the acuteness of the most sympathetic admirers."[31] More than any other, this play led to the establishment of Ibsen's reputation as a sphinx, uttering riddles for his public to solve. Those who looked for a fixed identity in Ibsen were surprised and even antagonized: this man seemed to be contradicting himself.

Bernard Shaw read the play in his own way: Ibsen had performed "a tragi-comic slaughtering of sham Ibsenism," which made his "astonished victims plaintively" declare that the play was a satire on his former works.[32] Happily Shaw could also savor its superb dramatic potential. After an 1897 performance, he characterized it as "not a diversion, but an experience deeper than real life brings to most men, or often brings to any man."[33] As we shall see later, Ibsen had here succeeded in raising the prose drama into the realm of poetry. It shocked those who had ticketed him as a propagandist for radical and "immoral" ideas; but it became the basis of a reevaluation of Ibsen's work that has occupied critics ever since.

The Elusive Playwright

Ibsen had at last achieved a true drama at once embodying the tragedy and comedy of human life. From here on he would write less about social issues than about man's condition, viewing it from various angles, as one masterpiece followed the other: *Rosmersholm, Lady from the Sea, Hedda Gabler, The Master Builder, Little Eyolf, John Gabriel Borkman, When We Dead Awaken*. These contained shocks of their own—the furtive eroticism of Hedda, the hints of incest in *Little Eyolf*, the frankly sexual symbolism of *When We Dead Awaken*. But Ibsen had achieved his heights, and from this eminence he could biennially issue a play respectfully awaited by the literate public. His shock treatment had won him the attention of the world he wished to reach. One could discuss his characters and his craftsmanship without vituperation or apology. Those who received these works had reason to be grateful to Ibsen for creating such towering if enigmatic figures as Rebecca West and Johannes Rosmer; Ellida Wangel and her understanding husband, Doctor Wangel; Hedda Gabler and her lover-genius Ejlert Løvborg; Hilde and her Master Builder Solness; Asta, Rita, and the ineffectual philosopher Allmers; Gunhild and Ella battling over John Gabriel Borkman; and finally, the dramatist himself figured in the sculptor Rubek, flanked as always by his two women.

Ibsen began by shocking his public and ended by creating a new one. He saw to it that no one could any longer remain an "Ibsenite," member of a partisan group. But it was and is possible to be an "Ibsenian," a lover and admirer of his work.

By placing himself outside the society he was viewing, Ibsen was able to present new and startling views. He participated by not participating; he established his identity by developing a nonidentity. His strength (and some would say, his weakness) lay in his determination to be only an observer.

In his lifetime he was embraced successively by those who espoused revolution, nationalism, romanticism, idealism, realism, socialism, naturalism, symbolism, and psychoanalysis. But he wriggled loose from every embrace. No sooner had he been labeled this or that than he shocked the labelers by moving on to something new. "Where I stood then, when I wrote my various books, there is now a fairly compact crowd, but I myself am no longer there; I am somewhere else, I hope in front."[34] The greatest shock of all to most readers of Ibsen is that he eludes all labels. His protean nature is best expressed by his own words about Earl Skule: he "doubts his own doubt." Robert Brustein elegantly formulated this reflexivity of Ibsen's: "The real quintessence of Ibsenism is total resistance to whatever is established, for his anarchistic iconoclasm extends not only to the current conventions of his time, but even to his own current beliefs and convictions."[35] Even this keen perception can be challenged; we shall try to do so by showing exactly what Ibsen does communicate in his production.

The process of reevaluation has gone on long after his death warrant as an artist was signed and sealed. Still his plays keep being revived, sometimes for the wrong reasons, if any reason for reviving them can be said to be wrong. We are told that *Peer Gynt* was extraordinarily popular in Germany during World War I. This was largely due to its adaptation by the mystical writer Dietrich Eckart (a proto-Nazi), who turned it into an expressionistic dream play, in accordance with the taste of the times.[36] *Peer Gynt* no doubt lends itself to such treatment, being a prefiguring of Strindberg's *Dream Play* (1902). But when we are told that Germans saw themselves in Peer as "the creative, world-administrating god-man" type, battling the materialism of the West personified in England and America, we can only shake our heads.

Radicals have more generally taken him to heart. In the Russia of 1905 *An Enemy of the People* was hailed as a revolutionary play.[37] In Germany and America he was a favorite of the Yiddish theater. In 1950 Arthur Miller rewrote *An Enemy of the People* to bring it into line with his own left-wing views.[38] The recent surge of a new feminism has been the occasion for a flurry of performances of *A Doll's House*. We shall look more closely at his reception by various audiences in chapter 6. That Ibsen can be read in more than one way is actually a tribute to the diversity and breadth of his writing. It implies an enduring quality that enables him to communicate with ever new audiences. Ibsen was a challenging writer from the start, and he seems not to have lost that quality.

But what exactly is the nature of his message? Not one of the many analysts of Ibsen has explored his work as *communication*. It is clear that like any serious writer he is communicating something, but what is it and how does he do it? In the following chapters I shall suggest some answers to this question.

READINGS AND REFERENCES

The definitive Norwegian text of Ibsen's writings is Henrik Ibsen, *Samlede verker*, ed. Francis Bull, Halvdan Koht, and Didrik Arup Seip, 21 vols. (Oslo: Gyldendal, 1928–58), known as *Hundreårsutgaven*. An edition of the plays and poems alone, in modernized spelling, is *Samlede verker*, ed. Didrik Arup Seip, 3 vols. (Oslo: Gyldendal, 1960), also available in paperback ("Fakkel-bok," 1962).

The basic English translation is *The Collected Works of Henrik Ibsen*, ed. and revised by William Archer, 12 vols. (London: Heinemann, 1906–12). A modern English version is *The Oxford Ibsen*, ed. James Walter McFarlane, 8 vols. (London: Oxford University Press, 1960–77). *The Oxford Ibsen* contains not only new translations, most of them by McFarlane, but also comprehensive introductions to each play, Ibsen's drafts and notes (if any), commentary by Ibsen and others. There are also lists of English productions and selected bibliographies of the biographical and critical literature. A new American version of the last twelve plays is Henrik Ibsen, *The Complete Major Prose Plays*, trans. and introd. by Rolf Fjelde (New York: Farrar Straus and Giroux/New American Library, 1978). This also includes a selected bibliography and a survey of professional American performances of Ibsen's plays. Selections from Ibsen's nondramatic prose writings are gathered in *Ibsen: Letters and Speeches*, ed. Evert Sprinchorn (New York: MacGibbon and Kee, 1965). For further English translations see the Bibliography.

Anthologies of critical essays on Ibsen are *Ibsen: A Collection of Critical Essays*, ed. Rolf Fjelde (Englewood Cliffs, N.J.: Prentice-Hall, 1965), and *Henrik Ibsen: A Critical Anthology*, ed. James W. McFarlane (London: Penguin Books, 1970). Early English-language criticism from 1872 to 1906 is collected in Michael Egan, *Ibsen: The Critical Heritage* (London: Routledge, 1972).

A Model for Communication

THE MODEL that will be used as the framework for our discussion is a modification of the one developed by Roman Jakobson, renowned scholar in linguistics and poetics. This model presents a generalized conception of how people communicate in everyday life. It applies also to the sending of messages by telephone and telegraph, and it can easily be adjusted to fit the work of poet and writer, trying to communicate something beyond bits of information.

In any act of communication there is an *addresser* and an *addressee*, also known as *sender* and *receiver*, *source* and *target*. In conversation the addresser and the addressee function alternately as speakers and listeners. In a literary work the addresser is the *author*, who is the sole speaker, sending his or her message as a monologue to addressees who are the potential *audience*, whether readers or (for plays) listeners. Ibsen as playwright was striving to express something of himself, sending a more or less *expressive* message to a more or less *receptive* audience.

Each act of communication or message *refers* to something in the real or imaginary world, something that we may call the *context* of the participants. The author is talking *about* something, a *topic* that he or she hopes will be understood by the audience. Ibsen clearly drew on the life of his own times whether the material was historical or contemporary.

The addresser must adopt a *channel*, a medium through which the message can reach the audience. In speech this is the air that we agitate

16

with sound waves, in telegraphy the wires or the air that transmits electrical impulses. For Ibsen, the channel was the *drama*, as performed in a theater, imaginary or real, in the latter case by actors on stages under the guidance of stage managers and directors.

Before it can be transmitted by the channel, a message must be encoded by the addresser in a particular *code*, a language that can then be decoded by the addressee. In telegraphy this may be the dots and dashes of the Morse code, in speech and writing a natural language that is shared by addresser and addressee. But it is the essence of a literary work that there is a code behind the natural language, a second code, a cryptic mode of expression containing a deeper level of content. Ibsen's natural language was the cultivated (Dano-)Norwegian of his day. But it will be shown here that behind this language there was a symbolic code with deeper meanings.

Finally, the message has a *form*, imposed on it by the addresser, that is appropriate to its purpose. A simple, informational message has a simple, straightforward form, whereas one that is intended to give esthetic pleasure is modeled into a form that is likely to impress the addressee as poetic. An author's style is a matter of form, a selection from the options open to a user of the language. We shall try to show not only that Ibsen was deeply conscious of the importance of form but that his form in all its various guises was basically poetic, in a way eminently suitable to a modern drama.

This makes six aspects of communication, each of which will be discussed in a separate chapter of this book: author, context, channel, code, form, and audience. Mnemonically it may be helpful to set them up in tabular form:

2 CONTEXT (Topics)

3 CHANNEL (Drama)

1 AUTHOR (Expression) → MESSAGE → 6 AUDIENCE (Reception)

4 CODE (Symbolism)

5 FORM (Poetry)

No such model can hope to uncover all of what Jennette Lee in 1907 called "the Ibsen secret," in her book of that title. Any work of art carries its own mystery, in large part impenetrable to criticism. But at least we can follow Peer Gynt's example in Egypt when he contemplated the Great Sphinx. He studied it aft and fore, through his lorgnette and his cupped hand, and proceeded to make his notations —though, to be sure, he later "arrived at other conclusions."

READINGS AND REFERENCES

For an account of the original model on which ours is based see Roman Jakobson, "Linguistics and Poetics," in *Style in Language*, ed. Thomas A. Sebeok (Cambridge, Mass: Technology Press of M.I.T., 1960; New York and London: Wiley, 1960), 350–77.

Jennette Lee's 1907 book was *The Ibsen Secret: A Key to the Prose Dramas of Henrik Ibsen* (New York: Putnam's).

1

Who Was Henrik Ibsen?

Everything that I have written has the closest possible connection with what I have lived through—even if I have not actually experienced it. In every new work I have aimed at my own spiritual emancipation and purification—for no man can escape the responsibilities and the guilt of the society to which he belongs.

Ibsen, letter to L. Passarge, 16 June 1880.[1]

ON THE OCCASION of his seventieth birthday in 1898, Ibsen declared his intention of writing a book "that will link my life and my writings together into an explanatory whole."[2] Happily for his many interpreters, he never fulfilled this intention. Nor is it really necessary: the man stands out clear and strong in the works he left behind. One could almost write his biography by using as a source the message that is his work.

For writers of earlier ages the lack of sources makes this a necessity: of Homer's life we know nothing, of Virgil's little, of Chaucer's something, of Shakespeare's more, though virtually none of it relates to their writing. The man whose grave we venerate in Stratford-on-Avon was the pillar of his community, not the man we perceive in the sonnets or in *The Tempest*. Only in relatively recent times did writers become public figures in their own right, and so the object of biographical scrutiny, on a level with politicians and other performers.

Even today the average consumer of literature is relatively unin-
terested in its authors, aside from the fact that the name provides a
trademark identifying a certain type of product. "A. Conan Doyle"
or "Georges Simenon" assures the reader of a psychological mystery,
"Ernest Hemingway" of male adventure in and out of the bull ring;
even "Shakespeare" is largely a label for an awesome evening in the
theater purveyed in beautiful, only half-understood accents.

In this chapter we shall explore the topic of what kind of *persona*
is concealed under the label "Ibsen." The first question we ask about
a message is who sent it. If we are to understand the significance of a
message, it is important to know the name and nature of its sender.
A wire summoning one to Washington could have an entirely different value if it came from the president rather than from some jocose
friend!

With Ibsen we are not limited to his works. We can explore in some
detail the relation between the known or rumored facts of his outward
life and the products of his art. There are letters, speeches, interviews,
and the observations of many whose lives he touched, and from these
huge biographies have been written. Ibsen himself was not generous
with personal information; he prized his privacy and complained when
critics, as he put it, added him to the characters of his plays.[3] He sel-
dom appeared in public, and he often disappointed those who tried
to approach him. Many who met him found him to be a rather different person from what they had imagined while reading him. Saving
most of his communication for his writing, he was often taciturn, at
times downright uncivil. Yet on occasion he could be garrulous, as the
words tumbled forth and he poured out his feelings. Although rejecting
easy familiarity and finding friendships burdensome, he did make
friends to whom he could be almost pathetically devoted and open-
hearted.

The Transformation

This duality is significantly revealed in a minor episode from the summer of 1869. The art historian Lorentz Dietrichson, a Norwegian who
had recently been made a professor in Stockholm, received a letter in
a hand he did not recognize. It proved to be from Ibsen, with whom
he had struck up a great friendship five years earlier, while showing
off the art treasures of Rome to the eager young dramatist, then just
arrived from Norway. Dietrichson knew well the plain and rather un-
distinguished scrawl Ibsen had used down to that time, but now Ibsen
had adopted a copperplate backhand that not only was clear but cal-

ligraphic. In his next letter Ibsen included a new photograph of himself, which showed that he had trimmed down the bushy black beard, which had been his trademark, to two neat, aristocratic "mutton-chop" sideburns. Dietrichson later commented that it was the first time he had seen Ibsen's tightly compressed lips.[4]

The transformation had actually taken place three years earlier, when Ibsen began presenting to the world a facade that was calculated to impress. His "bohemian" years as the struggling artist were over, and he took up his role in the bourgeoisie, with a dash of aristocracy that grew over the years. His new dignity is revealed also in the contents of his first letter to Dietrichson, a request that he write a biographical sketch of him for the German reading public. "Please dash off something suitable for the Germans, as well-disposed as your conscience permits," wrote Ibsen. "But it won't do any more to write about my poetic poverty. Tell them instead that the government and parliament have given me a poet's stipend, that I travel, that I am living 'in dem grossen Vaterlande,' etc."[5] He was no longer to be presented as a struggling, impecunious poet but as a successful and well-established writer. His outer image would henceforth reflect this sea change: goodbye to Bohemia, welcome to the Bourgeoisie. From now on he was the impeccable gentleman, velvet-coated, on occasion be-medaled and top-hatted.

The paradox is that in the years to come this very bourgeois would write a series of plays that seemed to many to rock the very foundations of middle-class society. The writer who in one poem declared that he would be happy to "place a torpedo under the ark" (Noah's) was also at home in the salons of the mighty.[6]

Bourgeois or Bohemian?

In 1868 Ibsen settled down with his family in Dresden, Germany, after four exciting and nomadic years in Italy. With his twin dramatic poems, or poetic dramas, *Brand* and *Peer Gynt*, he had won a large reading public and status as Scandinavia's most promising dramatist. For the first time in his life he could feel free of economic worries. And that winter he turned away definitively from romantic dramas for reading to realistic plays for the stage. The change in his outer appearance corresponded to that of his dramatic form, giving almost the impression of two different Ibsens. Yet all he did was to build a bourgeois shell around a bohemian self, and they are both essential parts of his identity. The bourgeois is accounted for by his birth and his background, as we shall see, the bohemian by his personal revolt against that background. The conflict between them produced the drama of his life and gave life to his dramas. It was the real psychological content of the "war between trolls in the chambers of mind and heart," which became his definition of living.[7]

"Bourgeois" in its widest sense, as applied to Ibsen, includes his role as a responsible citizen, a man of orderly habits, seeking economic stability in a precarious world, even a social creature hoping for the love and respect of his fellows, and determined to do his duty toward them. As a bourgeois he tended to be personally dignified, imperturbable and disciplined, sexually inhibited, undeviatingly systematic, confident, and firm.

As a "bohemian," on the other hand, he was an artist struggling for self-expression, in quest of that liberation of the human spirit which he called for again and again in his writings. In this role he could be garrulous, argumentative, excitable, immoderate in drinking, sexually active, personally a bit on the unkempt and indecisive side. Either character may seem more than enough for one man, and together they proved almost too much even for Ibsen. But they enabled him to people a whole theater by what he called "self-anatomy," the dissection of his inner self.

Outwardly he was unimpressive—short, dark, gnomish—for which he compensated by extreme foppishness: high heels, a long frock coat, a top hat with a mirror inside.[8] Yet, as he matured and aged, those who saw him, and especially those who painted or modeled him, found him impressive; the Danish author Herman Bang once compared the look in his eyes (in particular the left one) to the piercing glance of a lion.[9] That a writer of bourgeois (or lower) birth should yearn for royal recognition is not without precedent: the fairytale writer Hans Christian Andersen and the immortal Geheimrat Johann Wolfgang von Goethe were both eager to hobnob with princes. Ibsen himself became a favorite of the Swedish-Norwegian kings Carl XV and Oscar II, and he found his best patron in Duke Georg II of Saxe-Meiningen. All three rulers decorated him, to his sardonic delight; and he was glad to be made an official delegate of Norway-Sweden at the opening of the Suez Canal in 1869.

The ambivalence is most apparent in his attitude toward his kin. From the day he left his birthplace Skien for good in 1850 at age 22, he appears never to have seen again either his parents or any other of his relatives, although they lived on for many years. When his father died in 1877, Henrik wrote to his uncle, Christian Paus, explaining why he had given the appearance of "voluntarily and deliberately estranging myself from my family." His chief reason was that he could not be of help to them because of his own straitened circumstances. To this, one could say that it need not have kept him from at least writing to them. The real reason is suggested by a later sentence in the same letter: "I felt a deep desire to avoid contact with certain attitudes which prevailed there, and with which I was out of sympathy. I wanted to avoid the unpleasantness or at least the bad feelings that might have resulted."[10]

Yet in 1882, only five years later, he could remind Georg Brandes, his benevolent Danish critic who had belittled his family background, that "my parents were members on both sides of the most respected families in Skien. The town's representative in the parliament over many years, Justice Paus, and his brother, Chief Magistrate Paus, were my father's half-brothers and my mother's cousins. Equally closely related with my parents were the families Plesner, von der Lippe, Cappelen, Blom, in short, just about all the patrician families who then dominated the place and its surroundings."[11] There is more than a touch of pride in his bourgeois background in this enumeration of names whose very form associates them with the more or less foreign ancestry of the Norwegian upper middle class.

Let us step back and look at the position of this class and the kind of world they created around Ibsen's childhood and youth.[12]

The Social Order

Henrik Johan Ibsen was born on March 20, 1828, when the French Revolution and the Napoleonic disaster were still freshly in mind. New revolutions and wars—but no world wars—were to dot the period of his life. He began writing at mid-century and stopped at the end, becoming remarkably representative of the critical half-century from 1850 to 1900. In England the age is called "Victorian," and Ibsen's family did have its Victorian aspects. However, the major innovation of the period was the hitherto undreamed-of expansion of the known world through mechanical invention and industrial capitalism. Political dominance on the European continent shifted from France to Germany, while the whole continent played second fiddle to imperial England. On the eastern horizon loomed somewhat dimly a developing Russia.

Ibsen was born and lived the major portion of his life in Norway, a country on the very northern margins of the European continent, remote from the classic centers of European culture. When Ibsen's work erupted in England, Edmund Gosse described Norway as "a land unknown in the literary annals of Europe."[13] But the ferment that had reshuffled the map of Europe around 1800 had also placed Norway firmly on the path to full nationhood. That the country did not yet have it in 1850 was due to the dispositions of the great powers. They had detached Norway from a four-century-old dynastic union with Denmark and had handed it over, like so much chattel, to the tender mercies of Sweden. Norwegian leaders succeeded in ameliorating the terms of the Swedish union by gathering a constitutional assembly at Eidsvoll to protest the move. On May 17, 1814, a democratic constitution in the spirit of the times was adopted and independence declared. Sweden, under the leadership of Prince Carl Johan Bernadotte, a former Napoleonic general, wisely accepted the constitution, in return for Swedish control of foreign affairs and the royal house. It proved to be an uneasy union, during which Norwegians bent their energies to finding (or refinding) a national identity that would not be politically Swedish or culturally Danish. Ibsen, dying in 1906, barely lived to see the 1905 rupture of the union, so the issue was constantly before him.[14]

The class structure of the new country was simple enough. By 1814 the native Norwegian nobility had virtually been wiped out, and it was no great upheaval in 1821 when their titles were formally abolished. Their functions had long since been assumed by royal officials, including the military, clerical, and civil authorities. They stalk proudly through Ibsen's dramas in such figures as General Gabler, Hedda's father; in Brand's Dean, who tries to neutralize the rebellious young pastor; and in Chamberlain Bratsberg, the gray eminence in *The League of Youth*. Their higher echelons constituted the aristocracy of the country, to which might be admitted shipowners like Karsten Bernick in *Pillars of Society* and proprietors of ironworks and sawmills like Haakon Werle in *The Wild Duck*.

The great masses of the people were country folk like those we see in *Brand* and *Peer Gynt*, a farming and fishing class that constituted the backbone of the population. They had their own social hierarchy, from the independent farm owner (the *bonde*) down through the renter (*leilending*) and the cotter (*husmann*) to the landless hired folk (*dreng, taus*) who functioned as servants. The urban middle class considered the farmers, especially the *bonde*, backward but picturesque. Now they were beginning to flow off the farms into the towns, where they gradually constituted much of what would become the laboring classes, an incipient urban proletariat.

The Ibsen Family

By birth Ibsen was automatically entered into the middle class, a petty bourgeoisie, which was neither independently wealthy nor firmly rooted in the soil. Between the university-trained officials and the proprietors on the one hand and the relatively stable peasantry on the other stood a growing middle class of uncertain status. With luck, talent, and persistence its members were in a position to climb into the ruling classes. But they were also highly vulnerable to fluctuations in the economy, being both upwardly and downwardly mobile.

Such a one was Henrik's father, Knud. When Henrik was born, he had his own business, which included operating a general store and a distillery and trading in foreign imports, especially from France, Germany, and England. He made a good match by marrying Marichen Altenburg, whose father was well-to-do. Knud's income enabled him to move from the substantial Stockmann house in the center of town, where Henrik was born, to the even finer Altenburg house, which had been his mother-in-law's. He kept open house for friends and family, entertaining lavishly; and he bought a country house outside town, at a place called Venstøp.

The genealogies of the Ibsens and Altenburgs went back to a long line of skippers and merchants, branching into Germany and Denmark (with a dash of Scotch). The name Ibsen was a Danish patronymic-become-surname, Ib being short for Jacob. But the family had been in Norway for a long time and considered themselves as firmly Norwegian as did Henrik himself.[15] Henrik, the oldest living child, was six when his father's luck began to fail. Knud had to give up his enterprises one after the other, and he ended by retiring with his wife and four children (a fifth on the way) to the Venstøp estate, which had been planned only as a summer home. In a town of three thousand, as Skien then was, such a failure would count far more heavily than in a larger place. Skien was a busy seaport and lumbering town, where social status was closely correlated with commercial success. It is not exact to say, as some biographers do, that Ibsen was "déclassé." He was still one of a clan of well-to-do kinsmen, though the ties were weakened.

The chief problem was not so much the family failure as Knud's own failure as a father and a family man. The setback was such a blow to his pride that he became a broken and embittered man. Knud could not bend under misfortune: in his later years "he found people unjust and ungrateful and struck back with the only weapon he had left—his sharp tongue. When misery got the better of him, he sought oblivion in the bottle and dreamt of the day when he should regain the social position which befitted him."[16] He grew quarrelsome and litigious, at home moody and incalculable, at times close to brutal. His wife,

Marichen, once a lovely girl, spontaneous and artistic, responded by intensifying her care for the children. She became a recluse, doing her best to offset her husband's weaknesses. Eventually she converted to a pietistic religious view that gave her comfort.

In what can hardly have been a happy or harmonious home, Henrik escaped into his own world of fantasy. Neither homelife nor genetic inheritance can account for genius, which can arise in the most unlikely places. But at least we can say that some of the first symptoms of Henrik's talent were present already in childhood. He was the ugly duckling of the family who became its swan.

Memories of Ibsen's Childhood

Our information about Ibsen's early years is pieced together from his own aborted childhood memoir as well as more or less reliable gleanings from the recollections of his townsmen after he had become famous. These recollections suggest a child with an unusually well-developed inner life. He avoided ordinary child's play and made up his own games by painting make-believe figures on bits of wood. He would then arrange them in patterns of imaginary action that caused him to "sit laughing silently to himself, so that he shook," enough "to distress his siblings."[17] He ran puppet shows for the neighborhood and even learned to do conjuring tricks. He showed a talent for drawing and (for a boy in those days) an inordinate fondness for dressing up. When teased, he fought back, but otherwise he was gentle. At dances the girls liked him and were pleased when he asked them to dance.

In these scattered reports there is enough to prefigure the bohemian in him—standing apart from his group, leading a life of make-believe, projecting himself and his fantasies on puppets, being a bit of a trickster and a magician.

Indeed, his talents were such that had the means been available, he would have been sent off to school and university. As it was, he got two years at a local private school, giving him a foundation in ancient history, Latin, and German, all of which he would put to good use. He also took lessons in painting and began to dream of a career in that art. He read avidly, including the Bible, of which he was always fond. It is not known exactly what else he read, or what he saw of theater, but Skien offered opportunities for both, however limited. It *is* known that at an early age he determined to get to the university and study medicine. In 1843, perhaps as a way station to this goal, he accepted a job offered him as an apothecary's apprentice in Grimstad, a seaport down the coast, even smaller than Skien.

The Apothecary's Apprentice

So he emerged into the world, pushed out of the nest by economic need, relieved to escape from a home he had already rejected. At the apothecary he lived his real life in the night, reading, writing, drawing. He remained wholly outside the "society" of the town and put himself even further beyond the pale by fathering a son on one of the maids, a country girl whom he did not marry.

Yet he soon became the center of his own circle of young men, where he was known for his "bubbling humor." His wit and his paradoxical views made him a focus of merriment, which combined with his status as an outsider to attract like-minded young people and bring out the bohemian in him. Meanwhile he began preparing for the entrance exams at the university by writing compositions for a tutor in Christiania. One of the few preserved was prophetically entitled "On the Importance of Self-Knowledge." Penned at age twenty, this essay presented views from which he would never deviate: "Even if a man, by acquiring this self-knowledge, gets to know his worst characteristics and so finds himself required to humble himself in his own eyes, such humiliation can in no way impair his self-respect, since it provides evidence of a strong will and an honest quest for what should be man's goal in life—the development of his spiritual gifts and a care for his temporal well-being."[18]

The best of the friends he made in Grimstad were a customs clerk, Christopher Due, and a student, Ole Schulerud. To them he could reveal his ambitious plans and radical views. They shared a common poverty, which led Ibsen to scorn those who had "empty brains with full wallets."[19] His heretical views on religion, love, and morality were already arousing attention. The February Revolution of 1848 in France was an electrifying event to our bohemian rebel, and he applauded the uprisings that threatened the European order established by Metternich. We have seen above how he expressed his feelings in verse and eventually in the verse drama *Catiline*. Its fiery opening lines can stand for Ibsen's own determination to reform himself and his society:

> I must! I must! Deep down within my soul
> A voice commands, and I will do its bidding;—
> I feel I have the courage and the strength
> To lead a better, nobler life than this—
> One endless round of dissipated pleasures![20]

Rome is corrupt, its citizens either power-mad or pleasure-seeking, i.e., bourgeois like Cicero or bohemian like Catiline. But now Catiline resolves to purify Rome and restore the city to its pristine virtues. Unhappily his own irresponsible past rises up like a ghost in the shape of Furia, the dark woman whose sister he seduced, and she drives him on to ruin. The good in him, represented by his wife Aurelia, struggles in vain against his evil genius. He asks himself characteristically:

> Is life then not an unabating struggle
> Between the hostile forces in the soul?
> And in this struggle lies the soul's true life.[21]

Catiline's inability to resolve this struggle and win harmony destroys him in the end, as it will other Ibsen heroes in later and more mature plays.

Career and Marriage

By leaving Grimstad for Christiania in 1850, Ibsen took his second step into a larger world. For the first time he met people "of his own generation whose horizons were European."[22] The capital and its university were the goal of those who, like Ibsen, were hoping to find a place in the new cultural life of the country. For those who, again like Ibsen, were indifferent scholars, there were the diversions of the theater and journalism. One of Ibsen's was to join some student radicals in editing *Manden* ("The Man"), later known as *Andhrimner*, a short-lived literary and political magazine. He took a job at a workingman's Sunday school and almost got thrown in jail when its leaders were arrested as potential subversives. Journalism offered him opportunities to write dramatic criticism, to draw cartoons, and to print political commentary. Less an ardent patriot than a Scandinavian unionist, he was willy-nilly swept up in the nationalistic movement as a protégé of Ole Bull, mentioned above. In Bergen he eked out his living by putting on plays that the public wanted, while programmatically required to write plays that the public rejected, perhaps because they were more pedagogical than entertaining, all for the national cause.

Ibsen did his bounden duty, turning out *The Burial Mound*, based on Viking romance, *St. John's Night*, drawn from folklore, *Lady Inger*, an episode of Norwegian history, *The Feast at Solhoug* and *Olaf Liljekrans*, using ballad themes, and *The Vikings at Helgeland*, from the Icelandic sagas. They all contain themes and situations that are recognizably Ibsenian, but except for the last they are little more than apprentice pieces. Ibsen was desperately trying to conform to the requirements of his job, suppressing the rebel in him, aside from an occasional flash. Only when he fell in love with a young girl, Rikke Holst, ten years his junior, could he impulsively pour out some of his real thinking. She later reported: "He could suddenly start to talk in a frenzied, ruthless torrent of words—paradoxes and wild truths, so that one walked bewitched beside the little man as he exploded savagely against all conventions."[23] He won her heart and courted her with poems, but when her father caught up with them, Ibsen turned tail and ran. The bourgeois father would have no bohemian for a son-in-law. In 1856, three years later, Henrik met Suzannah Thoresen, who proved to be the right wife for him—a woman with a firm character and progressive views, and one who was willing to put up with the bohemian and could also set him firmly on the path to his future career. By this time he had had his first success in the theater, and Suzannah's stepmother, the Danish Magdalene Thoresen, encouraged his suit. She herself had literary ambitions and sensed in her son-in-law a bohemianism akin to her own (she may have been a model for Ellida in his *Lady from the Sea*).

In ways we can probably never fully assess, marriage provided for Ibsen the focal point in which his warring selves could meet: freedom with responsibility. "Only after I was married," he wrote in 1870, "did my life take on serious meaning." "Her character is just the kind I need, illogical, but naturally poetic, with a great-souled way of thinking, and an almost violent hatred of all things petty."[24] In a poem expressing his gratitude to her, he wrote:

> Her kin is the shifting
> Pageant of shapes
> That stride through my song
> With banners aloft.[25]

Her thinking must certainly have influenced his handling of the themes of love and renunciation in the narrative poem "On the Heights" (*Paa Vidderne*) of 1859[26] and the verse drama *Love's Comedy* of 1862. In both of these the hero is faced with a choice between family responsibility, the bourgeois life, and an art that demands total commitment, freedom to create, the bohemian's detachment from life. In poem as well as play the ironic conclusion is that domesticity destroys creativity, so that the only way for the artist is to renounce love in reality and treasure it as material for art. In these works Ibsen succeeded for the first time in giving artistically satisfying form to the dramatic conflict between his own warring selves.

Ibsen won significant support from the friends he made on his return to Christiania, a bookish and critical circle of men who called themselves the "Learned Hollanders," with the litterateur Paul Botten Hansen as its chief luminary. Here he could release his bohemian self in a torrent of talk which earned him the nickname "Gert Westphaler," a reference to the talkative barber in a comedy by Ludvig Holberg.

The Call of the Heights

"On the Heights" may be described as a symphonic poem in nine parts, telling the story of a huntsman who sets off for the mountains

> With knapsack o'er my shoulder
> And rifle loaded on my arm.

He leaves his mother and his sweetheart behind, after many tender farewells, promising them to be back as soon as possible. But on the mountain heights he gains a new perspective on his life:

> Once more inspired here I stand,
> My blood is now so cool.
> I tread beneath my feet
> A life, not half—and far less whole,
> A life between remorse and sin.

Here he meets another hunter, a stranger who fixes him with his glittering eye and eloquently holds forth on the freedom the heights can give. Our hero decides to spend the winter, and he dreams of bringing mother and bride up to him in the spring, in order to

> Teach them all my newer wisdom,
> Wake their laughter at their home;
> Soon life mid ice-encircled wastes
> Will not seem strange to them.

This is not to be, for while he stays away, his mother dies when her cottage burns, and his bride-to-be marries someone else. He can see these events from the heights, and the strange hunter teaches him to look at them with detachment. He points out the esthetic effect of viewing them through his cupped hand, as pictures: see the fire in dramatic contrast against the snow or the bride's red skirt against the green birches! Our hero responds:

> Now I am steeled; I follow the call
> That commands me to strive for the heights!
> My life in the lowlands is lived to the end;
> Up here on the heights is freedom and God,
> While the others but fumble below.

In *Love's Comedy* the hero also chooses to follow the call to the heights, but only after a painful parting from his beloved. We are first entertained by a comic spectacle of engagements and marriages in all stages, where the edge of love is blunted by the petty considerations of bourgeois life. The only free spirits, with some of the daring of the bohemian in them, are Falk ("falcon"), a would-be poet, and the sensitive young Svanhild, whose viking name suggests some of the "great-souled way of thinking" that Ibsen attributed to his wife. Falk's indecision leads her to say to him:

> You're like two different characters,
> Unreconciled . . .[27]

Like the author, he is torn between his conflicting goals.

Falk invites Svanhild to join him courageously "in freedom," which he defines as "fulfilling one's calling all the way." He regards her calling as that of being his inspiration, but she coldly tells him that she is not interested in being the wind that inflates his poet-kite. Only when he shows her that he will break with the conventions of his society does she gladly join him in a battle for freedom and truth. At this point the merchant Guldstad ("Goldstead"), representing the practical, bourgeois point of view, offers Svanhild marriage based on the solid advantages of material comfort. He even generously offers them financial assistance if they should decide to marry, but only on condition that Falk assure Svanhild he will love her forever. When he is unable to do so, the lovers sadly part, realizing that only in this way can their love live on forever—as a beautiful memory. Falk goes on to fulfill his mission:

> As poet, yes; for every man's a poet
> In schoolroom, government or church,
> Each one, of high or low estate,
> Who in his task envisions the ideal.[28]

Off he goes with a band of fellow singers, merrily caroling as they climb the mountainside:

> What if I've run my vessel aground,
> How lovely it was to go sailing.[29]

In these two works, with their original blending of wit and wisdom, Ibsen found expression as never before for his own peculiar form of psychological dualism. The conformist in him values the stable advantages of bourgeois living, whereas the rebel proclaims the freedom of the bohemian artist. Home, mother, bride, all the social obligations of the well-adjusted citizen are pictured as confining and injurious to the free human spirit. The true artist breaks out of the shell, seeing life "through the cupped hand," seeking out the hardships of the heights, where he or she can roam at will and observe life from afar—as a drama that no longer concerns the artist personally. This is not done lightly: at first the artist has a bleeding heart, but then steels his or her will and does like the hunter in "On the Heights":

> The flood in my veins no longer streams,
> And I think I mark in the vaults of my heart
> The symptoms of petrifaction.[30]

Life or Art?

Ibsen had finally succeeded in making his inner conflict the theme of his art and thereby sublimating it. The mountains became a metaphor, a very natural one for an ardent hiker and lover of Norwegian nature, for the distancing from life that a poet needs in order to see life clearly. The mountains became an Archimedean point, from which one would move the world. They afforded perspective, though they were still within sight of humanity. We observe this rebellious bohemian again and again in Ibsen's later writing, always affording relief from the settled values of the social order. One recalls the dissipated genius Ejlert Løvborg in *Hedda Gabler* and the tattered, but buoyant Ulrik Brendel in *Rosmersholm*. Not only are they significant as characters, but they contribute spice and spirit to what might otherwise be a drab spectacle.

Gustave Flaubert, another great writer torn between conformity and rebellion, was writing at about the same time: "You can depict wine, love, women, and great exploits on the condition that you are not a drunkard, a lover, a husband, or a hero. If you are involved in life, you see it badly; your sight is affected either by suffering or by enjoyment."[31] In Shaw's *Man and Superman* Tanner says to Octavius: "The true artist will let his wife starve, his children go barefoot, his mother drudge for his living at seventy, sooner than work at anything but his art."[32] In 1950 Tennessee Williams wrote, "What choice has the artist, now, but withdrawal into the caverns of his own isolated being?"[33] The American poet Marianne Moore showed the world an "upper middle-American-spinster role," but within "she choose to house the radically innovative poet."[34]

Clearly Ibsen was not alone in his sense of conflict between life and art. But it was something he had to discover for himself, and the realization came just in time. He was at the ebb of his career, when his theater in Christiania was going bankrupt. He had left Bergen in 1857 to become artistic director of Christiania Norwegian Theater, a second theater in the capital; in 1862 it closed its doors. Ibsen is said to have become slovenly, alcoholic, inattentive to his work.[35] But the writing of "On the Heights" and *Love's Comedy* resolved his artistic problem and set him securely on the road to fame. In 1864, when he was at last enabled to go abroad and devote himself to nothing but writing, he found his Mecca, like so many other Scandinavian artists of the time, in Italy. Emerging from the Alps into the Italian sunshine gave him the feeling of being "released from the darkness into light, from the mists through a tunnel into the sunshine."[36]

Among the artists and writers of the Scandinavian Club (*Circolo Scandinavico*) of Rome, Ibsen could express much of his pent-up bohemianism. His first explosions took the form of indignant attacks on the prudent policy followed by Norway-Sweden in 1864 in "deserting" the Danish cause. Germany had crushed the Danish army and annexed the duchies of Schleswig-Holstein. Lorentz Dietrichson tells of a dramatic evening when Ibsen began speaking after a frugal dinner and a glass of wine under the summer sky: "His voice rang out, and in the evening dusk one saw only his burning eyes. When he had finished, no one cheered or touched his glass, but I think we all felt that this evening the Marseillaise of the North had rung out in the Roman night air."[37] Gradually Ibsen relaxed his anger and proved to be "sociable, cheerful, and friendly." His taste in art was for the baroque, above all Michelangelo and his school: "Those fellows had the courage to commit a folly now and then."[38] Taciturn he could be, but he was also loquacious, especially after some glasses of Falernian wine. Count Snoilsky, the Swedish poet, immortalized this phase of his life in some verses from 1898:

> I hear you speaking
> Into the night,
> Lightning flashing
> Beneath the big hat![39]

We need not trace here the endlessly varied forms in which Ibsen expressed his basic personality conflict in his plays. Nor will it be possible or necessary to pursue the obvious psychological or psychoanalytic aspects.[40] Although these are interesting, they can apply as well to madness as to genius, and it is a bit late to cure Ibsen's schizoid tendencies, even had we wished to do so. An interested psychiatrist cited by Meyer holds that "people of this temperament may be led into creativity because they (a) want to create an imaginary world in which everything can be controlled, and (b) want to avoid the unpredictability and spontaneity of real relationships with real people."[41]

Ibsen often complained of loneliness, which no doubt was accentuated by his love/hate relationship to Bjørnson, who had already made himself the popular poet of Norwegian nationalism. Perhaps by way of apology, Ibsen wrote to him, "I can never bring myself to strip completely. I have the feeling that where personal relationships are concerned, I can give only false expression to what I feel deep down inside, to my true self, and that is why I prefer to shut it up within me."[42] His status as a loner is reflected in his emphasis on the unique and the individual.

A May Sun in a September Life

Ibsen's loneliness was only intensified during his long exile abroad from 1864 to 1891, years in which his life comprised little else than devotion to his art. There was an inverse relation between his fame and his affability: the more famous he became, the more unapproachable he made himself. Besides his creative work, he had to supervise business matters connected with the publication, translation, and performance of his plays, work nowadays turned over to an agent by most authors. Not only was he personally frugal, but he also proved to have a sharp eye for finances and investments. He made occasional trips, chiefly to receive honors, and often vacationed in the Alps. He received a few personal friends and colleagues but limited his associations as much as possible. His wife destroyed most of their letters to each other, regarding their relations as "nobody else's business." We would know very little about his home life were it not for the chatty reminiscences of his daughter-in-law Bergljot. She shared with her father Bjørnson an outgoing nature that led her to write down and later publish what the Ibsens would no doubt have preferred to keep to themselves.[43]

In the earlier years, while they struggled together against poverty, Henrik would amuse his wife and himself by drawing fanciful bank notes payable to her in the future, decorated with figures playfully representing his wife. But as the years went on, his severe routine and her poor health quenched some of the fires within. As early as 1868 a young Danish friend in Rome had noted his "demonic pursuit of literary fame" and had speculated on the effect of this on their marital relations.[44] This problem was to be the theme of Ibsen's plays of old age, an experience he clearly had himself lived through.

However, the bohemian within could not be contained forever. In 1889 the inner self broke through its shell in search of a youth that burned within as hotly as ever. It happened while he was summering in the mountain village of Gossensass in the Tyrol after an absence of five years. He was now a famous man, and the villagers honored him by naming his old lookout spot the "Ibsenplatz" and by holding a grand celebration. Among the summer guests was a well-brought-up young woman from Vienna, Emilie Bardach, eighteen years old. To her astonishment and gratification the great man singled her out for special attention. She was overwhelmed and involved herself in a passionate, and for both of them a hopeless, whirlwind affair. Our evidence for what actually happened is scanty but sufficient to piece together an impression of its importance for Ibsen. We have seven letters to her from Ibsen, written after his return to Munich, and two from her to him. She later reminisced about it in print and orally, and released extracts from her diary to an American scholar. Deeply revealing are the words Ibsen wrote on the photograph of himself he sent her, two months later: *"An die Maisonne eines Septemberlebens"* —"To the May sun of a September life." In *The Master Builder* Hilde Wangel recalls the exact day when Solness kissed her ten years earlier: it was September 19, which was just eight days before Ibsen and Emilie parted. Could the date have been, as Koht suggests, a cryptic message to Emilie in Vienna?[45]

Ibsen never met Emilie again, but we seem to see her figure or some aspects of her character in the series of passionate young women in the plays that followed: Hedda, Hilde, Rita, Irene. Their passions are all frustrated by their men's concern for career. It is a curious fact that none of the four young women who are known to have been friends with Ibsen in his last years ever married. The most devoted of them was the Norwegian pianist Hildur Andersen, with whom he often appeared in public in the years after his return to Christiania. Irene in *When We Dead Awaken* accuses sculptor Rubek of having merely used her as a model. But when Brandes in 1895 sent Ibsen an essay on an infatuation of Goethe's old age, he responded warmly: "When I think of the quality that characterizes Goethe's work during that period, I mean the sense of renewed youth, I ought to have guessed that he must have been graced with some such revelation, some such reassurance of beauty . . ."[46]

Ibsen's duality is amusingly reflected in the two pictures Erik Werenskiold made of him in 1895. The official portrait is solemn, even majestic, painted against a background of the heights and peaks toward which he aspired. But one day during the sittings, Ibsen commented on a painter who had done his portrait in Rome, "He was in the habit of painting saints, so I was not a very good subject for him." He chuckled, and later Werenskiold made a drawing from memory of

"The Laughing Ibsen." Werenskiold was a famous fairytale illustrator, and his drawing makes Ibsen look like the old troll king of the mountains breaking into a smile. This, no doubt, is the smile that graced his stern face many a time when he began telling tales in the company of his bohemian friends.[47]

The answer to the question contained in the title of this chapter must be that within his person Ibsen housed at once a bohemian and a bourgeois. Much of the dramatic tension in his work comes from the way in which he dialectically expressed these two identities in his plays. It was not for nothing that he described the process of literary creation as "holding judgment day on one's self."[48]

READINGS AND REFERENCES

The major biographies of Ibsen in English are: (1) Halvdan Koht, *Life of Ibsen*, trans. Einar Haugen and A. E. Santaniello (New York: Blom, 1971). Koht, a Norwegian historian and statesman, published it as *Henrik Ibsen: Eit diktarliv*, 2 vols. (Oslo: Aschehoug, 1928–29). This was translated into English by Ruth L. McMahon and Hanna Astrup Larsen (New York: Norton, 1931). In 1954 a new, greatly revised edition was published in Oslo by Aschehoug; this is the edition translated by Haugen and Santaniello, in consultation with the author. (2) Michael Meyer, *Ibsen: A Biography* (New York: Doubleday, 1971). Meyer is an English writer and translator, whose work is less critical than Koht's but is more comprehensive and readable; it is a book to be grateful for.

A detailed treatment of Ibsen's personality split is in Charles R. Lyons, *Henrik Ibsen: The Divided Consciousness* (Carbondale, Ill.: Southern Illinois University Press, 1972), which the author calls "the first attempt to read Ibsen's plays primarily as explorations of consciousness." (Preface, p. xiv.) For psychoanalytic views see note 38 to chapter 1.

Books dealing with particular parts of Ibsen's life are Oskar Mosfjeld, *Henrik Ibsen og Skien* (Oslo: Gyldendal, 1949); Einar Østvedt, *Henrik Ibsen: Barndom og ungdom* (Skien: Rasmussen, 1973); Einar Østvedt, *Henrik Ibsen som student og blant studenter* (Skien: Rasmussen, 1971). Ibsenforbundet, founded 1948, has published since 1952 an Ibsen Yearbook (known as *Årbok* or *Ibsenårbok*) in which many biographical articles, as well as critical essays, have appeared. For a survey of its contents see Einar Østvedt, *Ibsenforbundet gjennom 25 år: 1948–1973* (Skien: Rasmussen, 1973); Østvedt was the founder of Ibsenforbundet and from 1952 to 1962 editor of its *Årbok*.

2

Topics of the Times

You ask if I would like Dagbladet *sent to Dresden. Yes indeed I would. . . . I wish to have the paper, not because of any vain curiosity about news, but because I am in this way drawn more closely and intimately to the life of my home and am strengthened in my work.*

Ibsen to his publisher, 10 October 1868.[1]

EARLY ENGLISH (and American) commentators on Ibsen's plays were fond of calling the author "provincial."[2] It is hard today to recapture exactly what they meant by this, though it seems to suggest a certain lack of sophistication. Even Henry James, who came to admire him, used the term.[3] It implies certain limitations, which hardly apply, for example, to a work like *Hedda Gabler*.

It may be bold to suggest that it was the critics who were provincial rather than Ibsen. The mainstream of British tradition was more insular than continental. Ibsen himself was firmly planted in the cultural tradition of the European continent, and its worthy heir, in spite of having grown up at its northern limits. For all his narrow, confining circumstances, he succeeded in gaining deep insight (almost by sheer osmosis, it seems) into the main currents of thought in his time. Even his plays with historical themes draw on the life of his day. He gave his figures shapes that were recognizable by his contemporaries. If they at first seemed strange in Victorian England, it could have been because of the insularity of the era.

In this chapter I shall sketch the context of reference against which we must understand Ibsen's plays. What kinds of topics did he select for treatment and embody in the speech and action of his characters? In short, what were his plays about—in a surface sense? We shall probe more deeply later.

At least five major traditions of European life and letters come together in Ibsen's plays and are often so intertwined that it is hard to disentangle them. I shall take them up in roughly the same order that they became dominant in Ibsen's thinking and emerge in the plays, explaining the concerns that animate his plots and characters. These five traditions are classicism, romanticism, Christianity, idealism, and realism/naturalism.

Classicism

When Ibsen started writing, there were still universities at which lectures were given in Latin. Although this was no longer true in Christiania, knowledge of Latin and Greek was required for admission (Ibsen failed his Greek, which kept him from becoming a full-fledged student). The heritage of Rome and Greece was potent even in a Protestant and Germanic-speaking country like Norway, which had never been occupied by the Romans and which had rejected Roman Catholicism in the sixteenth century.

As we have seen, Ibsen's reading of Cicero and Sallust provided him with hero and setting for his first play, *Catiline*. His early training in Grimstad was supplemented at the so-called Student Factory in Christiania. At this cramming school a classical enthusiast named Henrik Heltberg tried to pound more Latin into the heads of would-be university students, whom he called his "barbarians." One of them, the writer Arne Garborg, later portrayed him (in a novel) as holding forth on his beloved poet Horace and life in his grape arbor: "There they lived ideally! With wreaths of vine leaves in their hair they lay at table by the purling spring, drinking the sparkling Falernian wine to the accompaniment of the lyre."[4] This may even have been Ibsen's source for Hedda's romantic concept of beauty, the "vine leaves in the hair," which she tried to force upon Løvborg at his bacchanalia. Ibsen also used the image in *Emperor and Galilean*, where Julian the Apostate wears them as a symbol of pagan beauty.

Catiline was a figure of the Roman republic, a pagan nobleman; Julian was emperor of the Roman empire, a Christian who tried to restore paganism. But they were not alone in reflecting Ibsen's classicism. Ibsen claimed that he conceived the form of *Brand* in St. Peter's

Church in Rome (perhaps its magnificent dome suggested the "ice church" towering over the play), and it is significant that the voice on high which speaks through the avalanche at the end breaks into Latin when pronouncing judgment on Brand: "He is *deus caritatis*"— the God of love. Again, in Ibsen's final avalanche, at the end of *When We Dead Awaken*, as the lovers Rubek and Maja go down to destruction, the blessing on them is spoken in Latin: "*Pax vobiscum!*"—peace be with you.

We have seen that on his arrival in Rome in 1864, Ibsen's first interest was in baroque art. After some months his eyes were also opened to the beauty of classical sculpture, no doubt with the help of Lorentz Dietrichson. In a letter to Bjørnson he wrote enthusiastically of the figure of the Tragic Muse in the Vatican: "I venture to maintain that through this I have come to realize what Greek tragedy was. This indescribably exalted, calm, and powerful joy in its facial expression, this richly laureled head, with something ethereally rapturous and bacchantic about it, eyes that gaze inward and at the same time through and far beyond what they are looking at—just so was Greek tragedy."[5]

The entire fourth act of *Peer Gynt* takes place in the Mediterranean world, as a kind of comic *Odyssey* in reverse. Even though the world Peer observes is a North African, contemporary Moslem one, some of its chief monuments, like the Great Sphinx and the statue of Memnon, are from classical times. There is an amusing reference to Mount Olympus, abode of the Greek gods (his Englishman wants to extract water power from the Castalian springs of poetry), and they are all on their way to Greece to profit from the Greek rebellion against the Turks. The Odyssean parallel appears in the faithfulness of the waiting wives (Penelope and Solveig) and the roving eyes of the husband-travelers (Odysseus and Peer). In this act the Norwegian folklore themes of the preceding acts are given classical sublimation, as when the Dovre king is transformed into the Great Sphinx.

Ibsen also showed his fondness for classical mythology in a remarkable philosophic poem of December 1870, "Balloon Letter to a Swedish Lady." (Formally it was a thank-you note, conveyed by "balloon" in allusion to the beleaguered Paris commune of that year.) Ibsen contrasted the gods of Greece and Rome favorably with those of ancient Egypt, where he had recently been a delegate. The gods of Egypt, he wrote, are now mere "nameless corpses in their crypts":

> None received the call to live,
> None the privilege of sinning,
> Or to rise and sin no more.

By contrast the classical deities live on in human memory as real personalities:

> Where personality is absent,
> Where the form does not convey
> Hate, anger, ecstasy, or joy,
> The beat of pulse, the throb of blood—
> There the whole magnificence
> Is but a skeleton's dry rattle.[6]

Romanticism

By the time Ibsen began writing, the romantic movement in other European countries had already peaked. But in Norway it still flourished in a form derived from Germany, one which emphasized its nationalistic aspects. More than in England, romanticism in Germany and Scandinavia took the form of an assertion of native values against classical influence and foreign, especially French, domination; it was an important force in welding the many small German states into a single nation. The equivalent in Norway was what has been called "the Norwegian myth." The newly reestablished Norwegian state needed to find again its historical and cultural identity. Exactly how this should be done was a matter of concern and debate during Ibsen's youth.

The upper middle class described earlier, the "establishment," declared its loyalty to the united Norwegian-Swedish monarchy, which meant the king of Sweden, and simultaneously maintained cultural ties with Denmark by following Danish models of writing. A number of idealistic young people, especially students, saw these ties as hopeful preludes to a united Scandinavia, politically as well as culturally. This dream was shattered, for a very long time at least, by the events of 1864, when Sweden and Norway prudently looked the other way while Germany seized the disputed Danish provinces. We have seen evidence of Ibsen's bitterness at this "treachery."

Even within a Scandinavian union there would be room for a Norwegian identity, and the romantics were eager to cultivate the treasures of the Norwegian past. They saw history as a guide for the future and drew on writings of the Middle Ages for inspiration, above all the sagas and poems of the Old Norse period. They also followed Rousseau in seeking out the values of nature and the simple life among the unspoiled common people. The poet Henrik Wergeland (1807–45) was a pioneer in this work, and Bjørnson, as the great advocate of literary nationalism, followed him enthusiastically. Their work bore rich fruit, making nineteenth-century Norway culturally autonomous and innovative, no longer a blank spot on the European map but the home of a culture that could boast of world-renowned names.

Ibsen's role in this movement was of unquestioned significance, though in some ways against his will. He first contributed by writing plays for Ole Bull's Norwegian Theater in Bergen and then by directing the Norwegian Theater in Christiania. Unlike Bjørnson, he was not entirely at home in a movement that called for strong emotional attachment and political activism. He felt that much of the patriotic sentiment was sheer bombast. In his first original play from Bergen, *St. John's Night* (1853), he satirized a would-be poet, Julian, who spouts nationalist sentiments. Julian declares that he has fallen in love with a wood nymph, the so-called *huldre*, symbol of Norwegian folklore, but is now bitterly disillusioned on learning that she has a cow's tail! In *Peer Gynt* Ibsen will have great fun with the same concept, in the more appropriate setting of the hall of the Dovre king. Here Peer is enticed by the Greenclad Woman, only to discover on closer inspection that she and all her kin are ugly and animalistic: endowed with the bovine appendage as their hallmark.

Ibsen was not unpatriotic; he was just not a 100 percent superpatriot. He understood the value of the sagas as material for imaginative literature and even applied for stipends to collect folklore. He made one field trip for this purpose, hiking across the mountain divide between east and west Norway. In reviewing the performance of a folkloristic play, he formulated his own policy: "A national author is one who finds the best way of embodying in his work that keynote which rings out to us from mountain and valley, from meadow and shore, but above all from within our own selves."[7] The crucial words are the last: ". . . from within our own selves." From 1863 to 1867 he would write in rapid succession three plays based on materials that expressed his idea of the "keynote" of his nationality. *The Pretenders* recreated an episode from the royal sagas of Norway's medieval magnificence, when its kings dominated the north Atlantic. A cautionary tale on the dangers of sectional and partisan squabbling, the play gave a perspective on the past that was fully applicable to the present. *Brand* struck the keynote of life in the west Norwegian fjords, constricted, rugged, puritanical—as Ibsen had observed it on his folklore expedition. *Peer Gynt* rang out with an entirely different tone, the more relaxed, easygoing, relatively well-off life in an east Norwegian valley, humorous and lighthearted. Based as the play was on materials mostly collected by Peter C. Asbjørnsen, it reflected a comic spirit. Each of the three plays embodied healthy criticism of the complacency and self-glorification that can become the bane of all nationalism.

By holding up an honest mirror to his people, Ibsen contributed to the strengthening of their spirit. In *Brand* the hero tells the mayor that the Norwegians of his day had about as much in common with the Vikings as the Greek pirates of his day had with Homer and Euripides:

> A dwarf won't reach the stature of a man,
> Although Goliath was his ancestor![8]

Yet his *Vikings at Helgeland* is probably the best play ever written about Vikings. Saga characters like the heroic Sigurd and his friend Gunnar, or their respective wives Dagny and Hjørdis, as well as the poet from Iceland, Ørnulf, live in his play as intensely human personalities. *Lady Inger* deals with the sensitive problem of Norway's failure to win its independence from Denmark in the sixteenth century, when Sweden won its freedom. The problem is concentrated in the single personality of Lady Inger: she lacks the strength to be at the same time a national leader and a loving woman. In *The Pretenders* the outcome is ambiguous. On the one hand there is the delightfully villainous Bishop Nikolas, who not only plays the opponents off against one another but returns in Act V as a ghost, to prophesy the future of his countrymen. The bishop will always be there—

> Whenever hearts shrivel, whenever minds cringe
> And bend like willows before the wind—[9]

On the other hand there is the noble King Haakon, with his divinely inspired idea: "Norway was a *kingdom*, it shall become a *nation*."[10] National identity was an anachronism in the thirteenth century, but (as we have seen) a very lively issue in the nineteenth.

In *Peer Gynt* Ibsen made extensive use of folklore and ballad material but he did not sentimentalize it or even take it seriously. He wove it into a philosophical rhapsody so skillful and appealing that it *has* become a major symbol of Norwegian national identity. Professor Francis Bull, leading historian of Norwegian literature, once emphatically declared that if only one book could be taken with them abroad, many or most Norwegians would choose *Peer Gynt*.[11] Yet the picture of folk life is something less than edifying: the wedding at Hægstad farm is a riot of dancing, drinking, and wenching, climaxed by Peer Gynt's bride-snatching and his flight to the hills. Act II with the trolls in the mountains presents a still more grotesque caricature of the Norwegian people.

Even during Ibsen's deliberate exile from his country, lasting from 1864 to 1891 except for two visits home, his most productive years, he kept abreast of events in the North. After eight years abroad he wrote, "In the night and in my writing I am at home."[12] In his epigrammatic poem, "Burnt Ships" (1871), he subtly expressed a love of country that was worth many national anthems:

> He turned his prows
> Away from the North;
> Sought brighter gods
> Where he sailed forth.
>
> The snowland's beacons
> Were quenched in the deep,
> As fauns of the Southland
> Lulled him to sleep.
>
> He burned his ships;—
> Smoke of blue
> Like a streaking bridge
> To the Northland flew.
>
> To hearths of the snowland
> From sun-drenched tides
> Each night of the year
> A horseman rides.[13]

Christianity

The Christian tradition was an all-encompassing part of Ibsen's context, even when he rejected some aspects of it. No study of Ibsen's work should overlook the fact that he and his audiences were trained from childhood in the fundamentals of the Bible, the Lutheran catechism, and the rituals of the Norwegian Lutheran church. Christianity was established in Norway at the end of the Viking Age, after several vain attempts, by King Olaf Haraldsson, who was martyred in 1030 and became Norway's first and greatest saint. Five centuries later, in 1537, the king of Denmark-Norway abolished the Catholic church, sweeping away its practices and institutions, and set up a new church after the teachings of Doctor Martin Luther.

A major innovation was that the new Lutheran church was national, not international; each country had its own church, with the king as its nominal head. In this way the church became part of the state, and its ministers state officials. Not only was religion institutionalized, but it could become a supporter of national sentiment.

In Ibsen's plays the representatives of the Lutheran church do not come off well. The medieval Bishop Nikolas in *The Pretenders*, however villainous, is at least a personality of dimensions. The Lutheran pastors are, with few exceptions, defenders of the status quo, weak-kneed representatives of the establishment. In *Love's Comedy* the Reverend Strawman is a comic, if at times pathetic figure. The dean in *Brand* is a pompous authoritarian, who does his best to cool the religious fervor of young Pastor Brand. The Reverend Manders in *Ghosts* is childishly naive, easily taken in by sanctimonious talk, deeply shocked by any idea that is the least bit radical.

Brand embodies all that the rest of the clergy is not, and because he rebels against its temporizing, he is gradually driven out of the church. His rebellion is fired by ideals that the church itself proclaims —a sacrifice for Christ. In his speech to Agnes and Einar he scorns the usual idea of God as an old man:

> . . . grey and bald, as old chaps are,
> With a long silvery beard, like pendent ice?
> He looks good-natured, but he's stern enough
> To make a child at night afraid of Him.
> Whether you gave Him slippers on His feet
> I really couldn't say—we'll let that pass;
> But certainly skull-cap and spectacles
> Would be appropriate accessories.[14]

Brand's God, on the contrary, is "young, like Hercules, And not a grandpa-God, in life's decline." Behind Brand we glimpse that real-life rebel against the Lutheran church establishment, the Danish philosopher Kierkegaard. Brand's call for "all or nothing" seems a paraphrase of Kierkegaard's "either-or." In Ibsen's pastor we recognize the challenge of institution by individual, an important element in the doctrines of Jesus, one which led to His crucifixion by the authorities of His day.

Ibsen's ending, however, leaves it unclear whether Brand's mission has failed or succeeded. As the avalanche buries him, a voice cries out, "He is the God of love." This could mean either that by his sacrifice he has won God's love or that he has been unable to reconcile his ideals with divine charity. Like so many of Ibsen's epigrammatic conclusions, it is double-edged, ambiguous.

Even though Ibsen threw an unflattering light on the usual Christian clergy, he did so in the name of Christian ideals of perfection. His rejection of the church did not extend to his personal life. When his son married Bjørnson's daughter, Ibsen (against Bjørnson's wishes) insisted on a church wedding. The great Norwegian humanist and polar explorer Fridtjof Nansen once testified that Brand's exhortations for the "wholeness of will" were a vital inspiration to him on his pioneer crossing of the Greenland ice. Having like Brand cut off all retreat, he could only go forward, staking everything on his personal strength and courage.

In *Peer Gynt* Ibsen created a play that can be (and has been) read almost directly as a Christian sermon.[15] The pastor who delivers the funeral sermon in act V even seems to speak with Ibsen's own tongue. He extols the man who had "been himself," in spite of early shame and humble circumstances, by living a life of quiet devotion to duty. As a builder and homemaker he had atoned for the cowardice that had made him cut off two fingers to escape the draft. Peer Gynt is passing by and stops to listen to the sermon. Self-deceiver that he is, he takes the pastor's praise to himself, an ironic act, since we know that he has violated every Christian precept in his own life. The sermon is one of the impulses toward Peer's ultimate self-realization. Eventually he is made fully aware of the emptiness of his life, which then enables him to receive the Christlike mercy of his beloved Solveig. As a symbol of divine love she receives and forgives him while the churchgoers are intoning the hymns of Whitsuntide.

The paradox has often been noted: the rascal Peer is saved, but the heroic Brand is sacrificed. This is not surprising in terms of Christian teaching. Elsewhere, too, Ibsen reflects basic concepts from his early religious training, e.g., in his puritanical attitudes toward sex as a sinful impulse to be restrained. He lays great emphasis on the confession of sins, as when Bernick, in *Pillars of Society* reveals his dishonest manipulations, or when Rebecca in *Rosmersholm* admits her complicity in Beate's death. Those who sin are required to atone for their sins through some kind of personal sacrifice. In the many contests between paganism and Christianity in his plays, Christianity appears to be the stronger. Yet he equates paganism with happiness, which the Christian ethic is forever destroying.

Idealism

In the Scandinavian and German world within which Ibsen spent most of his life, the dominant philosophy was the "idealism" of G. W. F. Hegel (1770–1831). We do not know what Ibsen had read of Hegel, but his one reference to him is such that he must have read something. In 1873, when Brandes sent him his 1869 translation of John Stuart Mill's *Utilitarianism* (1863), Ibsen rejected its "philistinism" and expressed amazement "that there are authors who write on philosophy without knowing Hegel."[16] Hegel's work summed up the whole idealistic tradition from Plato through Kant. His ideas were "in the air," having influenced the Norwegian Monrad, who reviewed *Catiline* favorably, and the Danish writer J. L. Heiberg, from whom Ibsen had learned a great deal. Kierkegaard protested certain aspects of Hegel but assumed knowledge of him as basic. Hegel's philosophy was closely allied to romanticism and Christian thinking, both of which, as we have seen, were important to Ibsen.

The play that most clearly reflects Ibsen's philosophical idealism as defined by Hegel is his mammoth historical play of 1873, *Emperor and Galilean*, ten acts divided into two plays.[17] It is a pivot in Ibsen's writing, coming at the exact center of his career, with twelve mostly "romantic" plays before and twelve mostly "realistic" plays after. He devoted more time to this play than to any other, working on it off and on for ten years. He called it "a world-historical drama" and announced that it would be an expression of his positive world view, which many of his readers had demanded. Although he kept insisting that it was his best play—perhaps because he had worked so hard on it—it is so overloaded with characters and elaborate philosophizing that it is probably his least-played and least-read drama. This is regrettable, for it is intensely revealing of Ibsen's thinking.

Although played against a vast panorama of the ancient world, with Constantinople as midpoint, the work is clearly intended as an allegory of the modern conflict between secular and religious views. We shall look more closely at it as a play in the next chapter, considering it here as a vehicle for Ibsen's philosophical views. Julian was brought up as a Christian but chafes under the restrictions of its self-denial. He leaves for Athens to learn about the beauty of ancient Greece, only to find that "the old beauty is no longer beautiful." His attempts to restore paganism fail, and with the help of a mystic named Maximos he tries to create a synthesis of pagan self-expression and Christian self-denial, which will be the "third empire."

The notion of a "third solution," a "third empire," in which the contradictions of life will be resolved, is an old Neoplatonic idea, which was reenforced for Hegel by his study of the Greek tragedians. He saw history as a dialectic conflict between opposing forces, a "thesis," or thrust, that brought about an "antithesis," or counterthrust. These might be harmonized in a higher "synthesis," which again became the thesis of a new conflict, and so on ad infinitum. In *Emperor and Galilean* the conflict is between the empire of the flesh, i.e., of pagan beauty, represented by the Olympian gods, and the empire of the spirit, i.e., of Christian sacrifice, represented by the crucifixion of Jesus. Julian's failure to found a "third empire," which will harmonize the two, is Ibsen's way of saying that the conflict is perpetual and insoluble. Like Kierkegaard, he rejected the possibility of realizing a synthesis in life, which would be just another compromise.

Ibsen saw man as everlastingly split between a higher and a lower self, god and beast, struggling but failing to harmonize the two. In his art he could express this struggle toward the ideal positively in men like Brand, negatively in Peer Gynt. The ideal creates a tension between what we are and what we would like to be, between what is and what we want. In this tension he found the mainspring of dramatic action, a concept out of Hegel and Kierkegaard that corresponded to the conflict between his own two selves. As Brian Johnston (1975) has suggested, the influence of Hegel extends also into the later plays, the "Prose Cycle."

Realism/Naturalism

While plotting *Emperor and Galilean*, Ibsen experimented with a play in prose from the contemporary scene. *The League of Youth* (1869) has proved to be eminently playable, but it is of limited interest and impresses more as an exercise in method than as a great play. Angered by Clemens Petersen's review of *Peer Gynt*, which maintained that the play was not poetry, Ibsen vowed that he would try his hand at "photography." Bjørnson, who had been his model for the noble King Haakon, now recognized himself also in Ibsen's caricature of a liberal orator. He felt it as a stab in the back and relations between them cooled for a good while. Ibsen denied any such intention, suggesting that Bjørnson might have a "bad conscience," and pointed out that to interest the public, the characters had to have recognizable models in contemporary life.[18]

This turn to contemporary life and social problems was in keeping with the literary trends of Ibsen's time. The industrial and scientific development of the early nineteenth century revolutionized the social circumstances of men and women. It also led to widespread rethinking of the purposes of literature. Writers would no longer be entertainers of an idle hour—they wished to educate and inform their readers under the guise of depicting life in all its grim reality. Writers like Balzac and Flaubert in France had created a new realistic novel.

August Comte had laid the foundations of a positivistic world view, one in which Hegelian speculation was replaced by empirical observation of reality. In England the novels of George Eliot and Charles Dickens, with the philosophical-scientific writings of Charles Darwin and John Stuart Mill, contributed to a new, earthbound, but essentially progressive and optimistic view of man's perfectibility.

In Scandinavia many of these new ideas were funneled through the brilliant young critic Georg Brandes (1842–1927), who introduced a new literary epoch by his lectures at the University of Copenhagen. They were published as *Main Currents in Nineteenth Century Literature*, beginning in 1871. At first Brandes had been cool to Ibsen's work, for Brandes's views on esthetics had prevented him from understanding or appreciating Ibsen's poetic dramas from *Love's Comedy* to *Brand*.[19] But Ibsen was delighted by Brandes's critical essay on his work written in 1867, and after they met in 1871, they became fast friends. Their correspondence is the most fruitful of Ibsen's letter-writing efforts. To Brandes, Ibsen makes frank and detailed statements of his views on life and literature, apparently finding him a kindred spirit to whom he could pour out his thoughts more freely than to anyone else. Hand in hand they moved into the "modern" world of realism and naturalism, Ibsen as dramatist, Brandes as critic. They created the period known in Scandinavian literature as the "modern breakthrough."

Ibsen had just passed his fortieth year when these ideas began to germinate in him. With *The League of Youth* he drew blood, and once he got the incubus of his "world-historical drama" off his back, he settled down to writing his series of prose plays about contemporary themes. In *Ghosts* he went well beyond the usual realism into what would be called "naturalism," of which Zola became the chief exponent on the continent. No sharp distinction can be drawn between realism and naturalism, unless it be that the naturalists delved more deeply into the bitter and sordid aspects of life and were less hopeful of reforming the world.

In considering the extraordinary series of a dozen plays that began with *Pillars of Society* and ended with *When We Dead Awaken*, we are conscious that while they all bear the stamp of Ibsen's personality and (as we shall see) his technique, no two of them are alike. Each play is independent, and yet together they form a cycle that could be performed in sequence, as Ibsen wanted them to be read. Each play grows out of the preceding, unfolding like flowers from a common stem. They are naturally divisible into three groups of four each, the *social*, the *psychological*, and the *philosophical*, according to their dominant thematic elements. The most typically social plays (1877–82) are *Pillars of Society*, *A Doll's House*, *Ghosts*, and *An Enemy of the People*. The psychological group (1884–90) includes *The Wild Duck*, *Rosmersholm*, *The Lady from the Sea*, and *Hedda Gabler*. The philosophical (1892–99) are *The Master Builder*, *Little Eyolf*, *John Gabriel Borkman*, and *When We Dead Awaken*. Ibsen himself called these plays a "series" (*en Række*), which "constitute a whole, an entity," rounded off with his "epilogue." As noted earlier, we think of them as Ibsen's "Prose Cycle."[20]

The realism of these plays is evident in the way Ibsen made use of his personal experiences. The scene in *Pillars of Society* brings back Grimstad (just as *The League of Youth* is redolent of his birthplace, Skien).[21] Other issues in *Pillars* were distinctly contemporary: Unseaworthy ships were being debated in England, and the problem was equally sensitive in seafaring and shipowning Norway. The scene with foreman Aune, who represents the workers, reflects the growing restlessness of labor. The return of Lona Hessel and Johan Tønnesen from America reminds us that the late 1870s were a period of unparalleled emigration from Norway of young people looking for greater freedom and opportunities. One of these was the author and painter Aasta Hansteen, who returned from America and became a leading suffragette. Lona's (and Dina's) rebellion against a male-dominated society was also in the spirit of the pioneer woman's rights champion in Norway, novelist Camilla Collett. The feminist issue is foreshadowed in *League*, a secondary theme in *Pillars*, headlined in *A Doll's House*. Nora's story was based rather directly on the sad experience of Laura Kieler, a woman of Ibsen's acquaintance. Like Bjørnson, she felt exposed and exploited, but Ibsen could again have pointed out that a model is not the same thing as a portrait.[22]

After his fortieth year Ibsen did not read much literature, aside from the Bible. He had absorbed what he needed and concentrated on newspaper reading.[23] Newspapers brought to his ivory tower workshop the knowledge of contemporary life that he wanted. They were a new and evergrowing factor in the life of the times. With universal literacy the press could gradually extend its coverage to the entire world, bringing home to people the catastrophes and the comedies of humankind as never before. In the eighteenth century it took weeks for news of world events like the American and French revolutions to reach outlying areas. Ibsen's generation crossed a threshold into an information explosion about events remote from their personal lives. His plots are not all journalistic, of course, but they do include a great many situations that he had not experienced firsthand: divorce, incest, paresis, political corruption, suicide, poisoned drinking water, arson, murder, seduction, child neglect, and financial swindles. He used these themes, not for their own sakes, but because they gave his spectators the illusion of observing real events. They could be disturbing to the equanimity of readers but also exciting and even enthralling diversions in their often boring daily lives. One may object that such events have been the stuff of drama since Æschylus, which is true. But in the "realistic" Ibsen they are not packaged in mythical archetypes; they occur in settings that are recognizably contemporary, and they happen to people like the members of his audience, however exceptional some of them may seem.

Ibsen was keenly aware that he lived in a world of ferment, one in which the Industrial Revolution had provided new opportunities for entrepreneurs as well as politicians. In *An Enemy of the People* we observe in the newly established baths the infancy of Norway's tourist industry, since grown to vast proportions. Dr. Stockmann exclaims, "What a glorious age this is to live in! It's as if a whole new world were springing up all around."[24] But as the good doctor is about to discover, this new world is built on money, and money does not always mix well with morality.

One solution to this problem was socialism, an ideal of the revolution of 1848, widely advocated by writers like Friedrich Engels and Karl Marx. Ibsen's individualism was too strong for him to accept any kind of collective solution to the problems of the world, and many of his letters as well as speeches by figures like Dr. Stockmann suggest that his ideal society was more like that envisaged by the anarchists. But when Shaw identified him as a socialist, and a journalist conveyed this to him, his protest was mild indeed. He was surprised, he wrote, to learn "that I, who had made it my principal task to portray human characters and human fates, had, on certain issues—without having consciously or deliberately so intended—arrived at the same conclusion as that reached by the Social Democratic moral philosophers through scientific research."[25] Whatever this noncommittal answer meant, socialism did not become an issue in his plays. Hilde's insistence that the Master Builder stop sabotaging his assistant's promotion is an entirely different matter.

Ibsen has often been credited, as one of his principal contributions to the drama, with bringing the life of his age on the stage. It is not as simple as that, but he was certainly one of the pioneers. He was a modern, in the sense that his later years were lived in a world that had begun to assume the shape we know today. Ibsen felt no great enthusiasm for the new world of machines and sometimes expressed a fear that these would even further reduce the possibility for his highly valued individual development. Brand, in his final soliloquy, foresees a future in which

> A sickening fog of smoke from British coal
> Drops in a grimy pall upon the land,
> Befouls the vernal green and chokes to death
> Each lovely shoot, drifts low in poisoned clouds,
> And steals the sun and daylight from the place . . .[26]

Today Norwegian lakes are being poisoned by the fallout from German factories, waterfalls have been harnessed by hundreds of power plants, and oil rigs dot the North Sea.

Ibsen's apprehension in 1870 at the German military triumph over France is expressed in his "Balloon Letter," in terms that look forward prophetically to the two world wars he was spared from seeing:

> In Prussia's sword lies Prussia's scourge.
> There can come no exaltation
> From a simple calculation
> . . . .
> Doomed is the victory of numbers.[27]

Ibsen was a man who could be as critical of the world power of ancient Rome and modern Germany or Britain as he was of the pretensions to greatness of his own little Norway. His view of the world was dramatic and dialectic from the start. He saw the clash of forces, great and small, in human lives as the most provocative entry into an understanding of existence.

To sum up: Ibsen's study of the *classics* made him familiar with the great rebels Catiline and Julian. As a Norwegian he sought out themes offered him by the new *romantic* view of his country's history and folk traditions. As a *Christian* he rebelled on behalf of the ideals of the founder against the compromises of the church. As an *idealist* he found his countrymen, indeed men in general, lacking in integrity and high purpose, but in figures like Brand and Peer Gynt he provided them with a dual identity much like his own. First and last he saw the world in dialectic, Hegelian terms as an unending dramatic conflict seeking resolution in an elusive synthesis. The new *realism* suggested numerous examples of this conflict in the industrial, urbanized society around him.

Even now, a century or so later, Ibsen's context does not strike us as altogether strange, however dated some of his Victorian themes may seem. We live under the influence of the same trends projected out of the past—classicism, romanticism, Christianity, idealism, and realism. It is odd to think that some could use the word "provincial" to describe a writer who was to so high a degree a European and a citizen of the world.

READINGS AND REFERENCES

Brian W. Downs in his *Ibsen: The Intellectual Background* (Cambridge: University Press, 1948) provides a much more detailed account of the influences playing upon Ibsen's mind than I have been able to do in this survey.

Special studies of Ibsen's *classicism* include a pioneering article by Andrew R. Anderson, "Ibsen and the Classic World," *Classical Journal* 11 (1916), 216–25, and a book by Josef Faaland, *Henrik Ibsen og antikken* (Oslo: Tanum, 1943). Valuable analyses of the sources are found in James Walter McFarlane's study of *Emperor and Galilean* (*The Oxford Ibsen*, 8 vols. [London: Oxford University Press, 1960–77], 4.597–603); for *Catiline* there is an extensive bibliography in *The Oxford Ibsen*, 1.711–12.

Ibsen's attitude toward *nationalism* and Norway is discussed at length in Halvdan Koht, *Life of Ibsen*, trans. Einar Haugen and A. E. Santaniello (New York: Blom, 1971), 215–22. His treatment of *Peer Gynt* is seen as a purely Christian one by Finn Thorn, *Henrik Ibsens "Peer Gynt": Et drama om kristen identitet* (Oslo: Aschehoug, 1971).

Ibsen's *idealism* (in the Hegelian sense) is explored by John C. Pearce in "Hegelian Ideas in Three Tragedies by Ibsen," *Scandinavian Studies* 34 (1962), 245–57. Brian Johnston, *The Ibsen Cycle* (Boston: Twayne, 1975), argues that the underlying plan for the plays in the cycle was derived from Hegel's *Phenomenology of Mind*. Koht (*Life*, 234) claims that Ibsen studied Hegel during his first year in Christiania, but Michael Meyer counters that "we have no evidence that Ibsen ever read a line of Hegel" (*Ibsen: A Biography* [New York: Doubleday, 1971], 64). Hegel's centenary was celebrated in 1870, while Ibsen was living in Germany.

Special studies of Ibsen's *realism* are Daniel Haakonsen, *Henrik Ibsens realisme* (Oslo: Aschehoug, 1957), and Horst Bien, *Henrik Ibsens Realismus* (ms., 1969), trans. into Norwegian as *Henrik Ibsens realisme: Det klassisk kritisk-realistiske dramas opprinnelse og utvikling* by Frode Rimstad (Oslo: Universitetsforlaget, 1973). The latter is Marxist and an interesting testimonial to Ibsen's vitality even in the communist world. Its motto is a 1906 quotation from the Marxist critic Clara Zetkin: "Ibsen the rebel will live as long as there is a bourgeois society; Ibsen the artist will survive it."

3

The Play's the Thing

In the theater one learns to be practical, to admit the power of cir-
cumstance, and, when absolutely necessary, to abandon one's higher
ideals, for the time being.

Ibsen, report to annual meeting of The Norwegian
Theater, Christiania, 2 July 1859.[1]

THAT IBSEN's chief medium or channel for expression was the *drama*
is beyond argument. In his youth he wrote a great deal of verse, he
painted extensively, and he was prolific as a literary and dramatic
critic. Even then the writing of plays was his chief ambition, and soon
after he began his exile in 1864 and achieved success as a dramatist,
he gave up his other pursuits, devoting himself with single-minded in-
tensity to playwriting. His technique was founded on a combination
of dramaturgic theory and practical theater experience that no other
dramatist of his day could equal. We have to look back to Shakespeare
and Molière to find anything comparable. Yet it is debatable whether
we can speak of the *theater* as his primary medium, for his plays vary
greatly in their emphasis on the needs of the practical theater as
against the demands of the reader of literature.

On stage a play is a spectacle, something to be seen, which fits
remarkably well with Ibsen's 1874 definition of creative composition
(*at digte*) as being essentially "to see," that is, "to see in such a way
that whatever is seen is perceived by his audience just as the poet saw
it."[2] Practical dramatists have to project their inner visions as peep-

shows into the drama of their inmost lives. Dramatists differ from other authors by needing in a higher degree to master something of the crafts of the painter and the sculptor, the musician and the dancer. Their characters appear in the round, like sculptures (we think of Ibsen projecting himself into the sculptor Rubek), and they form a picture to be viewed as a painter's composition. They move in a dynamic plasticity that is choreographic, and at the same time they speak words with an inner music that reaches and moves the hearts of listeners. These figures must engage in action that gives life new meaning, action that imitates life without merely duplicating it, a plot that meaningfully alters characters' relationships from moment to moment and maintains the spectators' suspense.

Ibsen lived in an age when it had become possible to launch the printed play, in which a reading audience can create its own stage, one that need bear no relation whatever to the physical theater. In his day and ours Shakespeare's plays are more read than performed, and in Germany this is no doubt true of Goethe's *Faust* as well. Nineteenth-century poets like Byron and Shelley gave dramatic form to some of their major poetic works, to be performed on cosmic stages without relation to their dramaturgic potential.

Theatrical Experience

Ibsen's first play, *Catiline*, was written for a real enough stage but was characteristically launched in print, read with mixed feelings by critics, and not performed. It is invaluable as a portrait of the artist as a young man, though it preceded Ibsen's experience in the theater. The plays he wrote in Bergen were usually performed before they were printed, and some of them were not printed at all until after Ibsen had become famous. They were exercises in dramaturgy, apprentice pieces that attempted to meet the demands of the stage, in a period which Ibsen later described as "a daily abortion."[3]

Yet from the vantage point of our knowledge of his later career we can see that his good fortune in being attached to the theater in Bergen was one of those historical coincidences that boggle the mind. Impulsively hired by Ole Bull as "house dramatist," he was sent abroad by the more practical managers of the theater to study dramaturgy, a trade for which there was little precedent in his country. He got only as far as Copenhagen and Dresden, but at least he could see first-rate live theater and meet such leaders of dramatic art as the Danish J. L. Heiberg, author and critic, and his actress wife, Johanne Luise Heiberg, to both of whom he later offered homage. Most seminal was his reading of the newly appeared manifesto of the German writer Hermann Hettner, *Das moderne Drama* (1852). Hettner called for better theater, demanding that actors as well as authors take their profession seriously. Actors should go beyond declamation to the portrayal of human character, and authors beyond intrigue and coincidence to the unfolding of real life.

It is important to recall that in Ibsen's early years there were no theater directors as we know them. Ensemble playing was a novelty, if it occurred at all, for each player tried hard to inflate his or her role, and the stage manager was primarily responsible for making sure that the players knew their lines and pronounced the words correctly, and that the props were in position when needed. Ibsen is said to have been timid about correcting the actors, and especially the actresses, but he seems to have been successful, and the theater in Bergen did well during most of his time there. In Christiania the situation was different; here he assumed full responsibility for the productions, and he had to compete with the well-established and popular Christiania Theater. But in both cities the theater, then as now, was subject to the whim of its audiences. In his day this meant a steady diet of French comedies, especially by the ever-popular Scribe, and Danish "vaudevilles," a kind of musical at which Heiberg was a master.[4]

Painting and Stage Directions

When putting on these plays, Ibsen made use of whatever talents he had, some of which are reflected in his playwriting. Anyone who has read through his stage directions will have noticed his precise and exacting way of visualizing the scene in which his characters will move, the pictures that will catch the eye of his audience and establish the premises of his action. There is reason to believe that this is a result of his "painterly" eye. From youth he dreamed of becoming a painter, and only after a struggle with himself and at the insistence of his wife did he give it up. He took lessons in Skien, Bergen, and Christiania. At fourteen he was already doing watercolors in a naivistic style *à la* Henri Rousseau or Grandma Moses. In both Grimstad and Christiania he drew caricatures; he filled the walls of the apothecary's shop with small oil paintings. On his walking tours he painted majestic fjord landscapes, dramatically contrasting the sea with snowcapped mountains. For his play *Olaf Liljekrans* (1857) he painted figures in native dress to guide the costumers. In all, more than sixty of his paintings have been identified.[5] He was last seen at his easel in 1863, although Koht reports that he did some painting at Berchtesgaden in 1868. His son Sigurd once said, "The world can thank my mother that it has one bad painter the fewer and got a great writer instead."[6]

Bad (or merely conventional) painter he may have been, but there is a close relationship between his painting and his drama. We owe our deeper understanding of Ibsen's scenic vision to John Northam (1952), who concentrates on his scenic effects. One of his examples is the large white shawl that Rebecca West is crocheting in the opening scene of *Rosmersholm*. As she works, Rebecca and Mrs. Helseth talk about the dead and about the fabled white horse that warns of death. At each major crisis through the play she again picks up her crocheting. In the final scene she throws it around her head as a bridal veil when she and Rosmer pledge their troth. But it also becomes her shroud when she and Rosmer are seen standing on the bridge, and Mrs. Helseth again associates it with the white horse as they end their lives in the millrace.

Directors who stage Ibsen have often done so without taking into account his keen theatrical eye. It is regrettable that they feel at liberty to dispense with his directions and create settings that are far from his original intention. An example of Ibsen's care in this respect is his handling of the lighting in *The Wild Duck*; he pointed out that each of the five acts has a different lighting to correspond with the mood of that act.[7] Northam makes the point: "Visual suggestion can add unspoken information where strict realism inhibits open statements of feeling and motive. It can do more; by evoking simple, emotional responses to colour, light, darkness, it can help to steer the mind through many situations where dialogue alone presents merely a choice between conflicting interpretations of character."[8]

Those who know Ibsen only from some of the plays of his middle period, say *A Doll's House* to *Hedda Gabler*, may tend to think of him as the dramatist of the overstuffed, and indeed, stuffy Victorian drawing room. But a wider familiarity, even with his major plays, shows that as many, probably more of them, have outdoor settings, often richly varied with backdrops and glaciers. Ibsen once jestingly attributed the many night scenes in *Catiline* to the fact that he wrote it at night, the only time he could escape from his pill-mixing duties in the dispensary. The many outdoor scenes can similarly be accounted for by his passion for hiking, especially in his youth. He enjoyed the outdoors and tramped happily up and down the mountains of Norway, as well as those of Italy, Austria, and Germany. His was the generation when mountains were being discovered by urban dwellers as an escape and a resource of the spirit. The contrast between the con-

finement of culture and the freedom of nature was not lost on him
and is frequently reflected in his settings.[9]

Early Plays

Returning to the plays he wrote in Bergen, we are told that only one
of them, *The Feast at Solhoug* (1856), succeeded on first performance.
Aside from a certain lyric quality, this ballad drama has little to com-
mend it. *Lady Inger at Østråt* (1855) has proved to be more successful on revival. This play has all that a director wishing to please a romantic audience could ask for: a strong female lead, Lady Inger, a
noblewoman with the Ibsenian tragic flaw of self-doubt; a vivid Re-
naissance setting, complete with Gothic touches including eerie burial
vaults. The plot teems with high political intrigue and is kept moving
by a series of most incredible misunderstandings. Secret documents fall
into the wrong hands, and Inger becomes the instrument of her own
son's death. Her eldest daughter's seducer and betrayer, the Danish
nobleman Nils Lykke, manages to seduce her second daughter as well.
This witches' brew of intrigue, seduction, politics, and national pathos
is all distilled in the course of one night, thus observing most neatly
the (supposedly) Aristotelian unities of time, place, and action.[10]

The critical playgoer is more likely to be entertained by *The Vikings
at Helgeland*, in which Ibsen reached back into the Viking Age, in that
tenth century which stood at the transition from paganism to Christianity. Here one is in the world of helmeted and sword-wielding men
and women, who sail ships back and forth between Iceland and the
tempestuous shores of north Norway. The action is the last act in a fate
drama that began with a bride-snatching many years before. The Icelandic *skald* and chieftain Ørnulf of the Fjords lost his daughter Dagny and his foster-daughter Hjørdis to the redoubtable Norwegian Vikings Sigurd and Gunnar. We quickly recognize the love quadrangle,
or double triangle, of the *Volsunga Saga* (and Wagner's *Nibelungen*),
with its confusion of identity. The strong woman, Hjørdis (the Bryn-
hild of the Saga), is by mischance married to the weaker man, Gunnar. Her frustration (foreshadowing Hedda Gabler's) has turned to
vengefulness, triggering a plot of tragic dimensions. Misunderstandings
lead to multiple slayings, and finally the heroine's suicide, after which
she is wafted off on black horses to Valhalla, the pagan warrior's
heaven. Beneath the viking trappings these conflicts are human enough,
especially for Hjørdis, in whom love and hate contend, as expected in
a woman scorned.[11]

Ibsen created a more complex historical setting for *The Pretenders*, his great drama of Norway at the apex of its medieval glory, the reign of King Haakon Haakonsson (1217–63). The settings are a feast for the eye. From act to act Ibsen mobilizes a different staging of the conflict between Haakon and his father-in-law the Earl (later Duke) Skule—a pretender to the throne, who gambles on and loses his attempted rebellion. Here we have moved into royal palaces: acts I and II in Bergen, III and IV in Oslo, and V in Nidaros (Trondheim), the three focal points of power in thirteenth-century Norway. The cast is large; the play is long enough to require some cutting. It survives by virtue of the human clash between the self-assured Haakon and the self-tormenting Skule. Haakon sees himself as God's instrument in consummating a spiritual union of the Norwegian people, whereas Skule is forever looking for external signs to prove his right to the throne. In the end he succumbs to the forces of the nether world symbolized in Bishop Nikolas.[12]

Verse Drama

By this time Ibsen had already begun experimenting with his special form of verse drama in *Love's Comedy* (1862), later followed by the masterpieces *Brand* (1866) and *Peer Gynt* (1867). These plays are too rich in content and too long in performance to be easily assimilated on the stage; the two latter he called "dramatic poems." All three have actually proved to be popular stage pieces, especially in the original Norwegian, but also in German (and, in part, English) translations. The verse form itself creates problems, not only for the translator, but also for the performer. Ibsen's is a tightly rhymed verse, less naturally spoken than blank verse; a performer needs to play down the rhymes and modify the singsong effect of the strong rhythm so that the verse does not detract from the action. Any adapter or director will be faced with the dilemma of having to cut lines and whole scenes lest he or she overtax the audience's patience.

These plays have more than the verse in common: they are all contemporary (or nearly so) in scene, and they carry a heavy freight of philosophical rumination. There is free use of symbols and symbolic figures, typifying certain ideas and not necessarily individualized very far beyond what is needed to identify them as such. They point forward to the prose plays about contemporary life, while carrying over many of the romantic trappings of the earlier ones. They make excellent reading, especially to a reader who can simultaneously enjoy the verse, visualize the vivid stage action, and absorb the underlying ideas.

They have an operatic quality, *Love's Comedy* in the tradition of comic opera, *Brand* in that of grand opera, *Peer Gynt* in an inimitable conflation of both.

The idyllic setting of *Love's Comedy* is in the environs of Christiania, in the outdoors surrounding Mrs. Halm's villa, "a beautiful garden, irregularly but tastefully laid out; the fjord and the outlying islands can be seen in the background. . . . It is early summer; the fruit trees are in blossom."[13]

The poetic young man Falk entertains family, guests, and boarders with his original songs about the joys of the moment, while his listeners clink glasses or sip their tea. The action, as noted earlier, is minimal, consisting largely of Falk and Svanhild's aborted love affair. Most of the play is a series of tableaux, a pageant of comic figures, each of whom professes great devotion to romantic love as an ideal but betrays it in practice by being overly concerned with the domestic and unromantic aspects of engagement and marriage. In a witty, if over-long speech Falk compares love that results in marriage to tea that has been shipped overland from China: by the time it reaches the consumer it has lost its flavor. Confirmation of this satire comes when Pastor Strawman marches on stage, followed by his eight daughters in all possible sizes, one by one, with four more at home, and his wife bringing up the rear (carrying the thirteenth!). He is the ironic exhibit of love's comedy, a young man who had dreamed of becoming a poet but who drowned his poetry in the concerns of home and prelacy. When Falk gives up his love and goes off singing into the mountains, he at least retains his memory of love unsullied. But we are left with the typically Ibsenian question: what can he find there that will replace his loss?

Brand supplies one answer by showing what happens when an idealist loses touch with the real and seeks his ideal on the heights: he is destroyed, after being rejected by man and God. In this play the spirit is comic only in certain passages in which Brand confronts the officials of village and church. We are no longer gazing on the idyllic Oslo fjord but on the majestic, overpowering fjord country of western Norway, with its overhanging cliffs and menacing glaciers. The gloom is compact: "The mist lies thick and heavy. It is raining and nearly dark."[14]

Brand is making his way down through the chasms to his old home by the sea, where (contrary to his expectations) his life work awaits him. In the end he returns to the mountains, stoned by men, buried by the avalanche, a token of his own coldness of heart. The play is rich in thunderous, quotable soliloquies, as well as dramatic scenes in which men and women strive unsuccessfully to meet Brand's demand for "All or Nothing." *Brand* is, even more so than *Love's Comedy*, a play of paradoxes, a "Love's Tragedy," in which the most intense warmth of human love is embodied in Agnes, Brand's wife. She sacrifices all for love and is herself sacrificed on the altar of Brand's inhuman will. Yet Brand, too, is to be pitied: he is an archetype of the prophet crying in the wilderness, from John the Baptist to Savonarola. Reader and spectator alike can carry away the exaltation of high poetic vision as well as the catharsis of knowing that no man can attain perfection.

If *Brand* may be called a straightforward syllogism, *Peer Gynt* is a sinuous, slippery phantasmagoria, about as hard to wrestle with intellectually as is the Great Boyg with which Peer strives in the second act. "Go round about," cries the Boyg, an invisible and invulnerable creature of the dark which bars Peer's way on all sides. This is exactly what Peer does. The action of *Brand* is classic in its unity, whereas that of *Peer Gynt* is picaresque. Starting out as a kind of Sancho Panza to Brand's Don Quixote, Peer quickly becomes his own man as Ibsen keeps adding what he called "caprices."

Peer is a figure of folklore, and he brings with him the whole magic world of the folk. But this ne'er-do-well farm lad does not remain confined to the inland valley of Gudbrandsdalen where he was born. He makes his way into the world, earning himself a fortune in America, squandering it conspicuously in the Mediterranean, and returning home penniless as an old man to meet the Button Molder's judgment on his life. Like Faust, he is saved, not by his own efforts but by the love of a pure woman.

In reality there are three plays here: Peer's youth in acts I - III, including Peer's encounter with Solveig, his madcap adventures in the mountain, and his rejection of responsibility toward bride and mother; his middle age in act IV, set in the classical world of North Africa, from Morocco to Cairo; and his old age in act V, from his shipwreck off the coast of Norway to his last moments, resting his head on Solveig's lap. Any director who tried to present every line or every scene in one evening would not only lose the audience but also wear out the actor playing Peer. Ibsen at one time recommended omitting act IV in performance, but this would mean losing some of his most entertaining scenes. In Norway it was for years the rule to play acts I - III only, giving the drama a specious unity and reducing it to a mere spectacle.

As such, *Peer Gynt* has of course a great deal to offer: Peer dashing in and out as he plays the charming ne'er-do-well and soliloquizes about his dreams of future greatness; a country wedding complete with costumes, fiddlers, dancing, drinking, wenching, fighting; and Peer's romp up the mountainside with the bride on his back. Then come his abandonment of Ingrid and his encounters with the trolls, who turn out to be remarkably human, from the Greenclad Woman to the Dovre King, who propounds the riddle Peer is unable to answer: what does it mean "to be oneself?" Peer is rescued by Solveig, but when he tries to live with her, the past returns and drives him away. In a touching, much-acclaimed scene with his dying mother, he lulls her into final sleep with a fairytale ride into heaven, before he takes off for foreign parts.

Up to this point there is constant life and motion on the stage, a superb genre picture, which an imaginative director can shape to his or her taste. Of course any careful reader will realize it is a satire and far from any real reading of Norwegian folk life and folklore in the nineteenth century. But what is a director to make of the fourth and fifth acts? Thirty years have passed, and the rapscallion Peer has become "a handsome, middle-aged gentleman in an elegant traveling suit, with gold-rimmed spectacles hanging from his vest," with a yacht in the offing and four international guests for a most elegant dinner.[15] His Norwegian past is but a dim memory, to which he makes witty allusions in conversation with his guests. The transformation is startling, the scene static, and the conversation philosophical. A solution practiced for some years in the Norwegian theater was to use two different actors in the part—Toralv Maurstad as the young Peer and his father, Alfred, as the aging Peer. Some of the impact is lost, however; we should be able to see traces of the young man in the older one, and again in the elderly Peer of act V, after another decade.

There is more talk than action in both of the last two acts, with their progressive penetration into the meaning of selfhood. In act IV selfishness reigns, beginning with the guests representing the major powers of Europe, who steal his yacht, followed by Anitra of the Bedouins, true "daughter of Eve," who steals his horse and his ruby. Finally he meets Dr. Begriffenfeldt, the mad director of a madhouse in Cairo. Here he encounters characters who are "bottled up in the cask of self," as Begiffenfeldt puts it, and Peer is crowned emperor, ironic fulfillment of his old dream, for he is emperor of all madmen, who are "themselves" by virtue of being "beside themselves." These scenes are so grotesque that they require an expressionistic mode of playing, recapitulating in distorted form the events of his earlier life, but now in classical terms and in international perspective.

Act V also reads better than it plays. Once more Peer recapitulates his youth, but in the old home valley and in reverse order. In a significant scene he peels an onion, skinning off his various roles, only to find that there is no core within. He comes in time for Ingrid's funeral, only to discover that his name is already a legend. He meets the Dovre King who dejectedly reports that *he* has been deposed and is now on his way to the national stage as a character actor. One by one Peer's self-defenses crumble, until life peels the onion and does find a core, Solveig's undying love, the one thing that has kept him from being melted down into the mass of forgotten humanity. These scenes offer tremendous challenges for actors and directors alike. The wealth of invention and the poetry of the scenes can only be hinted at on the stage; it is the relish of the reader that makes the play artistically valid. No stage can do full justice to this blend of humor, fancy, pathos, and tragedy.

The Third Empire

Even before writing *Brand* and *Peer Gynt*, Ibsen had begun planning for the "world-historical" play that became *Emperor and Galilean*, which (as we saw above) embodied his Hegelian idealism. These three plays, all conceived soon after his departure from Norway, reflect his liberation from the demands of the stage. Now he could write for readers, not the fickle spectators, and "be himself," putting into practice the doctrine that these plays express more than any others. *Emperor and Galilean* is even more intractable on the stage than the other two. An attempt by Ibsen's granddaughter Irene to compress its ten acts into one evening's performance (which I witnessed in Oslo in 1955) was a painful travesty. Michael Meyer calls it the Ibsen play "most underrated by posterity."[16] We shall try to see what made it so.

Originally Ibsen conceived of it as three plays of three, three, and five acts each. Then he combined the first two into one, making two partly independent plays: *Caesar's Apostasy* and *Emperor Julian*. Julian is another Ibsenian Hamlet, whose "to be or not to be" is the choice between Christianity and paganism. In the first play he moves step by step from being an ardent Christian to a passionate pagan, with a mystic tinge. In the second play he tries as emperor to force upon the Roman Empire a restoration of the already half-forgotten rites of paganism. But he falls on the eastern battlefields at the hands of a Christian, as he utters his traditional dying words, "Galilean, thou hast conquered."[17]

The panorama unfolded before our eyes covers the last years of

Julian's life, A.D. 351–63. Scenically it skips from Constantinople, the capital, to Gaul and Persia, the western and eastern bounds of empire. Every act requires a new set, all of them elaborate and even lavish, and the list of characters seems endless. It is the kind of dramatic spectacle that only the modern film or TV theater could manage with any success, as in the historical films of Cecil B. deMille and his successors. It is somewhat odd that no one has so far discovered the play and exploited it.

One of Julian's troubles is that he is more philosopher than man of action. At every critical moment he seems to think he can solve his problems by writing another treatise about them. Even his wife refers to his "inky fingers," and there are hints of his sexual impotence. He is disillusioned by the personal behavior of both Christians and pagans, finding that "the old beauty is no longer beautiful, and the new truth is no longer true."[18] In oracular séances the mystic Maximos conjures up for him a role as founder of the "third empire." The first, or pagan, empire was based on the garden of Eden's Tree of Knowledge and embodied the beauty of self-expression. The second, or Christian, empire was based on the Tree of Crucifixion and embodied the spirit of self-denial. The third empire, yet unborn, would be based on both principles, combining into one harmonious whole these apparently antagonistic ideals.

Misled by the ambiguous omens of Maximos, Julian sees himself as the coming founder of the third empire and its first emperor. He accepts a political role as pacifier of Gaul and is successful in his first step toward imperial power. At the end of the first play we have a sense of great dramatic strength; Julian has gradually progressed away from the ideals of his youth to the belief that a divine kingdom can be established on earth. In the second play we are disappointed by an overburdened scene, with many short and uninteresting episodes, which precede Julian's tragic end in the East. The play does little more than demonstrate the apothegm that "power corrupts." When Julian meets resistance, he begins to apply force and soon becomes another tyrant. He is as blind to human love and mercy as Brand, though less consistent, and his policies are as irresponsible as Peer's, though less charming. In the end he fails because the real meaning of the omens was that he was fated to be the instrument of furthering Christianity, not by favoring it, but by opposing it. He was an instrument of the "world will," willing what he "had to will," like Cain and Judas another "victim on the altar of necessity."

Ibsen read his sources diligently to produce this dual play, but except for some brilliant scenes between Julian and Maximos, it does not come alive. Reminiscent of *Catiline*, it has some of the same weaknesses, yet it is also enormously more sophisticated.

The Retrospective Technique

Even while he was occupied with launching this massive man-of-war, Ibsen had retooled his medium by designing one of his most popular and playable comedies, *The League of Youth* (1869). A theme sketchily treated in the skit *Norma, or a Politician's Love* (published in *The Man*, 1851, and not intended for performance) is here staged with all the trappings of Scribean intrigue, in a setting painfully recognizable to his contemporaries. With all the virtues and defects of a good cartoon the play unravels the character of Stensgaard, who has been called a "Peer Gynt in politics." At its core there is the same searching for selfhood as in other plays of this period. It is a curtain raiser for the dozen prose plays that followed, but lacks their depth; the characters are superficial. There is little either in structure or in content to reveal the master; it is not vintage Ibsen. The play demonstrates what he could do for the stage in a style he had mastered as stage manager in Bergen and Christiania.

The League of Youth opens in the festive setting of an open-air celebration of May 17th, Norwegian Constitution Day, the national holiday. A local dignitary is concluding the obligatory oration of the day, toasting "our freedom, which we have inherited from our ancestors, and which we will maintain for ourselves and our sons!"[19] Into this politically static atmosphere breezes young Stensgaard, a lawyer recently arrived, eager to unseat the current establishment and promote his political fortune. Ibsen prided himself on having managed without the traditional asides or soliloquies, but otherwise the plot is kept moving by the usual comic errors. Stensgaard receives an invitation to the local high society by misunderstanding, and by misunderstanding he manages to get engaged to three different women at once. When the truth comes out, he leaves the scene in defeat and disgrace, with a roar of laughter behind him, plus the cynical prediction of one observer that some day he will no doubt return as a member of parliment or the cabinet.

At this midpoint in his career Ibsen had demonstrated that he could satisfy the demands of stagecraft and that he had intellectual depth, but he had rarely managed to fuse both in the same play. His chief contribution to the literature of the theater was that he was able to do so in his remaining twelve plays, creating a genre in which profundity of thought could be embedded in stageable forms. By concentrating on the same domestic, bourgeois family that he had lightly dismissed in *Love's Comedy*, he could create microcosmic masterpieces with macrocosmic implications.

On the stage they are manageable because they bring us only the last act in a long series of events, a technique often called "retrospective." The opening scene usually presents a situation in which the characters appear normal and happy, going about their daily affairs. In *Pillars of Society* Mr. Rørlund is congratulating the women in his pious reading circle on the high moral tone of the society in which they live. Nora in *A Doll's House* cheerily enters her living room with her arms full of Christmas gifts and is greeted with endearments by a busy husband working in his study. Mrs. Alving in *Ghosts* is overjoyed at having her only son home from Paris for the dedication of a children's home in honor of her late husband. Dr. Stockmann in *An Enemy of the People* is eagerly awaiting the results of a test of the town's bath waters, which may enable him to save the town from disaster and strengthen his own position.

But our author does not wait long to introduce a discordant note that suggests an underlying disharmony and excites the spectator's curiosity. In *Pillars of Society*, least subtle of the plays, we learn at once that something is wrong in Bernick's shipyard, and the women's gossip hints at murky doings in the Bernick past. Nora reveals by her furtive munching of macaroons that she is hiding small secrets from her husband; only in a following scene do we learn that she is also concealing a major secret. In each play a stranger or an old friend arrives to bring out the past and precipitate the revelation of the real situation behind the glossy surface. Veil after veil is drawn back from the past, until the truth (or is it the truth?) stands nakedly revealed before us. Then the leading characters can do nothing but find a way out of their insoluble dilemma. They must somehow patch up a compromise or take the logical path to the "third empire," in a hereafter that we cannot know.

It is as if Ibsen had now decided to write only the fifth act of his plays. In *Peer Gynt* we can imagine how he might have recapitulated all the events of Peer's youth and manhood through reminiscence and conversation. Had he used the earlier technique in *A Doll's House*, he might have started with Nora's father, the ne'er-do-well, introduced young Helmer as her suitor and shown his guilt in condoning her father's defalcations, pictured their wedding and the trip to Italy, which involved her in secret negotiations with Krogstad to obtain money, and so on. With the new technique we learn all this and more in the course of three short acts, mostly in passing hints, and it is for us as spectators or readers to put it all together into a meaningful whole. We are forced to ask: what is this Nora really like? Is she a featherbrain, ignorant of all except the way to a man's affection; or is she a serious woman, who plays a part until she is awakened by his actions into a realization of her shameful position as a plaything? There is enough ambiguity in the text to call forth both interpretations among critics. Actresses have been faced with the same dilemma. Ibsen produced a text so challenging that reader or performer is required to find his or her own Nora, giving to actress (and eventually to the director) a freedom that has tempted great performers ever since.

There is much more to be said about Ibsen's stage technique than can be rehearsed here. What one would like to see more thoroughly treated in the literature is the actual results of this technique on the stage, in short, a detailed stage history of Ibsen's plays. Those writers who classify his plays as "well-made plays" sometimes use the term disparagingly, perhaps by way of contrast with the more loosely structured expressionistic theater that followed his. The materials for a stage history are available in reviews, reminiscences, and theatrical histories. We cannot take the space to pursue it here but will take up a few interesting instances that suggest some general principles.

Ibsen on Stage

If one reads critiques of Ibsen performances rather systematically and sets aside the reviews by critics who are simply anti-Ibsen and find fault with him and all his works, one is struck by the fact that the performers are often quite severely judged. In reviewing a performance by Janet Achurch, the first English Nora and one of the greatest, William Archer, the proto-Ibsenite, wrote that "she is *a* Nora and a very beautiful one, though not quite *the* Nora."[20] But who could possibly be *the* Nora, who would satisfy the expectations of every critic? Anyone who has read the play with any thoroughness, as of course translator Archer had, and who has worked out the tight web that Ibsen has woven around her, is not likely to find any Nora who will fully live up to his or her expectations. This is of course even more true for such inscrutable personalities as Mrs. Alving, Rebecca West, Ellida Wangel, Hedda Gabler, Hilde Wangel, Rita Allmers—and, not to be wholly sexist, Dr. Stockmann, Gregers Werle, Johannes Rosmer, Hallvard Solness, John Gabriel Borkman, and Arnold Rubek.

The reader has the advantage of being able to turn back the pages and ruminate over the contrarieties in their characters. He or she can try to decide when they are telling the truth—if ever—and can penetrate into Ibsen's ironic, often suspicious, attitude toward his characters and ferret out those seemingly innocent little statements that reveal what the speakers would as lief conceal.

In the theater the opportunities for conveying all these nuances are more limited, since there is no way of turning a performance back. Both directors and actors have a heavy responsibility in selecting what will be underscored so that the audience receives the message, and what may be more lightly touched. As a channel for communication the theater is sensitive to distortion, a defect which in communication theory is known as "noise in the channel." We perceive it as interference in our radios or TV sets. In the theater the author's message may be almost totally drowned out by the combined operations of translator, adapter, director, and actors. Translators, of course, equally affect readers. But few directors are happy today with the classic translations by Archer, however honest and faithful. They lack something of the verbal magic of the original, even in the prose, and they are typically rewritten by each director into more contemporary dialogue. A number of versions have actually been made by persons who know no word of Norwegian. Those by competent translators, like McFarlane's Oxford versions or Meyer's freer efforts, have adopted contemporary British forms, making it necessary to have special American verisons like those by Eva Le Gallienne or Rolf Fjelde.

The most famous and successful Ibsen adaptation is the one by Arthur Miller of *An Enemy of the People*, which in America has virtually replaced the original. What Miller essentially did was to play down or eliminate Ibsen's ambiguity, those endearing qualities in Dr. Stockmann which made Ibsen write about him: "Dr. Stockmann has a more muddled head on his shoulders than I."[21] Miller set out to Americanize what he calls Archer's "impossibly pedantic English" and to abbreviate the play where it seemed long-winded. But he also eliminated opinions expressed by Stockmann with which he did not agree, some of which he calls "fascistic."[22] Here he is thinking of Stockmann's "muddleheaded" mixture of genetic (animal) breeding and social (human) breeding, overlooking that Stockmann does not believe that aristocrats necessarily result from genetic breeding, since he flatly points to his own brother as an example of "vulgarity."

Miller's changes are at least partly explained by his no doubt good intentions in reviving Ibsen in 1951. During a time of witch hunts by the McCarthy Committee on "disloyal" persons, one of whom was Miller, he found an ally in Dr. Stockmann. But in doing so, he shifted characters (e.g., Morten Kiil) around, added speeches that are out of place in Ibsen, and rewrote the last two acts almost in their entirety. Dr. Stockmann's lighthearted game with the Mayor's hat and stick is replaced by a sermon: "I just wanted you to realize, Peter, that anyone may wear this hat in a democracy, and that a free citizen is not afraid to touch it." Ibsen's "the majority is never right" is emended to read, "the majority is never right until it does right." Issues that are ambiguous are made clear and Stockmann awaits the stoning mob at the end of the play as the shining hero he has become.[23]

Miller was a professed admirer of Ibsen and so, clearly, was Adrian Hall, who in 1978 directed *Rosmersholm* in a high-level production at the Trinity Square Repertory Company in Providence, Rhode Island, a production billed as a "new adaptation" by Richard Cumming. Ibsen's stage directions were disregarded, his dual scene being replaced by an open three-story stage that required the characters to be forever running up and down stairs. The crucial dialogues between Rebecca and Mrs. Helseth were replaced by gossipy conversations between a servant girl, introduced for the purpose, and Mrs. Helseth. That is, a trite stage convention was substituted for the scenes in which Ibsen established Rebecca's position in her environment. She is excluded from learning the local folklore of the white horse, which is part of the symbolic net that Ibsen wove around her. The concept of "nobility" and the contrast between the Christian and the pagan will was eliminated, apparently because it was assumed that the audience would not understand them. On the other hand, the gentle hints that Ibsen dropped about Rosmer's impotence and Rebecca's incestuous relations with her stepfather were changed to blatant statements. A quotation from the much later writings of Sigmund Freud was written into Rebecca's dialogue, making her her own analyst. All that is left of Ibsen's cosmic clash is a melodramatic tale of two high-strung individuals unable to adjust their fears and guilts to each other's demands.[24] The *New York Times* critic, Richard Eder, rightly concluded that for all its skill the production "cheapened the grave rhythm" of the play.[25]

Actors, Actresses, and Directors

The ultimate success of any play on the stage depends on the ability of the actors to make something out of the parts they are given to play. Ibsen did not usually participate in the actual staging of his plays in later years, but his letters to various stage managers are full of suggestions which show that he kept a sharp eye on productions. In the later plays he constantly emphasized the importance of natural acting; especially in the social plays he urged that the tempo be speeded up to that of normal speech.[26] He expressed alarm when Christiania Theater planned to use actresses to play Dr. Stockmann's sons. He wanted the boys trained so that the audience could tell their characters apart, and he urged that they be given "big, ugly boy's shoes" to wear.[27]

Directors were often genuinely baffled when confronted with a new Ibsen play. The Swede August Lindberg wrote to a friend, right before tackling *The Wild Duck* for its very first performance: "I feel dizzy. Such extraordinary tasks for us, the actors. Never before have we been faced with anything like this."[28] Ibsen gave very specific instructions about the play; for example, he wanted Hjalmar Ekdal played without a comic tinge, completely sincere and without affectation. He advised against the diva system, whereby the older actresses played the best parts—he wanted his young women played by young actresses: "We must abandon our fear of giving difficult parts to the young actors."[29] He urged the actress playing Rebecca to portray her as a real woman in real life.[30] Bjørn Bjørnson, son of the poet, was one of the first directors to realize Ibsen's intentions. He speaks of the importance of silences in many of Ibsen's dialogues, "the silences that were to lift the words."[31] In the one American production of *John Gabriel Borkman* that I have seen, the director would have done well to keep this in mind. The dialogue of the two Rentheim sisters was fired off at machine-gun tempo, when the situation clearly called for silences that would give time for the absorption of unspoken thoughts.

In 1891 a festive speaker thanked Ibsen on behalf of the actors for having created so many fine roles, to which he growled: "I have never written roles."[32] But of course he did, and particularly female ones. His plays called forth a new style of acting that did not permit posing and declamation and required that the actor enter into the life of the personality portrayed. Stanislavsky (1863–1938), the famous founder and director of the Moscow Art Theater (from 1898), placed Chekhov and Gorky above Ibsen. But he was inordinately fond of playing Dr. Stockmann, and when working out his well-known "method" he was strongly influenced by his experiences with this character: "In my actor's perceptions I felt myself more at home on the stage than in any other role in my repertoire."[33]

The list of actors and actresses who have made Ibsen roles a vehicle of their stardom is considerable. We need mention here only Eleonora Duse in Italy, Alla Nazimova in Russia, Janet Achurch and Elizabeth Robins in England, Minnie Maddern Fiske and Eva Le Gallienne in the United States. In 1906 Richard Mansfield toured America with a magnificent *Peer Gynt*; in 1927 Walter Hampden did the same with *An Enemy of the People*. Of course, there have been disasters as well. One of them was an early television performance of *Hedda Gabler* by Tallulah Bankhead, which I saw in 1954. (It was sponsored by U. S. Steel, presumably because of the pistols.) The reason for mentioning it at all is in connection with the review by Philip Hamburger in the *New Yorker* magazine, which called forth this reminiscence: "The first time I saw *Hedda Gabler*, Nazimova played Hedda, and, believe me, it was a wonderful experience, especially for a growing boy with vine leaves in his hair. Nazimova *was* Hedda, every last, deep, devious, frustrated particle of her." As for the Bankhead performance, all he could say was: "Poor public, poor Tallulah, poor, poor Henrik Ibsen!" The review was headed: "Hedda Get Your Gun!"[34]

Despite such aberrations, we must agree with Elizabeth Robins in her moving tribute, *Ibsen and the Actress*, that "without the help of the stage the world would not have had an Ibsen to celebrate; and without Ibsen the world would not have had the stage as it became after his plays were acted."[35] She fully recognized the "chasm" between "the literature of the drama and the literature of the stage," but she said, in giving the Hogarth Lecture on the occasion of the Ibsen centennial in 1928, that "Ibsen, more than any author I have known, comes to the rescue of the actor in this misery. He never deserts you, if you trust him."[36] She played the first English Hilde in 1893 after doing Hedda in 1891. That Hedda can still stimulate workers in the theater is evident from a brochure *About Hedda Gabler* (1970), inspired by the work of New York director Eli Siegel.[37] This reports on the intense discussions of The Opposites Company before producing the play. Rebecca Thompson, who played Hedda, saw her as "essentially good," a woman "who was trying to be honest." Contrary to the many critics who had condemned her, this company agreed with Elizabeth Robins that she is "pitiable in her hungry loneliness" and with Mrs. Patrick Campbell that she "is essentially a good woman." It is all a question, clearly, of which Ibsen clue one picks up, but in Ibsen's notes to the play there is good evidence for their views: "Hedda's despair is that there are doubtless so many chances of happiness in the world, but that she cannot discover them."[38]

Great directors have also seen in Ibsen's plays a challenge to their abilities. The Danish William Bloch, who directed the first *Enemy of the People* in Copenhagen in March 1883, was a pioneer in developing a naturalistic set. Just for the mob scene in act IV his prompt book ran to more than a hundred pages; a contemporary critic wrote that "the performance shone like a glittering and brilliant diamond behind the footlights." "The theater," he maintained, "should not be a mirror of life, but a reflection of the hidden life of the soul."[39] Bjørn Bjørnson, mentioned above, and the Swedes August Lindberg and Ernst Josephson did yeoman work in bringing Ibsen before the public.[40]

Many films and TV presentations of Ibsen plays have been made, especially of *Peer Gynt*, *A Doll's House*, *The Wild Duck*, and *Hedda Gabler*. The latest English-speaking Noras have been Jane Fonda and Claire Bloom (both in 1973); and Hedda has been portrayed by Glenda Jackson (1975).[41] We can only refer to these productions here, without further discussion; each has provided its own interpretation.

No doubt a certain amount of noise in the channel is not only inevitable but also useful. No one has devised a perfect system for communication, and there has to be room for innovation. The stage is highly sensitive to changing public taste. Ibsen as a stage manager learned "to abandon his higher ideals." Modern audiences are less patient than they were in his time, and it is not surprising if his plays occasionally need pruning in performance. But let it be a pruning of deadwood, not heartwood. Nearly everything in an Ibsen text has a purpose, and one cannot convey his message without fidelity to that purpose.

READINGS AND REFERENCES

The liveliest and most profound study of Ibsen's dramaturgy is John Northam, *Ibsen's Dramatic Method* (London: Faber, 1952; 2d. ed. paperback, Oslo: Universitetsforlaget, 1971); this is must reading for every Ibsen director. Important older studies are by William Archer, *Playmaking* (London: Chapman, 1913), and "Ibsen's Craftsmanship" in *Fortnightly Review*, July 1906; and by P. F. D. Tennant, *Ibsen's Dramatic Technique* (Cambridge: University Press, 1948). A German dissertation is by Johanna Kröner, *Die technik des realistischen Dramas bei Ibsen und Galsworthy* (Leipzig: Tauchnitz, 1935).

A fresh and enthusiastic view of Ibsen by one of the masters of the American theater is Harold Clurman, *Ibsen* (New York: Macmillan, 1977). In an appendix he offers some notes on how he would have directed *Rosmersholm*, *The Master Builder*, and *Little Eyolf* (setting forth the "spine" of each play and each character), after admitting that he has never had an opportunity to do so.

See also Rebecca Thompson, "On Playing *Hedda Gabler*," in *About Hedda Gabler* (New York: The Opposites Co. 1970); also included in the volume is "A Short History of *Hedda Gabler* Criticism, 1890–1970," by Alice Bernstein.

Hermann J. Weigand, *The Modern Ibsen: A Reconsideration* (New York: Holt, 1925) is a classic analysis of the major prose plays; he works out the psychological aspects of the characters and their interrelations, often in very original ways.

Besides the list of American productions in Henrik Ibsen, *The Complete Major Prose Plays*, trans. and introd. by Rolf Fjelde (New York: Farrar Straus and Giroux/New American Library, 1978), there is a brief discussion by Leonard S. Klein in Hans G. Meyer, *Henrik Ibsen* (New York: Ungar, 1972), 185–90. Michael Meyer includes the stage history of each play in the series of his Ibsen translations, published in London by Rupert Hart-Davis and in New York by Doubleday as Anchor Books.

4

Under the Surface

GINA: *Wasn't that a queer business, his wanting to be a dog?*
HEDVIG: *I'll tell you something, mother—it seemed to me he meant
something else by that.*
GINA: *What else could he mean?*
HEDVIG: *I don't know—but it was just as if he meant something else
than what he said, all the time.*

Ibsen, *The Wild Duck*, Act II.[1]

READERS AND viewers of Ibsen's plays, especially his later ones, have
often come away from the experience with a feeling akin to that of
young Hedvig after her conversation with Gregers. Some early critics
were so baffled that they tended to be belligerent about it. When *The
Master Builder* was first performed in London in 1893, one critic
wrote, "What this extraordinary piece of work may mean, Dr. Ibsen
alone can know."[2] Another flatly declared that when the play "is
not prurient, it seems to be meaningless."[3] Predictably more perceptive, Henry James wrote that "the mingled reality and symbolism of
it all give us an Ibsen within an Ibsen. His subject is always, like the
subjects of all first-rate men, primarily an idea; but in this case the
idea is as difficult to catch as its presence is impossible to overlook."[4]
Max Nordau, physician, popular writer, and Zionist, found Ibsen's
symbols to be evidence of his pet theory that Ibsen (as well as Wagner
and the French symbolists) was mad. Mental patients typically used
mysterious phrases, "freely coined by the speaker, or endowed by him

with a peculiar sense, deviating from that usually assigned them in speech."[5] Nordau failed to add that poets do the same, as Shakespeare was well aware when he wrote in *Midsummer Night's Dream*:

> The lunatic, the lover, and the poet
> Are of imagination all compact
> . . . .
> The poet's eye . . . . gives to airy nothing
> A local habitation and a name.[6]

It remains to be shown that Ibsen was a poet, something we shall consider in the next chapter. Here we are concerned only with what may be called his "dramatic code." By this I do not mean primarily his Norwegian, though this was his basic language, but an idiom of the theater, which can be transposed more or less intact into any other natural language. Belgian dramatist Maeterlinck noted (and admired) what he called the "dialogue of the second degree" in *The Master Builder*.[7] One English critic and Ibsen translator, R. Ellis Roberts, called Ibsen's symbolism "a perfect language."[8] Another English translator, C. H. Herford, speaks of the "dialect" in which Ibsen expresses the core of *Brand*'s thought.[9]

That these writers used such terms as "dialect" and "language" is significant, and we shall ask to what extent they are applicable. If it is true that Ibsen developed a dramatic language of his own, the study of his plays has something in common with the learning of a foreign language. Those who have not mastered his "language" will either misunderstand, as people do on hearing a strange dialect, or be baffled and even angered, as some are when they hear a foreign tongue. Perhaps Ibsen, when he advised his readers to take the plays in chronological order, was in effect suggesting a course in language learning. As in any good course, the early lessons are simpler than the later ones, and we learn as the language gradually unfolds.

From this point of view each Ibsen play is a text that contains a hidden meaning, more or less consciously encoded in it by the author. Only by careful and penetrating study of the text will the reader be able to "crack the code," as cryptographers say, and decode the message. Here it helps to have an abundance of texts, another good reason for reading as many Ibsen plays as possible when analyzing any one of them. As far back as 1907 an American professor of English, Jennette Lee, tried to come to grips with the subject in her book *The Ibsen Secret: A Key to the Prose Dramas of Henrik Ibsen*.[10] It is interesting to note that she finds the key to Nora in the tarantella dance. At this point she touches hands with a recent student of the same topic, Inga-Stina Ewbank, who sees in the dance "an action-symbol which fuses, for the audience, all the various 'parts' of Nora, all the different visions of her," since it "means one thing to her and a different thing to each of her spectators."[11]

The following discussion is written without direct reference to Ewbank's illuminating study, but like hers is intended to show how Ibsen's use of language "serves to link the surface with the underlying symbolical structure" (Ewbank, p. 101), "takes us under the photographic surface of realism," "through the physical landscape into a spiritual one," and "places a particular (realistic) action in a wider (symbolic) context of meanings" (Ewbank, p. 98). Or in Rilke's words from 1910 (quoted at the beginning of this book), how "things tangible [are] used for the sake of expressing the intangible."[12]

If we take a sentence like "Krogstad threatens Nora," we can by simple rules transform it into the passive, "Nora is threatened by Krogstad." These two sentences have a general meaning in common, namely that a person named Krogstad is performing an action known as "threatening" to a person named Nora. In modern linguistics this relationship may be described by saying that the two surface sentences have a deep structure in common, which of course can be expressed in various ways, e.g., "Krogstad's threat to Nora." For a work of art this structure is still very shallow, and one needs to plunge deeper into the uncharted sea of language to find the real "meaning." Like Gregers, we have to be good hunting dogs to bring it back up again from "the depths of the sea." The critics cited above seem to be declaring that there is nothing there, no bottom and no game, merely an abyss. James, finding Ibsen's idea elusive, added, "The whole thing throbs and flushes with it, and yet smiles and mocks at us through it as if in conscious supersubtlety."[13] The danger to be avoided is of course that one may read into the play something that is not there, as Ibsen occasionally complained that his critics were doing.

The Social Plays

Our decoding will begin with the plays here identified as "social" (p. 48) because they are primarily concerned with society and the pressure it applies on the individual.

Pillars is located in "a small coastal town," not unlike Grimstad; *A Doll's House* in an apartment house, presumably in Christiania; *Ghosts* on a country estate by a western fjord, somewhere around Bergen; *Enemy* in "a coastal town in southern Norway," no doubt Skien. Money is crucial in all of them and is generally detrimental to morality.

Bernick in *Pillars* is a shipowner willing to send out unseaworthy ships if he can make money on them. Nora in *A Doll's House* has had to borrow money secretly to save her husband's life and in doing so has had to forge her father's signature. In *Ghosts* Mrs. Alving married a dissolute husband for money and is now salving her conscience by building an orphanage in his name. In *Enemy* community leaders are willing to conceal the presence of polluted water in the local baths in order not to lose their investment. The thesis that money corrupts is in itself not startling; we are reminded of the teachings of Jesus as transmitted by the church, whether in His parable about the rich or in His driving out the money changers from the temple.

Even in Norway Ibsen was not the first to perceive the dramatic values of economic corruption: Bjørnson had explored it two years earlier in his epoch-making play *A Bankruptcy* (1875). Ibsen's advance consisted in the skillful way he was able to picture a whole social order through the story of one man, Bernick, in *Pillars of Society*. The opening stage set is "a spacious conservatory" in Consul Bernick's home. As in many other Ibsen sets, there is an opening to another world backstage, here a garden seen through the conservatory windows, and beyond that a street with houses and a corner shop, where people are seen walking and chatting. This is the small town, the little world in which Bernick is king.

The scene is full, even overloaded, and Ibsen would not again try to squeeze so much action into his opening. In the course of the first act the audience learns a good deal of the past, of old scandals that are being hushed up, as well as of a major enterprise that is being plotted by the businessmen, the bringing of a railroad to town. There are hints of rebellion in Dina Dorf, a young girl living with the Bernicks, and in Olaf, Bernick's son, who is incited by his uncle Hilmar to run off to America, more as a joke than anything else. The whole situation explodes by the end of the first act when Lona Hessel, Mrs. Bernick's stepsister, unexpectedly returns from America with the "black sheep" of the family, Johan Tønnesen, who is Mrs. Bernick's younger brother. By this device of the unexpected and usually unwelcome visitor, which Ibsen was to use often again, an apparently normal situation is turned into an abnormal one, with high dramatic potential. Lona herself is not just the past personified, however; she is also a keenly delineated and unforgettable character, a woman of the new age. She brings with her from the great plains an atmosphere of freedom, and her first action is to draw the curtains aside to "let in some fresh air" on these women "sitting here in the dark sewing all these white things" that look like shrouds.

Among the "old, unhappy" things we learn is the fact that Bernick had once rejected Lona in order to marry for money and that the scandal blamed on Johan was really Bernick's doing. Bernick's position in this society proves to be based on a series of ruthless exploitations and calculated deceptions. Only when he realizes that his crimes have come very close to making him the involuntary murderer of his own son is he willing to listen to Lona's demand that he publicly confess his misdeeds. Ironically, the occasion is provided by a torchlight procession in his honor. At the end of the play Bernick is relieved to be free of his burdens of conscience, and he now has "a long and hard day's work ahead." He may be less of a moral pillar of the community than before, but Ibsen gives him a second chance. He has been left in possession of wife and property, as well as the beneficent influence of Lona, who brings down the curtain with the oft-quoted aphorism: "The spirit of truth and the spirit of freedom—those are the pillars of society."[14] Having ceased to be a false pillar, Bernick now has a chance to live by this maxim and become a real pillar.

Torvald Helmer in *A Doll's House* is probed more deeply and given far less of a chance. Ibsen was clearly not satisfied to give his next play a happy ending. He also made a drastic reduction in the number of characters and the complexity of the setting. Again he begins with a normal, even festive occasion: Christmas eve, which has vivid and heartwarming associations for all Scandinavians. We see a comfortable home with the Christmas tree trimmed for the evening celebration, a pretty young wife dancing in with newly bought gifts for their three children, a successful banker-husband working in his study off the living room, delighted to flirt with his "lark," his "squirrel." Besides these two and the children there are only three characters, all of whom call in the first act: Mrs. Linde, an old schoolmate of Nora's, now widowed and looking for work—a foil for Nora's happiness; Dr. Rank, the family physician-friend, who proves to be secretly in love with her; and finally the unwelcome visitor, Nils Krogstad, who brings out the hidden past that will produce the dramatic tension of the play.

We need not pursue the plot further but should note that Nora's character has given rise to endless debate, springing from Ibsen's deliberate effort to characterize her as subtly as possible. She evokes our sympathy by her charm and beauty, by her childlike dream of perfection, by her moral strength during the crisis, which enables her to walk out of her home determined to find out who she really is. Yet, as Hermann Weigand (and before him, Georg Groddeck) showed, a careful analysis of Nora's actions suggests that she loves to playact and show off, that she lies very readily, and that she has no realistic understanding of her husband's position. Her weaknesses serve only to make her the more believeable, and the final scene, for which Ibsen once admitted he had written the whole play, is one of the masterpieces of world literature.[15] (When she doffs her Capri costume in which she had danced the tarantella at the Christmas ball, she also doffs her role of "child wife." Her everyday clothes reflect the mood of reckoning accounts with her husband: her love is dead because he saw in her only the doll and failed to meet the demands of the woman. Her dream of "the miracle" that would have made their life together a true marriage may be a mirage, but Helmer had failed even to make an effort to understand the situation. Not until she has slammed the door does it begin to dawn on him that a miracle is indeed what is needed.

"After Nora Mrs. Alving had to come," Ibsen once wrote.[16] He often emphasized that writing *Ghosts* was an absolute necessity for him. This is not to say that the two women can be equated. Mrs. Alving's reasons for leaving her husband were a good deal weightier than Nora's. Yet, unlike Nora, she returned, on the urging of her pastor, to bring up her child. Ibsen was defying those critics who insisted that Nora should have done the same.

The single setting is a garden room, from which we look into a conservatory beyond. This device obviates the need for changing scenery, at the same time setting the stage for dual action, one in the foreground, another in the background. Beyond the conservatory is a "gloomy fjord landscape" and a steady rain that is at once realistic and symbolic, an apt metaphor for the kind of world in which this tragic action is about to take place. Yet the opening scene is broadly comic, bringing on stage the vulgar Jacob Engstrand and the less than kind reception he gets from his daughter Regine, the Alvings' maid. We learn that it is a day of great expectations and rejoicing. A newly built orphange is to be dedicated in memory of the late Chamberlain Alving, and his artist son Osvald has returned from Paris to crown the happiness of his mother, who has been living alone on her great estate in western Norway.

Engstrand, a carpenter who has worked on the orphanage, is the first visitor. His crippled leg lends him a satanic touch, which is confirmed as we learn that he plans to open a so-called hotel for sailors, with his daughter as its "hostess," and that he is fishing for support from the Reverend Manders to help him achieve his goal. Manders arrives next, prepared to dedicate the orphanage, but taken aback by Engstrand's schemes. By the end of act I we have learned that Manders was the man Mrs. Alving fled to from her husband and that her reason for doing so was Alving's dissolute ways. One of the results of Alving's indiscretions was Regime, whose mother was hurriedly married off to Engstrand. Osvald was sent off to Paris, ostensibly to become an artist, actually to remove him from his father's influence. Now he has returned and starts a flirtation with Regine, not knowing that she is his half-sister. The key word "ghosts" is uttered in horror by Mrs. Alving as she sees (or rather hears) Osvald and Regine reenact the same scene that she overheard between her husband and Regine's mother.

The plot is as tightly woven as anything in Ibsen and moves with the inexorable quality of a Greek tragedy, with which it has often been compared. The lives of the five characters are intimately related, and in the end Mrs. Alving is left to cope with a situation she had never even remotely contemplated. She is thoughtful, well intentioned, serious-minded, surrounded by grotesque characters, ironically and at times even humorously portrayed, who are trying to take advantage of her. The orphanage burns, uninsured, and Osvald reveals that he, too, is burning up. His French doctors have told him that he is *vermoulu*, worm-eaten, and he refuses to believe them when they attribute the illness to his father. The dialogue is sharply chiseled, at once realistic and symbolic, engaging the breathless interest of the spectator as veil after veil is drawn back from the present, and the past in all its horror is revealed at the sunrise that coincides with Osvald's lapse into paresis. He calls for "the sun—the sun" with his expressionless face, and the mother's scream rings in our ear like Nora's slamming door, but more terrifying by far. Nora walked out on her children, but she was not asked to chloroform them!

An Enemy of the People rounds off the social plays by returning to a scene and providing an ending that is more consonant with the first of the plays than were the intervening two. There is a great deal of comedy, although the life situation in which Dr. Stockmann finds himself is serious enough. Dr. Stockmann's living room, with the inevitable room beyond, in this instance the dining room, and the doctor's study off to the right, is "simply but tastefully furnished." A constant stream of casual visitors as well as family members reflects the warmhearted, enthusiastic spirit of the doctor himself. He enters well after the beginning of the first act, laughingly bringing with him another unexpected guest for dinner, relying on the patience of his long-suffering but supportive wife. The only character who is out of sympathy with the good doctor's convivial spirits is his brother, mayor of the town, who obviously finds his kinsman something of a trial. Hints are dropped of a great and wonderful discovery which the doctor has made, and by the end of act I we know what it is. Stockmann has discovered and has now had it confirmed by expert opinion that the baths, on which the town is depending for its future prosperity, are infected and must be closed. Encouraged by the sycophants at his board, he looks forward to the plaudits of his fellow citizens for the service he has rendered them.

This time the unpleasant visitor who complicates the situation is his brother, the mayor. He not only distrusts Dr. Stockmann's discovery but rejects the idea of closing the baths and convinces the citizens that such action will adversely affect their pocketbooks. Step by step Dr. Stockmann is forced to retreat before the weight of public resentment. After having enthusiastically expressed his belief in the people, he is driven into denouncing "the damned compact majority" and announces his newfound doctrine that "the minority is always right." In the great public scene in act IV he even goes so far as to insist on a mixture of genetic and social reasons for the failure of the masses to follow his lead. In spite of Ibsen's playful disclaimers, we do find some of these ideas in *his* letters as well. But the figure of Stockmann is made so naive and at times ridiculous that Ibsen guarded himself against being identified with him. Stockmann's house is stoned; but he decides to stay in the town and open a school for the "mongrels" whom he had just condemned. He believes that in the long run he can make "free and high-minded men" out of them.

The play is a parable about a man who comes out of the wilderness to bring a healing message of good news to his fellow men but who is crucified for his pains by the authorities who feel themselves threatened by it. One reason for the appeal of this play is surely that behind it we glimpse the messianic myth, the archetype of the savior of humanity. Just as Jesus proclaimed that the world was sinful, so Stockmann announces that the waters are poisoned. Some who have nothing to lose receive him with enthusiasm, but the Pharisees denounce him. He is isolated and stoned, becomes a "dead" man in the community, deserted by those whom he came to save. But he rises from the "dead," gathers his immediate family around him, and asks for a dozen disciples whom he can train to be "free men" who will chase the "wolves" away and who will have the courage to risk their lives for the truth. Stockmann is a secular savior, to be sure, but he clearly sees himself in the role of a chastiser, whose role it will be to chase the money changers from the temple of society.

The common element in the social plays is that the audience is asked to identify with a person who has the courage to violate social norms on behalf of an ideal of freedom and truth. It is significant that three of them are women. Lona Hessel, Nora Helmer, Helene Alving, and Thomas Stockmann have in one way or another broken conventions and won the disapproval of those who value these conventions. They are supported in their revolt by minor characters like Dina and Martha in *Pillars*, Mrs. Linde and Dr. Rank in *A Doll's House*, Osvald in *Ghosts*, Petra and Mrs. Stockmann in *An Enemy*. But the fate of those who defy society can be disapproval, ostracism, even death. *Ghosts* has been described as a fate tragedy, but unlike the Greek tragedies, it has society take the place of fate. The individual is like Laocoön in the famous Greek piece of statuary, entangled in the coils of a great serpent from which he is unable to free himself. In these social plays the serpent is society, i.e., the web or network of relationships in which each of us is enmeshed. Most people feel reassured and comforted by this web, but surely everyone has periods when he or she would be happy to break out.

Ibsen made full use of the tricks of the theater he had learned from Scribe and other writers of "well-made" plays. But he filled them with ideas and meanings that gave them a deeper perspective. Nora's tarantella is a dramatic and picturesque scene, but its significance is revealed when her husband, alarmed by her passion, says, "You're dancing as if your life were at stake."—and she replies, "It is."[17] The audience understands because it knows of Krogstad's threat; but there is also an underlying implication for those who realize that the tarantella was originally a dance used to rid oneself of the deadly tarantula's poison. Ibsen's plays have something of the mystery story about them: the crime has already been committed, and it is now a question of untangling the events that have led up to it.

These plays also offer an innovative blend of humor and tragedy, which makes it difficult to classify them into the traditional genres. Even a tragic play like *Ghosts* has its humorous aspects: Engstrand's unflappable egotism is humorously revealed in the glaring contrast between his unvarnished, even juicy talk to Regine and his sanctimonious verbiage when the pastor is present. Dr. Rank's tragic loneliness is ironically displayed in a flirtatious scene with Nora, and his somber exit is blended with Helmer's inebriated lustfulness in a scene that calls simultaneously for tears and laughter.

The Psychological Plays

The blending of the comic and tragic reaches its heights in *The Wild Duck*, where Hedvig's death becomes the pretext for her father's hollow rhetoric and Dr. Relling's cynical confrontation with Gregers. As early as 1875 Ibsen declared that his writings dealt with "at once both

the tragedy and the comedy of mankind and of the individual."[18] After an 1898 performance of *The Wild Duck* in Copenhagen, he told
an interviewer that the play "is to be tragi-comedy, or else Hedvig's
death is incomprehensible."[19] In 1921 Shaw wrote that "Ibsen was
the dramatic poet who firmly established tragicomedy as a much
deeper and grimmer entertainment than tragedy."[20] In a monograph
on tragicomedy as a genre, Karl Guthke largely agreed with this judgment, after analyzing in detail the shifting elements of the comic and
the tragic in *The Wild Duck*. He suggests that tragicomedy is a pecu-
liarly modern concept, with roots in romanticism but typical of the
modern theater.[21] Here, too, Ibsen was a pioneer.

Ibsen was well aware, as we have seen, that he was embarking on
something new when he wrote *The Wild Duck*: "This new play in
many ways occupies a place of its own among my dramas; the method
is in various respects a departure from my earlier one."[22] He did not
specify the method, leaving it to the critics to find out. Although the
characters and settings are familiar enough, and the veils that conceal
the past are gradually dropped, there is a new type of psychological
interaction. The central event is not so much Gregers's revelation of
his father's sins, as the way in which he wins the confidence of Hedvig and a measure of control over her mind. The wild duck of the title
is his instrument, not physically but verbally, with which he establishes
in Hedvig's mind a metaphor that equates her with the duck. When
he imposes on her the obligation of sacrificing the duck to appease
her wrathful father, it is as natural for her to replace the duck with
herself as it conversely was for Abraham to replace the sacrifice of
Isaac with that of a goat when the Lord so commanded.

Besides the central metaphor there are numerous other suggestive
scenic allegories, which are part of Ibsen's dramatic language. The
settings of acts I and II form a significant contrast between the two
worlds of the drama. At the Werle's house a glittering party is in progress, with slightly inebriated dinner guests circling around a handsome, provocative woman and her friend, the host, a successful business
entrepreneur. At the Ekdal's house we are in a modest, lower middle-
class home, an attic apartment which doubles as living room and
photographer's studio, dimly lighted by a single lamp, where mother
and daughter are reckoning their skimpy household accounts. The
contrast reflects a gap between conspicuous consumption and respect-
able frugality, a topic of the times which a revolutionary writer might
have turned into a flaming critique of society. Ibsen was not concerned
about this but about the human bonds that tie these homes, more
closely than its members generally suspect.

Right: Ibsen the bourgeois. Woodcut of the photo sent to Lorentz Dietrichson in 1869. From *HU* 20.63. *Below*: Ibsen's later handwriting. From the draft of *When We Dead Awaken* (1899). (See pp. 20-22.)

Peer Gynt. Above: Lithograph by Edvard Munch (1896) used as a frontispiece of *La Critique* (Paris) to announce a performance in Lugné Poe's Théâtre de L'Oeuvre. Solveig and Mother Åse are posed before a Norwegian landscape prominently featuring a church. Reproduced by courtesy of the Munch Museum, Oslo. *Left*: Peer's return in the last scene. Production at Det norske teatret, 1962, with Solveig played by Liv Ullmann, Peer by Lasse Kolstad, and The Button Molder by Johan Nordlund. Photo by Sturlason, reproduced by courtesy of Det norske teatret, Oslo.

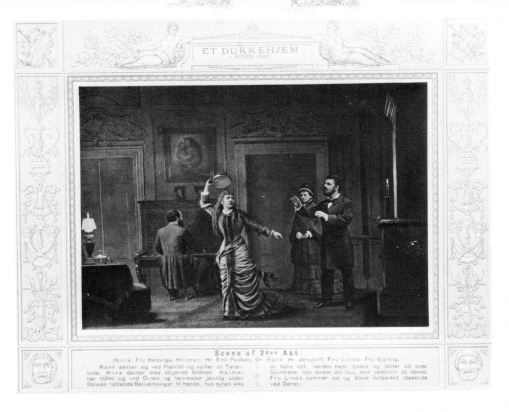

ET DUKKEHJEM
af HENRIK IBSEN

Scene af 2den Akt.
(Nora: Fru Hennings, Helmer: Hr. Emil Poulsen, Dr. Rank: Hr. Jerndorff, Fru Linde: Fru Gjørling.
Rank sætter sig ved Pianoet og spiller en Taran-   at høre det; hendes Haar løsnes og falder ud over
tella. Nora danser med stigende Vildhed. Helmer   Skuldrene; hun ænser det ikke, men vedbliver at danse.
har stillet sig ved Ovnen og henvender jævnlig under   Fru Linde kommer ud og bliver forbauset staaende
Dansen rettende Bemærkninger til hende; hun synes ikke ved Døren.

A Doll's House. Above: Posed scene
(ca. 1879) from act 2. The first Nora:
Mme. Betty Hennings, Helmer: Mr.
Emil Poulsen, Dr. Rank: Mr. Jerndorff, Mrs. Lind: Mme. Gjørling. Rank
sits at the piano and plays a tarantella.
Nora dances with increasing passion.
Helmer has placed himself by the
stove and keeps making remarks to
her during the dance; she does not
seem to hear this; her hair loosens and
falls out over her shoulders; she pays
no attention but continues to dance.
Mrs. Linde comes in and remains
standing, astonished, by the door. Reproduced by courtesy of Teaterhistorisk Museum, Copenhagen. *Right*:
Jane Fonda as Nora and David Warner
as Helmer in a film directed by Joseph
Losey (1973). Reproduced by courtesy of World Film Services, Inc.

Henrik Ibsen som Tugtemester.

"Henrik Ibsen as Chastiser." Cartoon in *Vikingen* (Christiania), 9 December 1882. In the first picture the conservatives (Høire) applaud when Ibsen attacks Stensgaard, the liberal politician. In the second the liberals (Venstre) guffaw when he exposes Bernick, the capitalist. In the third both parties scatter in terror as he lashes out in all directions in *Ghosts*.

"Henrik Ibsen, Receiving Mr. William Archer in Audience." Cartoon by Max Beerbohm, renowned English caricaturist and author. As translator, editor, and ardent advocate of Ibsen's dramas, Archer took a good deal of ribbing. Note the pattern in the wallpaper. From Max Beerbohm, *The Poet's Corner* (London: Heinemann, 1904).

Right: "The Ibsen Rock by Grimstad." Fantasy by Theodor Kittelsen, Norwegian folktale illustrator, in his *Glemmebogen* (Christiania, 1892). *Below*: Ibsen as the aging dramatist back home in Norway, pondering some new "madness" over his daily coffee and newspaper at Grand Café in Christiania. Painting by Edvard Munch from 1906-10. Reproduced by courtesy of the Munch Museum, Oslo.

Right: "The Official Ibsen." Painting by Erik Werenskiold in 1895, now in the National Gallery in Oslo. The background, with its lightly sketched farm home in the valley below the towering mountains, suggests the dramatist's favorite theme, man's striving for "the heights." From *HU* 20.243, reproduced by courtesy of Jens E. Werenskiold. *Below:* "The Laughing Ibsen." Drawing by Erik Werenskiold, done while he was working on the official portrait above. He wanted to capture a moment when Ibsen chuckled at the thought of a painter who had done his picture in Rome. Werenskiold, famous for his fairytale illustrations in this style, scribbled Ibsen's remark on the drawing: "He was in the habit of painting saints, so I was not a very good subject for him." From *HU* 20.247, reproduced by courtesy of Jens E. Werenskiold. (See pp. 35-36.)

who can bring wild ducks up out of the mire. Only Hedvig dimly understands what he means.

Contact between them is established when he speaks of the duck as having been "in the depths of the sea," and she confesses that she has sometimes thought of the whole loft as being "the depths of the sea," a phrase she must have picked up from her romantic reading, although she quite realistically is aware that it is only a loft. The phrase (*på havsens bund*) is, in the original, no more than a poetic cliché, an old-fashioned way of saying "on the seabottom" (*på havets bund, på havbunden*). However, when it is embedded in a setting where it throws light on the imaginative life of the child, and by its verbal magic creates a bond between her and Gregers, it acquires an entirely new significance. In *his* usage it seems rhetorical, revealing that he thinks in stereotypes and is intoxicated with his ability to handle abstract terms and formulate ideas in words. At this point we cannot foresee the tragic consequences. We know only that he has descended from his heights and wishes to plunge into the dim world of the "depths of the sea," where, like a good retriever, he will bring the Ekdal family back up to his own exalted world, which he identifies with truth and reality.

The play is built around this spatial metaphor; Gregers sees his own and the Ekdal home from the heights, and all he can see is the murky depth. He cannot see his father's solid strength in making the best of a lonely existence, or the happiness of the Ekdals in managing to patch up the shreds of a dubious past and a difficult present. Both the heights and depths have special significance in Ibsen's dramatic language. Peer Gynt heads for the heights but finds himself in the depths of the mountain among the trolls. In his poem "The Miner" Ibsen figured his own poetry as bringing the ore of the underworld into the light of day. In the depths are many of the hidden meanings of life, good as well as evil. So when Gregers wishes to plunge into the depths and bring the wounded wild ducks to the surface, it is metaphorically no different from the task of Ibsen's miner, or of Ibsen himself.

Ibsen unquestionably felt a deep kinship with Gregers, but he would hardly have said of him, as he did of Brand, that he was himself in his "best moments." For now, in his fifty-sixth year, Ibsen found in the wild duck a way of expressing poetically a view of humanity that included the element of love. At the end of *Brand*, the hero is reminded that he lacked love; at the end of *Peer Gynt* the hero is saved by love. But these are debatable and somehow constructed finales. The wild duck is Ibsen's vehicle for saying that humanity is more to be pitied than condemned and that one can do so only if one loves people. Like the duck, man is a wild creature that has been domesticated, has lost its ability to fly to the heights or to dive to the depths, and has been confined to the four walls of its home. Even here it can be the center of joy and happiness, a comfort to others, an object of love and attention.

From the superidealist's point of view, this may be but a sad lot. The novelty in this play is Ibsen's demonstration that trying to change the inevitable may simply make things worse. Gregers is at every point forced into a confrontation with the cynic Dr. Relling, who serves to balance his influence. He describes the Ekdal's need for an illusion to live by as the "life lie." His own life is not much more impressive than Gregers's: he keeps the theological candidate Molvik and himself alive chiefly by drink, and we learn that he is a rejected suitor of Mrs. Sørby's, friend of the elder Werle. In looking for deeper meaning in Ibsen's plays, we must recall that he also used "lie" as a synonym for poetry. The "life lie" is the poem man creates around himself to give life meaning and value. Peer Gynt calls his own imaginative experience "lies and damned romancing" (*løgn og forbandet digt*). Picasso (as cited at the beginning of this book) defined art as "a lie that makes us realize the truth."[28]

Gina Ekdal is one character who seems to need no lie to survive. She serves as a touchstone of all the imaginative self-deceptions of the others. She is a no-nonsense woman who knows the truth and has learned to live with it. At the same time she is unmistakably characterized by her speech and background as uneducated and unimaginative. For her, it was a step upward to be married to Ekdal, to have her own home and her own child, after serving as maid and mistress to Werle. Her homely observations are always the true expression of a deep love for the realities of life. She humors Hjalmar and fears Gregers, all for the sake of Hedvig, her own wild duck. Two less appealing realists are the elder Werle and Mrs. Sørby. Like Krogstad and Mrs. Linde in *A Doll's House*, they have learned to adjust to things as they are; they have told each other the truth and can live with it. But in an Ibsen play this marks them as ordinary persons, not exceptional ones, like those who win his attention and the interest of the audience.

Gregers is an exceptional person, in spite of the tragic consequences of his intervention. Yet Brand's idealism caused more deaths than Gregers's, and Dr. Stockmann's disappointed ranting at the mob is more vicious than anything Gregers says. All three fail in their attempts to awaken people to a high mission. The death of Agnes is even more touching than that of Hedvig. These situations all express a vision of life as the battleground of opposing forces, none of which can ever win a definitive victory. The aspiration to the heights, the call from God, the mission in life are always held in check by the basic guilt, the lies and evasions, the restraints that arise from the depths within. Ibsen injects a universal conflict into his individual fates, and especially in his talented and exceptional persons. Whether they are personally charming like Stockmann or charmless like Gregers is of little consequence to the underlying idea. Just as Ibsen wrote that it made no difference whether Brand was a pastor or a politician, so it makes no difference that Brand is handsome and Gregers is ugly. Ibsen was capable of "making the same syllogism" about both, i.e., of involving them in life situations which showed that their effort to achieve an integrated identity was impossible in an imperfect world.

For it is of the essence of Ibsen's code that in all his mature dramas the underlying theme is man's struggle for identity in the universe. He lived in an age when the Christian identity that the church had imposed was crumbling under the impact of novel forces, which we discussed earlier. In *Emperor and Galilean* he summed it up as a conflict between Christian self-denial and pagan self-expression. In Ibsen's thinking these had become irreconcilable ideals, both desirable, but in real life harmonized only by compromise. Hilde in *The Master Builder* sets up her pagan "robust conscience" against the Christian "tender conscience" of Solness; their attempt to combine them results in disaster. It is, to be sure, a glorious failure, but still a failure.

We shall take a quick glance at some of the later plays to see how Ibsen invents ever new metaphorical ways of expressing this view. In *Rosmersholm* the conflict is given a political setting, in which progressive views strive with conservative ones. Rosmer, the exceptional man, and Rebecca, the exceptional woman, are working to achieve a union of their highest ideals: Christian nobility and pagan happiness. They interact by mutually influencing one another: she is transformed by the "Rosmersholm spirit" and he by her "free spirit." Rosmer expresses this in his dream of going out into the world to create a race of men and women who will be both "noble" and "happy." But their attempt to create a new future for themselves ends in disaster because of the power of the "ghosts" in their own past. The metaphor used here is that of the "white horse," a folk tradition based on a variant of the nixie-merman (in the shape of a horse) that lures its victims into perilous waters. In *Rosmersholm* it represents the fate that hovers over anyone who attempts to defy the limitations of mortality. Life is one unending struggle between the sins of the past and our dreams of the future. Rosmer and Rebecca can have one glorious moment of union, but only at the price of death in the millrace.

In *The Lady from the Sea* the struggle that the heroine, Ellida, has to live through is the conflict between her desire for love and understanding from her husband and his daughters on the one hand and her fascination for the unknown, represented by the returned seaman, on the other. She struggles to clarify her own wishes and succeeds because, unlike Nora, she has an understanding husband. As a doctor—Ibsen's favorite profession and self-projection—he is a man who eventually learns to accept his wife's need for freedom and self-determination. By giving her a free choice, he enables her to cope with what we today recognize as a psychotic fixation. The "happy" ending has made the work less dramatic than the other plays of the period, but on close study I think anyone will agree with Francis Fergusson that "it is beautifully composed in every detail, so as to embody a single action, or motive, as Aristotle said any good drama must be." Fergusson identified (in Stanislavsky's terms) the "spine" of the play as "separation": "All of the characters we meet in Dr. Wangel's household feel that they are missing out; that they are somehow separated from the life and the love they need and cannot find."[29] He recognizes in Ellida the gifted person, like those I have described above, who feels alienated from life because he or she is possessed by a demon that pushes him or her "to creative or destructive action." Ellida's stranger is one such demon, and he can be exorcised only by a voluntary sacrifice on the part of her husband.

Ibsen's next exceptional woman, Hedda Gabler (1890), is less fortunate in her choice of a mate. Legally, though not emotionally, she is now Tesman's wife; in her feelings she remains General Gabler's daughter. She has a passionate inner nature but remains untouched by the life around her. She rejects the proffered bourgeois love of her husband, the scholar, and his family, as well as the illicit advances of the ever-willing Judge Brack. She resents the fact that she is about to become a mother, with all the responsibilities of motherhood. She longs for freedom and beauty, and, finding neither, she sets out to manipulate her environment. Her only hope in this direction lies in the bohemian genius Løvborg, but her attempts to make him into a Greek god "with vine leaves in his hair" are unsuccessful. She sees everything she touches turn ugly. In the end she is trapped between a Christian-bourgeois domesticity and a pagan-saturnine liaison, and chooses the freedom of death, as "beautiful" an end to a useless life as she can manage. The central metaphor here is embodied in the pistols: they represent her heritage; they are her playthings, her defense, and ultimately her release. Like her, they are cold and hard on the outside, fiery and dangerous inside. One could say that they enable the demon within her to shoot its way out.

The four plays examined in this section belong to Ibsen's greatest and subtlest creative period. They do not carry any obvious social message but penetrate deeply into psychological states, as seen against his basic view of the cosmic struggle between the two halves of the self. Ibsen described them as portraits, but like Rubek's busts in *When We Dead Awaken*, they have "something equivocal, something hidden within and behind . . . something secret that people cannot see." When he defines this secret as "the dear old barnyard animals . . . that man has corrupted in his own image," we perceive a new variant of the troll metaphor that dominates *Peer Gynt*.[30] Life is a struggle between the trolls that draw man down into the depths and the true humanity that aspires to the heights. Each person must strive to find his or her self, but this must not be identical with selfishness; in the Button Molder's words: "To be oneself is to slay oneself."[31] Many of his characters quite literally find that slaying themselves is the only solution. Selfless love like that of Dr. Wangel is a rare escape.

The Philosophical Plays

These are plays of old age, written after Ibsen's return to Norway, and they reflect a common theme that obviously concerned Ibsen very deeply. Briefly, it can be stated as the conflicting claims on a genius of his vocation, his art, and of his responsibility to those who love him. In these plays Ibsen showed that he could "make the same syllogism" about four different types of creative personalities: an architect, a philosopher, a financier, and a sculptor. Each of these is, or has dreamed of becoming, a creative personality aspiring to the heights. But each has some flaw, which he discovers too late, that either destroys his dream or leaves him unsatisfied with what he has achieved. The flaw in each instance is the failure to incorporate love with his art. If we identify the calling with his bohemian urge to create, we must see in love his bourgeois longing for social responsibility. In one way or another each of these creators has failed to harmonize these demands, and either compromises them (as in *Little Eyolf*) or is destroyed in trying to synthesize them.

In *The Master Builder* Solness has reached the top of his profession, but he broods over the cost in terms of the loss of his wife's affection and the damage his success has done to her. His career began with the building of churches, for the honor and glory of God. But for the last ten years he has built only homes, for men and women. The underlying message of this crucial change is complex: on the one hand it is autobiographical, and we think of Ibsen's change from writing poetic-philosophical plays of aspiration like *Brand* to social plays like *A Doll's House*. It also involves the Christian-pagan conflict, for when Solness built his last church, he realized that God wanted him to spend his entire life building for Him. Then he defied God and declared: "Listen to me, Almighty One! From this day forward, I too will be free. A master builder free in his own field as you are in yours." He turns to the building of homes, secular structures, only to discover "that people have no use for these homes of theirs. It doesn't help them to be happy."[32] So now he is going to combine homes with churches by building homes with high towers, and he has begun by building one for himself. Again an Ibsen character is trying to combine the contrasts into a synthesis, and we know that it is going to be impossible. But Solness is fascinated by the impossible, which includes hanging the wreath on the spire: except for that one time ten years ago, when he built his last church, he has never been able to climb a spire without getting dizzy.

Behind this spire we glimpse the tower of Babel, which according to Genesis was built by men who wished to reach up to heaven and be equal to God. Of course they failed, and so does Solness. However, the symbolism goes deeper, for the direct stimulus to his defiant action is Hilde, the woman to whom he had promised a kingdom ten years earlier and who now has come to claim it. She is a new Nora, demanding the miracle of her man, but in this play she tells him outright what she expects. In these terms the tower is also phallic, for Hilde awakens Solness's dormant sexuality and makes him long for his lost youth. He has feared youth, because it might topple him from his eminence. But now it comes to him as a loving, if demanding young woman, who expects him to live up to her ideal. When he is at the top, waving his hat, she hears him disputing with the Lord; there is singing in the air, and she waves back with a white shawl, crying, "My—my—master builder!" She brushes aside the fact that he crashes to the ground, for the important thing is his attempt: he *wanted* to do the impossible, and tried. However tragic, his death is also triumphant.

This is not true of *Little Eyolf*, where the ending is a quiet, yet moving resignation of the ideal. Like *The Lady from the Sea*, it is the only play in its group that fails to end in death and gives its characters a chance to go on living. One result is that they seem less dramatic, less exceptional, but they are no less intricately studied for their inner lives and philosophical implications. The writer-philosopher Allmers has two women about him in the familiar Ibsen pattern: his half-sister Asta, who offers him inspiration, and his wife Rita, who offers him passion. Each corresponds to one side of his character, and he is torn between them. Among these three Ibsen has woven one of the most complex webs in his production. Its verbal and visual symbols strongly suggest the constraints on achieving human goals. For ten years Allmers has been writing "a big book on human responsibility," but to do so he has evaded responsibility by going to the mountains, and he has been unable to make any progress on it. Instead, he has come back down with a mission: to make a man out of his crippled son, Eyolf. However, Eyolf, whose lameness is due to the parents' neglect, is again neglected and drowns. Allmers's freedom of creation has worked to the neglect of his responsibility, and he has not been able to synthesize the two. When he turns to Asta for support, she rejects him. Rita and Allmers, who are now left alone, resign and stop trying to unite the opposites. They accept the compromise of working together on behalf of a good cause. The poetically balanced finale sounds almost like a requiem: "Upwards—toward the peaks. Toward the stars. And toward the great silence."[33]

John Gabriel Borkman is a return to Ibsen's more natural and more powerful kind of grand tragedy. John Gabriel (as he is always known) is a financier who had great dreams, dreams of the human happiness he could bring about by his enterprises. But they were built on a lie, the betrayal of Ella, the woman who loved him. He also betrayed the trust of his investors, by stealing the assets of the bank to cover his debts, and was driven into bankruptcy by the very man to whom he had yielded his beloved (who steadfastly refused to marry). Confined to their old estate, now owned by Ella, he and his wife live apart, she on the first floor, he pacing the floor above her head like a caged wolf. He confidently expects to be restored to his "kingdom," but this is clearly just a "life lie," in which he is temporarily sustained by the visits of another broken man, the would-be playwright Vilhelm Foldal. Ella, who is his wife Gunhild's twin sister, returns to take up the battle with Gunhild over the life of Borkman's son, Erhart. But Erhart chooses his own life, leaving the three old people to themselves. John Gabriel's dream of greatness was in the mines, down in the deep dark shafts where his father had worked. He tried to bring the treasure up for the benefit of mankind (and his own power), but because he had failed to combine his craft with love, he lost. In the end he goes out to die in the snow, where the two rival sisters can at last join hands, "we twin sisters—over the man we both loved; we two shadows—over the dead man." Every aspect of the setting and the dialogue contributes to point up the futility of trying to unite love and calling in the same life. "The cold had killed him long ago."[34]

Finally, in *When We Dead Awaken*, the artist is a sculptor. Rubek, like Solness, is successful and famous. The play has been called a "picture of the artist as an old man," and we are inevitably reminded of Ibsen's own career. As with Solness, there are three phases in his creativity. First a youthful, genuinely inspired period, when he created his masterpiece, "The Resurrection," in the form of a beautiful young woman "untainted by the world, waking to light and glory, and having nothing ugly or unclean to rid herself of."[35] But this sense of sheer Christian purity yielded to his bourgeois realization of what the world is like, so he "created an area of cracked and heaving earth. And out of the cracks swarmed people, their faces animal beneath the skin." The movement from the first to the second phase clearly corresponds to Solness's shift from building churches for God to homes for people. In the third phase Rubek introduced himself into the group, "a man . . . bowed down by guilt . . . remorse for a lapsed life . . . He's harrowed by the thought that he'll never, never succeed. In all eternity he'll never be free to experience resurrection. He'll sit there perpetually in his own hell."[36]

Rubek, too, has his two women: a young wife, who means little more to him than a plaything bought by his wealth, and his old model Irene, who comes back as a mental patient guarded by a nun. Irene accuses him of having killed her soul by refusing the love she had proffered him. She calls him a "poet," "because you are soft and spineless and full of excuses for everything you've ever done or thought."[37] To this he replies, "I am an artist, Irene." She bitterly tells him that this was her tragedy: "You were an artist, merely an artist—and not a man!"[38] Although to her their relationship was her whole life, to him she was only an episode, an inspiration. She has thought of herself as dead ever since, while he has never been able to create again.

Now, in their new meeting they see the hope of a true resurrection. Rubek's wife, Maja, happily consoles herself with a more earthy man, who will not keep her caged in halls of statuary. But the gifted, exceptional ones, the man and the woman who were made for one another, and who have never been able to unite, make a last effort to do so. They climb the heights to see the sunrise, and once again Ibsen grants his aspiring human beings an end in glory. As the sun rises, they are buried in an avalanche, while Maja and her hunter survive. She sings

I am free! I am free! I am free!
No longer this prison for me!
I'm as free as a bird! I am free![39]

Over the avalanche a blessing is spoken by the nun, an appropriate blessing on all the exceptional people who in Ibsen's plays struggle to achieve their full human potentiality both in love and in creativity and invariably fail: *Pax vobiscum!*

These were Ibsen's final words spoken over his dramatic characters, and I cannot think how they could be bettered. He portrayed the struggles of men and women with the forces within them, those that draw them upward to humanity and those that draw them downward to trolldom. Now he can wish them peace, surcease from their struggles, the repose that comes only with death.

The Code

By going through Ibsen's prose cycle we have found a code that constantly works with opposing and essentially irreconcilable human aspirations. Ibsen saw the lives of men and women as part of a universal, even cosmic, conflict between the two halves of their own selves.[40] These halves he portrayed in a remarkably complex and subtle language, drawing on folklore, biblical tradition, literary predecessors, and his own creative invention.

On the one side was the stern demand of the *calling*, the single-minded rejection of the earthly self, in its most exalted form an isolation from the world, an artistic celibacy, an ascetic solitude, a "distancing" from life. Ibsen's metaphors for this calling naturally included high places—mountains, castles, heights, the upper atmosphere, places appropriate for the "superego."

On the other side there was the categorical imperative of love, the companonship of others, the sharing of life with one's beloved, participation in human responsibilities. Ibsen, in the puritanical tradition of his countrymen, symbolized this aspect of life as lower, a part of himself closely related to the animal, hidden away in the murky depths of the sea or the mountains. In *When We Dead Awaken* Rubek says to Irene: "I was obsessed with the idea that if I touched you sensually, my mind would be profaned and I would be unable to achieve what I was striving to create."[41]

Ibsen knew well enough that most people accepted a bit of each, trying to make out as best they could. In *Brand* he had castigated this lack of wholeness, the disintegration of character, but in his greater maturity he looked with sympathy on the illusions that people live by—one of them being poetry. Yet right to the end the struggle between earth and heaven, love and calling, forms the basic pattern which his imagination could vary endlessly.

I have not tried to interpret very many of Ibsen's cryptic symbols, only to present a key to his code. He used the ordinary words of the language, the actions of his characters, and his settings to express an identity crisis that not only was his but was common to many of his most gifted contemporaries. What he could not solve in his own inner life he expressed in this code. On the surface he presented human characters for the stage, but the perceptive and knowing reader, who has learned his language, can perceive the demon, the troll that lurks within.

READINGS AND REFERENCES

Inga-Stina Ewbank, "Ibsen's Dramatic Language as a Link between His 'Realism' and His 'Symbolism,'" *Contemporary Approaches to Ibsen*, ed. Daniel Haakonsen (Oslo: Universitetsforlaget, 1966), 96–123, is a seminal study of Ibsen's code. Two recent books are devoted to the study of mythic patterns: Orley I. Holtan, *Mythic Patterns in Ibsen's Last Plays* (Minneapolis: University of Minnesota Press, 1970), and James Hurt, *Catiline's Dream: An Essay on Ibsen's Plays* (Urbana: University of Illinois Press, 1972).

The critical literature of earlier years teems with discussions on the meaning of Ibsen's symbols. Jennette Lee, *The Ibsen Secret* (New York: Putnam's, 1907) was the product of an American professor of English at Smith College.

More recent discussions may be found in the volumes of *Ibsenforbundet*; e.g., in the volume *Contemporary Approaches to Ibsen 2*, ed. Daniel Haakonsen (Oslo: Universitetsforlaget, 1971), see Daniel Haakonsen, "'The Play-within-the play' in Ibsen's Realistic Drama," 101–17, and Mitsuya Môri, "Ibsen's Dramatic Irony," 118–39.

An excellent study of the "inner development" of Ibsen's dramas and the puzzling contrasts in his thinking is Jørgen Haugan, *Henrik Ibsens metode: Den indre utvikling gjennom Ibsens dramatikk* (Oslo: Gyldendal, 1977), published too late to be considered in this book. One hopes that it will be translated into English.

A model text edition and critical analysis of *The Wild Duck* is the one by Dounia B. Christiani (New York: Norton, 1968).

5

Poetry in the Round

My poem's like the heather-covered slope
That rises steadily above the peasant's farm.
Behind the slope—if you are standing free—
You gaze upon a ring of snow-clad peaks.
My lute is tuned to play a muted song;
But deeper strings lend color to the chords.
Within the poem thus a poem is concealed;
And he who fathoms this will understand the song.

Ibsen, *The Epic Brand*, st. 9[1]

IN A MOMENT of unusual candor, when he was angered by critic Clemens Petersen's claim that *Peer Gynt* was not poetry, Ibsen wrote to Bjørnson: "My work *is* poetry; and if it is not, it shall become so. The concept of poetry in our country, in Norway, shall come to conform with this book."[2] His prediction, which must have seemed rash to Bjørnson, has been fulfilled. It has increasingly been recognized, not only for *Peer Gynt* and not only in Norway, that he *was* a poet, not only in verse but also in prose. This development sustains his own judgment, as expressed to the Women's League on his seventieth birthday: "I have been more a poet, less a social philosopher, than people generally seem inclined to think."[3] These two statements show him battling on two fronts, in defense first of his verse, then of his prose as poetry. It was hard for his contemporaries, and for many of his critics down to the present, to recognize a poetic genre that was neither lyrical nor epic but essentially dramatic. Francis Fergusson called it "theatrical poetry," a "hidden poetry, masquerading as reporting; it is a 'poetry of the theater' (in M. Cocteau's phrase) and not a poetry of words."[4]

In this chapter I shall focus on the formal qualities of Ibsen's message that give it validity as poetry. Especially in his "social" plays Ibsen is often thought of as unpoetical, because he was echoing the "flat" speech of everyday conversation. Here we must first discount the distortions of translators who failed to reproduce the nuances of his language, either because they were unaware of them or because it was not possible to reproduce them in English. We have seen that Ibsen's language is often ambiguous, carrying in addition to its surface meaning some deeper sense. According to William Empson, ambiguity is one of the weapons in the armory of poets, without being in itself poetic.[5] Ambiguity is inherent in all natural language, which is the despair of scientists, who strive to be precise (by definitions, formulas, mathematical logic); but it offers the poet an opportunity to make his or her language richer and more suggestive of a variety of meanings.

In the special Ibsen genre I have here called "dramatic poetry," he has to give form not merely or primarily to the words spoken but to the dramatic structure as a whole. His "cryptogram" has to be wrapped in a form that will convey his message without apparent distortion. In verse, with its severe requirements of rhyme and rhythm, this is obviously true, but in prose it is less easily perceived. It is not too much to describe Ibsen's prose dialogue as a masterpiece of poetic cryptography, as hard to write and as astonishing in its perfection as anything he wrote in verse. The topics may fade and the ideas age, but the poetry remains, as modern critics have increasingly been willing to recognize. Even when the paint on his statues cracks and peels, the grace of his sculpture remains.

Ibsen, being also a literary critic, was quite clear and even insistent on the importance of form in poetry. In a poem of his youth, "In the Picture Gallery" (1859), he made a major critical statement: "The *form* it is that makes my verses poems!"

> Do not forget that in the realms of art
> It is the *form* alone that ranks;
> If you would judge the singer's scales,
> Attend to *how* he sings, not *what*.[6]

Rhyme as Form

In Ibsen's youth, verse was the prime language of dramatic literature, all in good romantic fashion. From the Greeks and the French to Shakespeare and Goethe and on to their Danish epigones Oehlenschläger and Heiberg, the grand tradition called for serious plays, especially tragedies, to be written in verse. *Catiline* was, not surprisingly, written in verse greatly reminiscent of such predecessors as the Norwegians Wergeland and Welhaven. Ibsen's earliest preserved verse is from 1847, and with it the nineteen-year-old amazed his companions in Grimstad. He brought this talent to perfection in *Brand* and *Peer Gynt*, but it does not carry over well in translation, especially since rhyme is in disrepute in the modern lyric. But rhyme is the lifeblood of Ibsen's verse, giving shape and dignity to his serious passages and a light touch to his humor (as in Thomas Hood, W. S. Gilbert, or Ogden Nash).

The year 1859 was a turning point for Ibsen in his technical skill as a rhymester, as in so much else.[7] He then initiated the so-called Ibsen strophe, a nine-line, alternately three- and four-beat stanza, usually rhymed a b a b c d c c d, known from "On the Heights" and his popular narrative poem "Terje Vigen." In the succeeding years he wrote three of his most interesting dramas entirely in rhymed verse: *Love's Comedy* (1862), *Brand* (1866), and *Peer Gynt* (1867). These are not in strophes, but in sharply chiseled lines, often run-on, with the rhymes intertwined. He used a mixture of masculine and feminine rhymes, with a sprinkling of trisyllabics, as in *Peer Gynt's vandene, strandene, vikende, skrikende* (which are the despair of translators). In *Brand* he spiced the satire of the mayor by letting him rhyme such absurdities as *pesthus, arresthus, festhus* ("pest house," "arrest house," "fest house," i.e., hospital, jail, and banquet hall, to be built under one roof to make a "community center").[8] In *Love's Comedy* an iambic five-beat line is used throughout, except in the interspersed songs. *Brand* is written in a four-beat line, some two-thirds iambic, the more elevated passages trochaic.[9] In *Peer Gynt* the rhymes and rhythms run riot. Nearly every scene has a different line length or rhythm, iambic or trochaic, three-beat or four-beat, with the rhymes intertwined and often witty.

Translation problems also bar recognition of his lyric poems, which are restricted in form and theme but are often intensely moving. In 1871 he was prevailed upon to publish his one collection (*Digte*), but only after a severe pruning and rewriting which left a mere fifty-five poems. Nine were added in later editions, and one can now read every scrap in the centennial works of 1928. The best of them are pungent and epigrammatic, often expressing the poet's inmost feelings more directly than the plays. The theme may be ironic, as in "Building Plans," or bitter, as in "The Eider Duck," and it may be openly auto-biographical, as in "The Miner." A few longish poems, like his "Balloon Letter" or "A Letter in Rhyme," are versified essays on the state of the world, and others in narrative form are miniature dramas. The one concession to popular taste is his much beloved and declaimed "Terje Vigen," an episode from the British blockade of Denmark-Norway during the Napoleonic wars. As Koht emphasized, personal and patriotic themes are here effectively blended, the personal being Ibsen's struggle with and victory over himself in 1861.[10] A number of poems are purely lyrical and were found worthy of being set to music by Edvard Grieg, e.g., "A Swan," "With a Water Lily," "Gone," "Margaret's Cradle Song," "Solveig's Song," and the like.[11]

Having achieved mastery in versification, Ibsen proceeded in the early 1870s to abandon it totally. As noted earlier, this represented a real sacrifice for him. A decade later, having mastered the art of prose, he rejected a request from actress Lucie Wolf for a verse prologue: "I myself have scarcely written a single verse in the last 7–8 years, having exclusively cultivated the far more difficult art of composing in a plain, truthful, realistic language." His reasons were that the verse form, he thought, would not in the immediate future be used in the drama. Art forms, he suggested, were like the prehistoric animals (e.g., the dinosaurs) that had died out when their time was past. "A tragedy in iambic pentameter is even now as rare a creature as the dodo bird, a few specimens of which still live on an African island."[12]

As late as 1871 he could still define the importance of verse and his need for it in his "Rhymed Letter to Fru Heiberg":

> Prose is suited to ideas,
>   Verse to visions.
> Joy of spirit, woes of spirit,
> Sorrow like the snows of winter,
>   Anger flashing—
> Fullest life I freest give
> In bonds of verse.[13]

This poem would prove to be one of the last he wrote. Six years earlier he had supported Clemens Petersen's opinion that "versified form with a symbolic background is my most natural medium.[14] But in 1874 he turned a deaf ear to Edmund Gosse's disappointment that

Emperor and Galilean was not written in verse, "My new play is no tragedy in the old style; what I wanted to portray was people, and precisely for that reason I did not allow them to speak in 'the tongue of the gods.' "[15]

He had, of course, written prose in such plays as *St. John's Night, Lady Inger,* and *The Vikings at Helgeland,* but in a mannered, historical style. There is much living dialogue in *The Pretenders,* in spite of its thirteenth-century setting. Not until he wrote *The League of Youth* (1869) did he wrestle with the problem of creating believable contemporary dialogue. Few would be so naive as to think that this is the same as a real-life tape-recorded conversation, which is usually repetitious, only mildly structured, full of false starts and self-corrections, interruptions and changes of topics. Except to those who participate in conversations, they are usually boring and undramatic. Credible dialogue has to incorporate some of these features, but it must also further the action of the play and keep the audience awake.

The Nuances of Norwegian

At this point we may digress to say a few words about the spoken Norwegian of Ibsen's day. Within his social class a standard speech had evolved, which differed only in minor detail from city to city. This "cultivated" speech was not only a prestigious class marker but for people like Ibsen an entirely natural idiom. The anomaly was that although it differed profoundly from the corresponding cultivated Danish, it was identically spelled. In the course of their four centuries of political union, the citizens of Denmark and Norway had developed a common written language, which rendered both Danish and Norwegian speech in a very imperfect way. In 1814 this form of writing was called "Danish" in Denmark and "Norwegian" in Norway, but the growing nationalism of Norwegians soon began to identify it as "Danish." Agitation sprang up on behalf of developing a purely Norwegian written language, which would correspond to Norwegian speech and reflect Norwegian identity. Reforms began already in Ibsen's lifetime, but only after his death were sweeping changes instituted (1907–38) which made his spelling quaintly obsolete. Since 1960 his works have been reissued in a contemporary orthography that again makes it possible for younger people to read him with ease.[16]

From the almost pure Danish writing of his first plays Ibsen moved step by step toward the Norwegian speech that was natural to him. During his romantic period he adopted many words peculiar to Norwegian rural life, especially in plays with a rural setting like *Peer Gynt.*[17]

In principle, he was committed to a gradual Norwegianization, which effectively suffused his romantic plays with a richly poetic quality. "I have myself adopted words from the country dialects, if they are understandable and can enhance the esthetic effect. In this way I contribute to the enrichment and development of our language." But he sharply rejected the efforts of some reformers to replace his language with one based on the dialects: "I will not assist in the liquidation of the literature I myself have helped to develop."[18] In *Peer Gynt* the comic figure of Huhu is Ibsen's gibe at those who wish to restore "the language of the orangutangs," i.e., the Old Norwegian language. Ibsen agreed with the linguistic adviser at the Christiania Norwegian Theater, Knud Knudsen, that the language change should be an evolution, not a revolution.

Part of his problem in writing believable dialogue was that in a framework of Danish spelling and grammar he had to give the effect of bourgeois Norwegian speech. Within this norm he could vary from a formal to an informal style, the formal drawing on Danish, the informal on Norwegian. In his letters and articles the style is generally formal; in the plays formal style is limited to public orations and to the speech of persons characterized as bookish or pompous. Ibsen enjoyed lampooning the pomposity of politicians and officials by using a flowery, rhetorical style, which could be dangerously reminiscent of Bjørnson's oratory. In *The League of Youth* Stensgaard harangues the multitude, "I have observed talents glinting and glittering deep down among the people. I have also observed the spirit of corruption that weighs oppressively upon these talents and keeps them in subjection."[19] The words are hollow and amusingly pompous, particularly when one realizes that Stensgaard is really talking about his own "talents."

The ability to characterize his persons by small, but telling features of their style may not be considered a major poetic triumph. But the employment of appropriate registers of speech is one of the important formal features of dramatic dialogue. They are a problem for every translator in exactly the same way as rhymes in verse, as noted by Popperwell when commenting on McFarlane's translations in the *Oxford Ibsen*.[20] As a formal feature they do not reproduce reality, in the way phonetic writing might, but they stimulate the imagination to visualize the character and give the play an added dimension. Meyer rightly calls this feature "one of Ibsen's supreme strengths, and one of his main contributions to the technique of prose dramas."[21]

The prose plays from *Pillars* to *Enemy* are rich with examples of sharply characterized speech styles. Ibsen refers to the problem of style several times, e.g., in connection with a performance of *Enemy* in 1882, when he writes that journalist Billing must be sure to speak "East Norwegian."[22] This can only mean that his accent should reinforce the image he gives of himself as a man of the people. There is little evidence of this in the printed text, except for his frequent reliance on profanity. The only other character in the play who swears freely is Dr. Stockmann himself, whose surprise and anger at the opposition is picturesquely profane.[23]

Ibsen even anticipated the current interest in differences between male and female speech styles. He asked a casual visitor in Munich, "Have you ever noticed how in conversation a woman usually ends a remark with a word of two or three syllables, a man with a monosyllable?"[24] Linguist Alf Sommerfelt noted some of the differences in the dialogue of Ibsen's men and women: Hedda Gabler and Hilde Wangel are addicted to the word *deilig* "lovely" and generally prefer the form *isj* to *æsj* for "ugh, ick" (the same feature in Gregers Werle no doubt suggests a certain effeminacy, perhaps a part of his mother fixation).[25] Ibsen remarked to his Boswell, John Paulsen, "There are a thousand finesses in dramatic art. Have you ever thought of the fact that the lines in a play should have a different cast according to whether they are spoken in the morning or in the evening?"[26] In a letter to a prospective French translator of *The Wild Duck*, he wrote that it "presents very special problems in that one must be very closely familiar with the Norwegian language to be able to understand how thoroughly every single character in the play has his or her particular individual mode of expression, by means of which the degree of cultivation of that person is marked. For instance, when Gina speaks, one must at once be able to hear that she has never learned grammar and that she has issued from the lower classes. And so on in different ways for all the other characters."[27]

Dialogue as Form

As mentioned, natural dialogue tends to be interrupted and unfinished. In *The Lady from the Sea* Arnholm discovers on a return visit to the Wangel home that his former pupil Bolette has grown into a marriageable young woman. He follows her with his eyes and starts to say, "She's really a lovely—," but covers his embarrassment by starting over, "They're really lovely girls these children who have grown up now—." Later Ellida speaks to him about their onetime affair, "At that time Wangel was still—at that time the girls' mother was still alive."[28] The interruption allows her to avoid saying "still married" and suggests to the audience that she is troubled by her position as a second wife. When Edmund Gosse reviewed the English performance of *Hedda Gabler* in 1891, the form of dialogue in it was so novel that he did not quite know what to make of "this unceasing display of hissing conversational fireworks, fragments of sentences without verbs, clauses that come to nothing, adverbial exclamations and cryptic interrogations." He did admit that "on the stage, no doubt, this rigid broken utterance will give an extraordinary sense of reality."[29]

A sense of reality is of course not reality but part of the poetic illusion. So are the many *verbal echoes* in the dialogue, which can be compared to the use of musical motifs in the work of Wagner, a contemporary of Ibsen's. In *Pillars of Society* the word "society" is firmly planted in the opening scene and gets repeated in virtually every scene after that; no one can remain in doubt of what the play is about. But this key word is not without its poetic function. Each person who uses it has his own interpretation of it, and this ambiguity illuminates the thinking of the characters. When Krap asks foreman Aune why he agitates, his reply (in the original) is, "Det gør jeg for at støtte samfundet," literally "I do it in order to support the society." His words strike the keynote of the play by alluding directly to its title, *Samfundets Støtter*, literally "Supports of Society." The verb *støtte* "support" associates directly with the noun *støtte*, which can mean any kind of supporter, including pillars. The English title permits no such play on words, since *pillar* cannot be a verb. But it turns out that Aune is not talking about "society" in a wider sense, only the Workingman's Society which he heads. Krap misunderstands and quotes Bernick as having called Aune's agitation "samfundsopløsende," i.e., destructive of society, antisocial. To this, Aune quite properly replies that "my society is not Mr. Bernick's society," and Krap counters by telling him off: "Your obligation is to the society known as Mr. Bernick's firm, for that is what we all live on."[30] In four speeches the word *samfunn* has been used in as many meanings, illuminating the contrasting interpretations of worker and employer, and setting the stage for a wider interpretation that will go beyond the selfish interests of either. In addition, this Norwegian word suggests "communion," as in "the communion of saints." Such verbal associations and playful echoes are mostly lost in translation.

Other key words that echo through the play and stay in the minds of the spectators are "the spirit of truth and freedom" enunciated by Lona Hessel, Nora's "miracle of miracles," Osvald's "joy of life," Dr. Stockmann's "damned compact majority." When reviewing *A Doll's House* on its appearance in 1879, a perceptive Norwegian critic, Erik Vullum, noted the absence of traditional imagery in the text, concluding that Ibsen "no longer needs to resort to any graphic aid to natural dialogue."[31] For us the important point is that the whole play is a dramatic metaphor, as proclaimed in its title, *Et Dukkehjem*. In spite of the English translations, this title does not mean a house for dolls, which in Norwegian is *dukkehus*, or *dukkestue*. Before Ibsen, *et dukkehjem* was a small, cozy, neat home; his play gave it the pejorative meaning. Nora is a doll only in a metaphorical sense, having been spoiled by her father and now by her husband. Her home is therefore not a home for adults but a playhouse. When William Archer saw it performed for the first time, he wrote, "The play is not a mere realistic drama, but a poem, and its poetry should be emphasized to give it full effect."[32] In 1971, two decades after his prosaic rewriting of *An Enemy of the People*, Arthur Miller wrote that he now saw the play "rather as a poem, a symbolic demand for a new stage of human evolution."[33]

The Poetry of Prose

If this can be validly maintained for the "social" plays, as I believe it can, it grows increasingly true as we move into the world of *The Wild Duck* and the plays that follow. We have seen how the play is built around a deadly metaphor that takes root in Gregers Werle's diseased brain. He, too, suffers from a "sickly conscience," which Relling unfeelingly diagnoses as "integrity fever," or "rectitudinitis," as we might also translate Ibsen's matchless *retskaffenhedsfeber*. Nordau suggests that it is one of Ibsen's many versions of "original sin."[34] Gregers, as the Christian he is, believes in the value of confession, followed by forgiveness. But Gina refuses to confess and Hjalmar refuses to forgive. Gregers imposes the demand of Christian sacrifice on little Hedvig, as if Hjalmar were a god to be appeased. The author balances the absurdly comic rhetoric of Hjalmar against the absurdly tragic rhetoric of Gregers: both of them have a "mission" in life. Hedvig's death is itself a poem of love, a young girl's love for an unworthy father, who blindly allows her to be crushed between the harsh demands of the ideal and the real.

Poetic mood grows ever more prominent in the following plays. Both Rosmer and Rebecca are deeply poetic figures. Rosmer brings with him the delicate fragrance of an old, decaying tradition, Rebecca the passion of the bewitching North. "It swept over me like a storm at sea. Like one of those storms we sometimes get in the winter up North. It takes hold of you—and carries you off with it, you see—for as long as it lasts. It never occurs to you to resist."[35] The play opens and closes on a poetic folklore motif—the white horse that warns the folk of Rosmersholm that a death will occur. At crucial turns of the action comes Brendel, bohemian and would-be poet, whose every speech is in a comic-poetic mode: "The ecstasies I've relished in my time, John! The mysterious beatitude of creation—or, again, its equivalent—the plaudits, the acclaim, the celebrity, the laurel crowns— all these I've gathered in my grateful hands, trembling with joy."[36] The conversation of Rosmer and Rebecca as they go hand in hand to the millrace is as ceremonial and ritualistic as a church service:

> ROSMER. The husband shall go with his wife, as the wife with her husband.
> REBECCA. But first tell me this: is it you who go with me or I with you?
> ROSMER. That is something we shall never fathom.
> REBECCA. Yet I would so much like to know it.
> ROSMER. We two go with one another, Rebecca. I with you and you with me.
> REBECCA. I almost think that is so.
> ROSMER. For now we two are one.[37]

The title of *The Lady from the Sea* in the original is *Fruen fra havet*, a lightly rewritten form of *havfruen*, "the mermaid." Mermaids, being both fabled and female, are poetic by definition. The theme of fascination with danger is also an old poetic motif. Here it is worked out in several forms, from the not-so-childish games that Hilde plays with the tubercular artist Lyngstrand (it's so "thrilling"!) to the very real fixation of Ellida on the strange seaman with the fish eyes, her "merman" who would lure her back into the sea. As the moment of choice is upon her, the text grows lyrical:

> WANGEL (quietly and sadly). I see it so well, Ellida. Inch by inch you're slipping away from me. This hunger for the boundless, the infinite—the unattainable—will finally drive your mind out completely into darkness.
> ELLIDA. Oh, yes, yes—I feel it—like black, soundless wings hanging over me![38]

In *Hedda Gabler* one of the main figures, Løvborg, is another bohemian, a scholar so imaginative and unorthodox that he chooses to speculate about the future. His secret love, Hedda, is more fascinated than fond of him. In her spiritual confinement he represents to her the dream of beauty that she covets and that she misses in her own life. She spins a web of poetry around him in the hope that he will live out her dream for her. Her "vine leaves in the hair" is a classical motif, as we have seen, and it stands at the other end of the spectrum from General Gabler's pistols, which are cold, hard, and modern.

These two images define her character and suggest better than anything else the extremes between which she swings.

While working on *The Master Builder*, Ibsen wrote one of the rare poems of his later years, a sad little ditty about an elderly couple whose home has burned and who now are searching in the ashes for a jewel they lost:

> But even if they find, these burned-out folk,
> The precious, unconsumed treasure—
> *She* will never again find her faith,
> Nor *he* the happiness that burned.[39]

In the play the theme of the home that burned is at the root of Solness's and his wife's deep frustration in marriage, a symbol of the love that has burned out between them. Solness is weighed down by guilt and fears the retribution that is coming. To his doctor he says: "The turn is coming. I can sense it. I feel it getting closer. Someone or other is going to demand: Make way for me! And then all the others will come storming after, threatening and screaming: Make way, make way, make way! Yes, just you watch doctor. One of these days youth will come here, knocking on the door—"[40] This rhythmic, dramatically exalted speech is typical of the later plays.

The fact that youth does indeed knock on the door immediately after Solness has predicted it is so highly coincidental and so pat that no truly realistic play could tolerate it. But there is poetic justice and humor in the shape that youth takes—not the young rivals that Solness is thinking of but a radiant, trustful young woman, Hilde Wangel. She comes to claim the "kingdom" Solness had promised her ten years earlier. Both phrase and idea are poetic, arising as they do out of the world of fairy tale, and the fact that the episode may never have occurred only adds to its mystic charm. Ironically, she *is* the one who eventually destroys him by insisting that he live up to her ideal of him. The verbal dance that these two perform, the lonely artist and the lovely girl, is sheer dramatic poetry. We spoke earlier of the symbolism of the tower and its meaning. Let us now look at its poetic value. Solness served the ideal by building churches, the real by building homes; in old age he clumsily tried to fuse them by building a home with a spire. But he foresees that it will bring him no happiness, for he himself remains outside these structures, alienated from God, isolated from people. With Hilde he dreams of a new synthesis, again a mythic symbol, the "castle in the air," in which no one can live. So, when he succeeds in climbing the tower, he has to fall, as did Icarus when his wings melted, because death is the inflexible limit to man's earthly aspirations.

The Master Builder calls to mind, as we noted earlier, the Tower of Babel. But it also suggests another well-known folklore theme: the builder who is promised some great reward if he can finish a church. Ultimately, he is frustrated by forces beyond his reach, just as Solness finds that he is unable to complete the church of his own life. He calls on forces beyond reality, his "helpers and servers," who have served him well until the end, when they finally desert him. In his youth Ibsen wrote: "Since the subject matter of myth is timeless, its validity in time can never be so limited as to disqualify an author from laying another stone upon that mythical foundation."[41] In this play he added another stone to the builder's legend by making it into a metaphor for human striving and, by implication, for his own.

Ibsen's last three plays are built in much the same way, with allusions to mythical-poetic themes, in dialogues that are charged with poetic feeling, expressed in symbolic objects or phrases that stir the imagination.

In *Little Eyolf* the Rat Wife is a modern Pied Piper of Hamelin, eerily peering about for anything in the house that is "gnawing." We discover soon enough that there are plenty of "gnawing" things in the house, above all Allmers's relationship with his wife, Rita. They are alienated from each other and from their son, Eyolf, who is left to be lured "into the depths" by the fascinating Rat Wife, just as Hedvig was lured by Gregers. Allmers is a dreamer, another of Ibsen's unproductive poets, who longs for "the solitude up among the mountain peaks and on the great desolate open spaces."[42] These characters are all surrounded by magnetic fields of mystic fascination that draw them together and then push them apart as they approach one another.

John Gabriel Borkman is Ibsen's last and most majestic picture of financial failure, a monumental projection of his father's fate. In a setting of "faded splendor," John Gabriel is living out his aged alienation, mystically brooding over the possibilities for human happiness that he has dreamed of providing by his enterprise. The woman he had rejected for money and career tells him, "The Bible speaks of a mysterious sin for which there is no forgiveness. I have never understood before what that could be. Now I do understand. The great sin for which there is no forgiveness is to murder love in a human soul."[43] Like Hilde Wangel and Ibsen himself, he is looking for his "kingdom." He reaches the heights of poetic prose as he develops the myth of the hidden treasure that is found and then vanishes as it is about to be extracted: "But I'll whisper to you here in the silence of the night. I love you, lying there unconscious in the depths and the darkness! I love you, you riches straining to be born—with all your shining aura of power and glory. I love you, love you, love you."[44] John Gabriel's vision becomes a religious rite, studded with words from biblical terminology.

This is equally true of Ibsen's epilogue, *When We Dead Awaken*, which he at first thought of calling *Resurrection*. From the solidly realistic starting point in the small talk of Rubek and Maja on their return to Norway from the south, the play quickly takes off into the world of poetry. Even their talk is subtly mannered, in short, alternate thrusts that draw them out; the young wife is so bored that she can "hear the stillness." Emotional relief enters in the shape of a strange white-clad woman, who proves to be Rubek's old model Irene, and a faunlike huntsman who will function as the "he-man" Maja has missed in her marriage. Irene's conviction that she is dead, murdered by Rubek's rejection of her love, is reinforced by her shroudlike dress and the contrasting blackness of the nun that attends her. The dialogues are misty, poetic conversations around the theme of art and life, specifically the artist's exploitation of life and happiness as material for art. Rubek has begun to lose faith in the value of his art: "All the talk about the artist's high calling and the artist's mission, and so on, began to strike me as basically empty and hollow and meaningless."[45] In its place he would like to put what he calls "life," but now it is too late. The only life he can experience is death on the heights, in the avalanche, which now becomes the final shroud. The play is built around the theme of resurrection, which is symbolized by his statue, as well as Irene's aphorism, "When we dead awaken, we discover that we have never lived."[46]

So Ibsen ends in poetry, where he had begun fifty years earlier. The prose of his last plays is better poetry than the verse of his first. Although he shifted from verse to prose in mid-career, he never stopped writing poetry. But it was a poetry to suit the modern theater. Even at its most prosaic, his dialogue has a form that gives it dramatic shape. The elements in this form of poetry are the play of dialogue, the balancing of characters, the use of verbal echoes and keywords, and the invention of symbols to give centrality to the plays. There is always underlying patterning in these plays, which becomes apparent to the naked eye only with careful analysis but which can still be felt by reader and spectator as a pervasive quality.

The characters form constellations that we recognize as figures on the firmament of Ibsen's mythology. This is an archetypal pattern of men and women who are trying to harmonize the oppositions of life and finding it not merely difficult but ultimately impossible. They are looking for a harmony that will not be a compromise, and they strive for it even though (or because) it is impossible and will lead to their destruction. The verbal echoes sometimes are no more than mannerisms of speech, which on a realistic plane serve to identify certain characters and make them memorable. But they are also dramatically significant by giving poetic shape and continuity to the plays. Then there are the symbols, which are elements in Ibsen's code, as we saw, but which are also poetic in themselves: Brand's ice church, Gerd's hawk, Peer's madhouse in Cairo, Bernick's rotten ships, Nora's desperate tarantella, Alving's flaming orphanage, Stockmann's poisoned baths, Hedvig's wild duck, Rosmer's white horse, Ellida's eerie seaman, Hedda's fatal pistol, Solness's dizzying tower, Eyolf's floating crutch, Borkman's veins of gold, and Rubek's tainted Resurrection. These central symbols are only a few of the many Ibsen created. Together, the features described comprise a poetic statement about the glory and the frustration of being human.

They also tell us, when compared with Ibsen's explicit statements, something of his theory of art and his view of life. Having tried in his early years to combine artistic creation with social participation, he found his true calling in the creative life and virtually isolated himself from physical contact with the human race. After having supported (if a bit reluctantly) the ideal causes of his day—nationalism, Scandinavianism, internationalism, feminism, even socialism—he withdrew. Brandes wrote that "Ibsen became himself by becoming a solitary . . ." His poetry, he said, is that of "loneliness, portraying the lonely need, the lonely strife, and the lonely protest."[47] He became the "esthete" on the "heights," who defined the act of poetic creation as essentially "to see," believing that "life and its phenomena are best viewed by a writer at a distance, in both time and space."[48] By remaining uncommitted, he could capitalize on his divided self, enabling him to take the topics of the times, project them on the stage, give them an underlying significance, and make a poetic statement that could reach the hearts of women and men, and not only in his own time.

Ibsen's poetic quality is best summed up in the words written almost a half-century ago by the great English novelist E. M. Forster: "Ibsen was a poet at forty. . . . He was a poet at sixty also. . . . Not only was he born a poet—he died one, and as soon as we try to understand him instead of asking him to teach us, the point becomes clearer."[49]

READINGS AND REFERENCES

Ibsen's use of the Norwegian language has been explored by several linguists: see, for example, Johan Storm, "Ibsen og det norske Sprog," in *Henrik Ibsen: Festskrift*, ed. Gerhard Gran (Bergen, 1898), 147–205; Didrik Arup Seip, "Ibsens retskrivning og sprogform," in Henrik Ibsen, *Samlede verker* [*Hundreårsutgaven*], ed. Francis Bull, Halvdan Koht, and Didrik Arup Seip (Oslo: Gyldendal, 1928), 1.16–24, and "Henrik Ibsen og språket," in his *Studier i norsk språkhistorie* (Oslo: Aschehoug, 1934), 228–36 (originally published in 1928); Trygve Knudsen, "Phases of Style and Language in the Works of Henrik Ibsen," *Scandinavica* 2 (1963), 1–20.

On Ibsen as poet, one can now read John Northam, *Ibsen: A Critical Study* (Cambridge: University Press, 1973), who flatly states (p. 1) that "all of his books, early or late, in verse or in modern prose, are a form of poetry" and who goes on to demonstrate this for six plays. His views have been challenged by Ronald Gray, who contends that the claim is built on a misunderstanding of the Norwegian word *digte* (like German *dichten*). Gray's book *Ibsen—a Dissenting View: A Study of the Last Twelve Plays* (Cambridge: University Press, 1977) argues from a more traditional view of the meaning of "poetry." It may be regarded as a healthy antidote or reaction, but it represents a point of view that I believe cannot be sustained on the evidence.

Inga-Stina Ewbank illuminates the poetry of Ibsen's prose in her "Ibsen and 'the far more difficult art' of prose" (*Contemporary Approaches to Ibsen 2*, ed. Daniel Haakonsen [Oslo: Universitetsforlaget, 1971], 60–83). She speaks (on p. 76) of the fact that in *Rosmersholm* "the whole verbal tissue of the play has a peculiar density and ambiguity about it," which fulfills the ideal of the greatest dramatic poetry by suggesting "complexities of character which are beyond the scope of the most exacting discursive analysis" (quoting John Bayley).

6

Ibsenites and Ibsenism

Not only those who write are poets, but so are the readers; they are collaborators, who are often more poetical than the poet himself.

Ibsen, Speech, 26 May 1898.[1]

WE HAVE now pondered the major aspects of the message Ibsen issued to the world in his often controversial but still enduring plays. What can we say about the audience that received his message and how does it relate to the aspects we have discussed?

In the first chapter I noted that we could reconstruct much of Ibsen's inner life by studying his work carefully. In the same way we can deduce a good deal about his intended audience. Like attracts like, and we may guess that those who, like him, were social outsiders, inwardly divided, rebellious about conventions could best identify with his characters. Young people chafing under the need of adjusting to the rigid demands of social norms were more likely to hail him as a liberator than those who had long since accepted these norms. The very idea of a drama that was more dialogue than spectacle required an audience that came to listen rather than to look. I shall suggest that Ibsen's audience has been of two kinds: the youthful and the thoughtful. Not that these are in contrast; they strongly overlap.

My own experience in teaching courses about Ibsen has been that his name invariably has attracted large classes of young people. This was true in the early 1930s, and it remained true forty years later, in public and private schools, in small colleges and large universities.

Even though the students find some of his topics to be dated, his attacks on conventional ways, his call for individual thinking, and his emphasis on moral independence appeal to young people who are liberating themselves from too close a dependence on their home environment and who are trying to find an identity in the adult world.

The Ibsen Audience

The only available statistics about the Ibsen audience in recent years come from his homeland, Norway.[2] In 1968 the audiences at performances of *Brand* in the city of Bergen consisted of about two-thirds women and one-third men. The number of persons in their twenties was 28 percent, a disproportionately high figure. The percentage of unmarried persons was slightly higher than one would have expected. Half of the audience had *gymnasium* (junior college) education or better, five times as many as the average population of the city. Upper- and middle-bracket income groups were greatly overrepresented. In short, the audience was predominantly female, young, educated, and middle class.

In the decade 1965–75 there were 315 performances of Ibsen plays in Bergen, more than in any preceding decade. Over the past century the most popular plays in Bergen have been *Peer Gynt* and *Brand*, followed at some distance by *Ghosts* and *An Enemy of the People*. Interestingly enough, Bjørnson and Ibsen plays were performed about equally often until World War II; since 1945 Bjørnson plays have virtually disappeared from the stage. Norwegian theaters in the years since 1945 have presented performances of 355 plays by 170 Norwegian dramatists and 893 plays by 487 non-Norwegian dramatists. Of the grand total, Ibsen represents about 6 percent, his nearest rival, Shakespeare, about 3. Corresponding figures for Denmark rank Ibsen fifth, for West Germany eighth, for the repertory theater in Birmingham, England, third (between 1913 and 1963).

A roundup of Ibsen performances in the years 1970–75 showed that five of his modern plays had been performed in each of the countries of Romania, Czechoslovakia, and the Netherlands. In France only *Peer Gynt* had been played, but in German-speaking Switzerland, in Austria, and in West Germany there were between eight and twenty-nine different productions every year, with *An Enemy of the People* in the lead, and including even *The League of Youth*. In England there were seventeen productions, among them *Hedda Gabler* and *The Wild Duck* produced by Ingmar Bergman as well as an adaptation of *Hedda* by playwright John Osborne. In Canada eleven plays were given in

Toronto alone. In the United States there were numerous productions, notably the opening of the Kennedy Memorial Center theater with *A Doll's House*. The play was also performed in New York, with Liv Ullmann starring as Nora, and in Seattle, under the direction of Eva Le Gallienne. In Japan, where his plays have been popular over the years, the only production was by a visiting Norwegian company. It is evident that Ibsen is alive and well, at least in the English-, German-, and Scandinavian-speaking world.[3]

We mentioned earlier the burst of activity in the last two decades to bring Ibsen's text into line with current English usage, either by re-writing Archer or by starting afresh from Ibsen's original. A selected list of these will be found in the Bibliography. Among the more active English translators have been Norman Ginsbury, Una Ellis-Fermor, Michael Meyer, and Peter Watts, while James W. McFarlane has successfully completed his monumental *Oxford Ibsen* in eight volumes, to which we have often had occasion to refer.[4] In the United States important versions have appeared by Eva Le Gallienne, Kai Jurgensen, and others, but now the whole Prose Cycle is available in a complete, unified version by Rolf Fjelde. These are in themselves evidence of the continuing interest in Ibsen right down into the year of his sesquicentennial.

Books have been written about the spread of Ibsen's fame and writings in various countries, though most of these are now far out of date: for Germany (Eller 1918, George 1968), France (Reque 1930), Spain (Gregersen 1936), England (Franc 1919, Egan 1972), Russia (Nilsson 1958, Nag 1967), America (dissertation by Andersen 1937), Punjab in India (Sethi 1976); there are also numerous articles for these and other countries as far away as Japan (Sato 1962). These generally make entertaining reading, since there are both sympathetic and unsympathetic critics, and the clash of their views often throws interesting sidelights on the thinking of the times. Controversy today is less over Ibsen's importance as "father of the modern drama" than it is over his relevance in the present-day theater. Dramatic literature of the twentieth century has become so much less structured and so much more unconventional and shocking that from this point of view he seems more like a grandfather than a father of the modern drama. There is today a voluminous critical literature, only a small part of which it has been possible to consider in connection with this survey. The six blind men who wrote contradictory reports on the elephant can scarcely have differed more than some of the critics of Ibsen.

We know that Ibsen was concerned about his audience. On sending a copy of *Brand* to Bernhard Dunker, a liberal jurist and one of his benefactors, he wrote, "I look forward with suspense to your judgment, for you have been one of the few spectators I always see in my imagination sitting in the front row as the work has progressed."[5] To Countess Sophie Adlersparre in Sweden, he wrote that in *Ghosts* he had probably gone as far in scandalizing his audience as the public would stand: "A writer must not leave his people so far behind that there is no longer any understanding between them and him."[6]

Women and Youth

On a celebrated occasion at the Scandinavian Club in Rome, Ibsen singled out two groups for whom he had a special admiration: women and young people. The issue was the right to vote in the club, and when Ibsen's motion was voted down, he made an impassioned speech, declaring that women and young people "have something in common with the true artist, something that takes the place of practical ability . . . Youth has that instinct of genius that unconsciously perceives what is right. But it is just this instinct that woman has in common both with youth and the true artist. . . . What I fear is the men with the small tasks and the small thoughts, men with the petty considerations and the little anxieties . . ."[7] His attack on what he called *gammelmandsfornuftigheden*, "the prudence of old men," is diffused throughout his work. Even when his characters begin to reflect his own aging, they are still prepared to have a last youthful fling. Solness climbs his tower, John Gabriel Borkman breaks out of his house, and sculptor Rubek heads off into the mountains, all in the company of women who love them.

That women have responded strongly to Ibsen's work goes almost without saying. Not only was he willy-nilly identified with their "cause" through his portrayal of the women in *The League of Youth*, *Pillars of Society*, *A Doll's House*, and *Ghosts*, but throughout his work there runs a gallery of strong women, from the demonic Furia of *Catiline* to the mad Irene in *When We Dead Awaken*. Of them all, Hedda Gabler is no doubt the one that fascinates the most in all her repulsiveness; but she, too, is the victim of a society dominated by men. The Englishwoman who first translated *A Doll's House*, Henriette Lord, wrote that Ibsen "opens all the great gates of his poetry to noble, pure-hearted, loving, disappointed women." At the same time a conservative critic like Clement Scott could regret that such a "foolish, fitful, conceited, selfish, and unlovable" woman should be allowed to "drive from the stage the loving and noble heroines who have adorned it and filled all hearts with admiration from the time of Shakespeare to the time of Pinero."[8] One wonders what he would have thought of the fact that among the women who have felt akin to Nora was Madame Mao Tse-Tung, once the powerful wife of the architect of Chinese communism. According to her biographer, Roxane Witke, she played the part of Nora when she was a young actress in Shanghai in 1935 and "adored the role" because it gave her a chance to represent Nora as "a woman rebel," whose role raised many questions relating to the emancipation of women.[9]

The impact of the play is reflected by Somerset Maugham in an imaginative scene from his novel *Of Human Bondage* (1915). His hero Philip is living with a professor's family in Heidelberg at the time when Ibsen plays were first being performed, "amid the cheers of adherents and the hisses of decent people." The professor is a mild-mannered person, but *A Doll's House* impels him to raise his voice and roar that this "was nonsense and obscene nonsense." "It was the ruin of the family, the uprooting of morals, the destruction of Germany," and he concludes by saying, "I would sooner my daughters were lying dead at my feet than see them listening to the garbage of that shameless fellow."[10] The good professor need not have worried: in his speech to the League for Women's Rights in 1898, Ibsen emphasized that the major contribution women could make would be as mothers, who would awaken in their children "a conscious feeling of culture and discipline."[11]

In 1874, when the students at the University of Christiania honored him with a torchlight procession, he warmly replied that the young people of Norway had answered the question of whether he was in spiritual contact with them. "Students," he said, "have essentially the same task as the poet: to clarify for themselves, and thereby for others, the problems of time and eternity that agitate the age and the society to which they belong."[12] Eleven years later he told the students of Copenhagen: "I intend to remain a student all my life. On the day I am not, I shall consider myself unworthy to live."[13] When he left Christiania the same year, he shook Bjørn Bjørnson's hand, saying, "Give my greetings to all who are young in Norway . . . and tell them that I will stand with them as a pivot on their extreme left. What may look like madness in the young contains the seeds of the future. Be sure of that."[14] At his last torchlight procession, in 1898, he alluded to Solness as "a man in some ways akin to me . . . However, *I* am not afraid of youth. I have never been afraid of youth. I knew that it would come knocking on my door. It came, and I greet it now with joy."[15]

We have numerous testimonials to the effect that young people in many countries responded with enthusiasm. In Germany Paul Schlenther, who became one of his translators, wrote, "our young eyes were opened to the false and glittering tinsel of the theater around us. We were thrilled and we rejoiced."[16] In Sweden Gurli Linder, a woman writer, reported that in her youth "Ibsen showed us our problems, our doubts, the injustices of our age, how dead tradition survived in a living shape, our belief in the future, in a just world built upon truth."[17] In France, director Lugné-Poe noted that his production of *Rosmersholm* and *The Master Builder* was put on by a cast of ten players "whose total ages came to less than two hundred years."[18]

Joyce and Freud

One of the more famous youthful rebels who found Ibsen a revelation was the seventeen-year-old James Joyce (1882–1941). In Ireland he felt some of the same pressures as had Ibsen in Norway: Catholicism and the new Irish revival did for him what Lutheranism and the Norwegian myth had done for Ibsen. In *Stephen Hero* (1904), an autobiographical fragment (rewritten as *A Portrait of the Artist as a Young Man*), he declared his discovery of Ibsen to be "the most enduring influence of his life." "Ibsen had no need of apologist or critic: the minds of the old Norse poet and the perturbed young Celt met in a moment of radiant simultaneity." Captivated as he was by Ibsen's art, what moved him most was "the very spirit of Ibsen himself that was discerned moving behind the impersonal manner of the artist."[19]

Joyce proceeded in all his ardor to produce his first literary effort, a brilliant fifteen-page analysis of *When We Dead Awaken*, which had then just been published. The article appeared in the leading English literary journal, *Fortnightly Review*.[20] He also set himself to learning Norwegian in order to read the rest of Ibsen's plays. Eventually he wrote an enthusiastic letter to Ibsen, saying among other things, "Your battles inspired me . . . those that were fought and won behind your forehead . . . your willful resolution to wrest the secret from life gave me heart." The conclusion must have touched Ibsen: "As one of the young generation for whom you have spoken I give you greeting—not humbly, because I am obscure and you in the glare, not sadly because you are an old man and I a young man, not presumptuously, nor sentimentally—but joyfully, with hope and with love, I give you greeting."[21]

This enthusiastic outpouring by the still untried master-to-be was inspired by a message Ibsen had sent him by way of William Archer, thanking him for the review. Joyce's biographer Ellmann goes so far as to write, "Before Ibsen's letter Joyce was an Irishman; after it he was a European."[22] Several students of Joyce's work have explored the influence of Ibsen on his complex masterpieces, *Ulysses* (1922) and *Finnegans Wake* (1939); the fullest treatment is given in B. J. Tysdahl's *Joyce and Ibsen* (1968). Here it is possible to find numerous allusions to Ibsen, along with distorted scraps of Joyce's Norwegian. His abiding affection for Ibsen is reflected much later in a sardonic poem, "Epilogue to Ibsen's *Ghosts*," written after viewing a Paris performance of the play. In this we hear the voice of Captain Alving's ghost, saying (*inter alia*):

> My spouse bore me a blighted boy,
> Our slavey pupped a bouncing bitch.
> Paternity, thy name is joy
> When the wise sire knows which is which.[23]

Sigmund Freud (1856–1939) was another lonely and rebellious youth who found Ibsen a revelation. Freud was troubled by lack of understanding for his work, uncertainty in his own thinking, and a sense of being an outsider. It is not surprising that he wrote one of the more perceptive essays on *Rosmersholm* demonstrating how admirably and delicately Ibsen had handled an instance of the Oedipus complex as the deepest layer of motivation in Rebecca's two puzzling refusals of Rosmer's proposal.[24] He must also have found Ibsen's solution of Ellida's problem in *Lady from the Sea* interesting, as an example of a fixation that is brought to the surface and thereby resolved. Koht noted that the vogue of Freud's teaching in the 1920s gave new actuality to the play.[25] Meyer suggested that Ibsen's conception of man's need for "a revolution of the spirit" corresponds closely to Freud's later concept of "liberation from within."[26]

Freud was not the only psychoanalyst to treat Ibsen's characters as real people. Wilhelm Stekel analyzed *Peer Gynt* as a description of "how the soul, oppressed by the primal passions, struggles to escape the hell of the instincts."[27] The American analysts Smith Jelliffe and Louise Brink in a twenty-page study of *The Wild Duck* found (1919) that "Ibsen preceded the more modern spirit of therapeutic research which recognizes in every disability a form and a degree of illness . . ."[28] The Norwegian Arne Duve subjected all the plays to a thorough psychoanalytic interpretation.[29]

Shaw and Socialism

The chief "Ibsenite" in Britain (at least in his own view) was George Bernard Shaw (1856–1950), who had not yet written a single play of his own when he was introduced to Ibsen's writings by William Archer and Eleanor Marx Aveling (Karl Marx's daughter). He was still a music critic but soon turned to drama, making his debut as a dramatic critic with his lecture on "The Quintessence of Ibsenism" to the Fabian Society in 1890. Shaw's enthusiastic advocacy of Ibsen raised many hackles, but it also established Ibsen as a name to be reckoned with in English literary history. Shaw's lecture was expanded and published as a book the following year, and in 1913 it was revised to take into account Ibsen's later plays. Shaw's unconventional views and provocative style of writing has made it a favorite introduction to Ibsen ever since. As such it is hardly reliable, emphasizing as it does the surface themes rather than the deeper meanings. Shaw's biographer, Archibald Henderson, aptly described it as "an ideological distillation of Ibsen in the role of ethical and moral critic of contemporary civilization."[30] Shaw found in Ibsen what he wanted: emancipation from the sentimentality, the respectability, the uniformity, and the injustices of Victorian England. Shaw was also an outsider, an Irishman with all the wit that this implies, and a Puckish clown, who wanted to amuse as well as provoke. One way of doing this was to tell the English that Ibsen was superior to Shakespeare. In *The Saturday Review*, where he was dramatic critic after 1894, he made it his slogan: "Down with Shakespeare. Great is Ibsen; and Shaw is his prophet."[31]

When Shaw began writing plays of his own, they were in most respects unlike Ibsen's, both in style and in theme. In a minor play called *The Philanderer* (1893) he even poked fun at his own "Ibsenism." A character named Charteris describes a club called "The Ibsen Club," in which a condition for membership is that "the candidate, if female, is not womanly, and if male, is not manly." When a man asks a woman, "Does Julia belong to me?" she replies, "Certainly not. A woman belongs to herself and to nobody else." To this he answers, "Quite right. Ibsen for ever!"[32] The play is not good, and William Archer was disappointed by it. Not until Shaw wrote *Mrs. Warren's Profession* (1893) did he succeed as a playwright, in a play where the spirit of *A Doll's House* and *Ghosts* hovers over the characters. Shaw's view of Ibsen was one-sided, as we might expect, and it has been suggested that his book should rather have been titled "The Quintessence of Shavianism."

Shaw's annexation of Ibsen as a socialist was decisively rejected in 1906 by the brilliant founder and theoretician of Russian Marxism, G. V. Plekhanov (1856–1918). Many socialists were pleased by Ibsen's unmasking of the hypocrisies of bourgeois society in plays like *Brand*, *Peer Gynt*, and *Pillars of Society*. In Czarist Russia his plays were considered dangerously revolutionary, so that they were carefully watched by the police and warmly applauded by intellectual radicals. Even before Plekhanov, Friedrich Engels, one of the great theoreticians of socialism, was aware of Ibsen as a progressive force, but he pointed out to Paul Ernst in 1890 that one could not expect a man from an industrially undeveloped country like Norway to understand the plight of the proletariat.[33] Plekhanov, who confessed to great admiration for Ibsen's work, quite correctly identified Ibsen's bourgeois background and used this to explain his lack of interest in socialism. In a closely reasoned essay of more than fifty pages, he maintained that Ibsen's cult of individualism was the western intellectual's way of not having to grapple with the real social problems of the age. Ibsen, he claimed, saw the problem as "moral" rather than "political." To Plekhanov, Ibsen's "revolution of the human spirit" was an empty slogan without positive content.[34] His essay makes interesting reading, but history has thrown an ironic light on it. The revolution he had worked for in Russia made Plekhanov one of its first victims: according to his biographer, S. H. Baron, he died in Finland in 1918, driven out of Russia after having been "harassed by overzealous Red Guards as 'an enemy of the people.'"[35]

Dramatists and Critics

It was Ibsen's fate to move altogether too rapidly from being avant-garde to being old hat. By the time of his death in 1906 a number of critics who had always opposed him exorcised his spirit by declaring, wishfully, that he was "dead as a doornail." In Rilke's words (1910): "Loneliest of men, withdrawn from all, how rapidly they have overtaken you by means of your fame! But lately they were fundamentally opposed to you, and now they treat you as their equal."[36] Ibsen was quickly enshrined as the father of the modern drama; e.g., Johanna Kröner (1935) called him "The man who has had the most decisive, the deepest and most enduring influence on all European drama . . . Through Ibsen's influence European drama has experienced a powerful renewal and progress."[37]

Whether or not the dramatists who followed him either liked him or learned from him, his example encouraged them to try new ways of presenting literary content in dramatic form. August Strindberg was one of those who was inspired by Ibsen in his youth, but later he attacked Ibsen in words that suggest a paranoiac sense of rivalry.[38] Ibsen was not unaware of this in his later years. Some of the misty and demoniac quality in his own late plays may have been inspired by his fascination for "the madman's eyes" of the painting of Strindberg that hung in his study. Pirandello was impressed by Ibsen's retrospective method and carried his indecisive conclusions even farther, so that we are sometimes left uncertain about who his characters are, since each one is what others see. In 1893 the English playwright Henry Arthur Jones clearly felt himself threatened by Ibsen; he warned his readers not to "join the bleak Norwegian's barren quest . . . in some base strife of petty dullard's, soused in native filth." But by the time of Ibsen's death he had changed his mind and called him "a great destroyer; a great creator; a great poet; a great liberator: in his later prose plays he has freed the European drama, not only from the minor conventions of the stage, but from the deadlier bondage of sentimentality, of one-eyed optimism, and sham morality."[39]

Ibsen made large demands on his audience, which may be one reason he sometimes failed to get the understanding for which he often pleaded. One who responded enthusiastically, but not always understandingly, was H. L. Mencken, famous American critic and man of letters. He published his own versions of *A Doll's House* and *Little Eyolf* in 1909; in his preface to the former he cited "the words of an enthusiastic German," who (in Mencken's tongue-in-cheek rendition) called Ibsen "the deepest-down-divingest, longest-under-stayingest, most mud-up-bringingest" moralist of his time."[40] In his later, better-known essay on Ibsen, "Journeyman Dramatist," Mencken rejected Ibsen's thinking but praised him as "a play-maker of astounding skill."[41] "Down to the time he lost his mind—he was then at work on *John Gabriel Borkman*—he never wrote a line that had any significance save the obvious one, and never forgot for an instant that he was writing, not tracts, but stage-plays." "Ibsen's chief interest, from the beginning to the end of his career as a dramatist, was not with the propagation of ethical ideas, but with the solution of aesthetic problems."[42] Mencken, like Shaw, was brilliantly one-sided, and as a no-nonsense man, he would have no truck with Ibsen's philosophy or symbolism.

Against Mencken's blistering rhetoric we may set Eric Bentley's placement of Ibsen as a central figure in his book *The Playwright as Thinker* (1946). He agrees with the thesis advanced in this volume concerning the deliberate ambiguity of Ibsen's work, pointing out that "an Ibsenite sentence often performs four or five functions at once." From *The Wild Duck* on, "the world of trolls and goblins comes thronging back into his work," and "a complex, shifting symbolism is employed—to the dismay of those who expect symbolism to be either purely decorative or purely allegorical."[43] Although Joseph Wood Krutch in 1928 could deny *Ghosts* the status of a great tragedy,

using it as an example of "the tragic fallacy," Bentley would write in
1946 that Ibsen is "the greatest writer of tragedies, not in medieval,
but in modern dress."[44] Krutch felt that modern man had lost the
cosmic perspective needed for the concept of tragedy, "No ghost will
leave the other world to warn or encourage him; there is no virtue or
vice which he can possibly have which can be really important; and
when he dies neither his death nor the manner of it will be, outside
the circle of two or three people as unnecessary as himself, any more
important than that of a rat behind the arras."[45] Bentley, more hopefully, claimed that "most often, perhaps, the modern tragic writer
sides with the individual against the mass and sees the struggle as one
between greatness and mediocrity, the living and the petrifact . . ."[46]

Maurice Maeterlinck, the neo-romantic Belgian playwright, was in
most ways very different from Ibsen, but as we noticed earlier, he admired his later plays for their artistry. "'What is it,' I asked, 'what is
it that, in *The Master Builder*, the poet has added to life, thereby
making it appear so strange, so profound, and so disquieting beneath
its trivial surface?' The discovery is not easy, the old master hides
more than one secret from us. . . . Hilde and Solness are, I believe,
the first characters in drama who feel, for an instant, that they are living in the atmosphere of the soul. . . . Their conversation resembles
nothing that we have ever heard, inasmuch as the poet has endeavored
to blend in one expression both the inner and outer dialogue . . ."[47]

The last playwright we shall mention who received impulses more
or less directly from the study of Ibsen is Eugene O'Neill. His plays
are often reminiscent of Ibsen's, but in one of them, *The Iceman
Cometh* (1939), he has clearly adopted the theme of the "life lie."
However, *he* calls it "pipe dreams." Larry Slade, a character in the
play, refers to Harry's Bar, where the derelicts hang out, as "The Palace
of Pipe Dreams" but also as "The Bottom of the Sea Rathskeller,"
and lo, we are transported right back into the Ekdal loft.[48]

The most delicately worded tribute to Ibsen as a poet came in an
apostrophe anonymously addressed to him by the greatest of modern
German poets, Rainer Maria Rilke, in *The Notebook of Malte Laurids
Brigge* (1910). Like the whole book, it is a prose poem in itself, which
should be read in its entirety; we have used a passage from it as a motto
of this book. Ibsen he calls "a timeless tragic poet."[49]

It may have been a presumption on my part to call all these writers,
actors, thinkers, and dreamers "Ibsenites," a term that once was op-
probrious and in any case is constricting. My point is merely that they
are sensitive and thoughtful persons, stars on the firmament of the Ib-

sen audience. Among the many thousands who have passively enjoyed or at least endured Ibsen's plays, these have been stimulated to their own creative work by his great example. Ibsen has communicated doubly with them.

In 1973 a German critic could write, after a performance of *A Doll's House* in Berlin, "The evening proved that as far as Ibsen's thematic problem is concerned we are in truth not a hundred years wiser."[50] The reason for this is clearly that Ibsen not only "described human beings" but also, as he insisted, "described human fates." Even though the generations change and people become concerned about new topics, their fates have not really changed. Life and death are still the fate of all; women and men strive for a perfection that is not of this world and that cannot be reached in this world, but that is still worth striving for. It is good to know that a century or so ago a Norwegian dramatist was able not merely to formulate this timeless dilemma but to body it forth in characters that can still live on the stage.

READINGS AND REFERENCES

The basic bibliographies for the student of Ibsen are Hjalmar Pettersen, *Henrik Ibsen bedømt af samtid og eftertid* (Oslo: published by the author, 1928), and Ingrid Tedford, *Ibsen Bibliography, 1928–57* (Oslo and Bergen: Norsk bibliografisk bibliotek, 1961), vol. 20. Later bibliographies, since 1954, are in the *Ibsenårbok*, a publication of Ibsenforbundet, founded in 1948. The yearbook first appeared in Skien in 1952; since then it has been published usually but not always annually. Three books have been issued under an English title, *Contemporary Approaches to Ibsen* (1965/66, 1970/71, 1975/76), containing reports on international Ibsen seminars held in Oslo (1965), Cambridge (1970), and Bergen (1975).

The books and article referred to on p. 112 reporting on Ibsen's reception in various countries are: William Henri Eller, *Ibsen in Germany, 1870–1900* (Boston: Badger, 1918); Miriam A. Franc, *Ibsen in England* (Boston: Four Seas, 1919); Dikka A. Reque, *Trois auteurs dramatiques Scandinaves Ibsen, Bjørnson, Strindberg devant la critique Française, 1889–1901* (Paris: Champion, 1930); Halfdan Gregersen, *Ibsen and Spain* (Cambridge, Mass.: Harvard University Press, 1936); Nils Åke Nilsson, *Ibsen in Russland* (Stockholm: Almqvist, 1958); Martin Nag, *Ibsen i russisk åndsliv* (Oslo: Gyldendal, 1967); David E. R. George, *Henrik Ibsen in Deutschland: Rezeption und Revision* (Göttingen: Vandenhoek and Ruprecht, 1968), *Palaestra* 251; Michael Egan, *Ibsen: The Critical Heritage* (London: Routledge, 1973); S. S. Sethi, *The Theatre of Ibsenites in Punjab: A Critical Study* (Patiala: Madaan, 1976); Toshihiko Sato, "Henrik Ibsen in Japan," *Edda* (1962), 3–20.

No major study has been made of the Ibsen reception in the United States and Canada. Annette Andersen, "Ibsen in America," *Scandinavian Studies* 14 (1937), 65–109, 115–46, is only an annotated bibliography, valuable if incomplete; more recent bibliographies have appeared irregularly in *Scandinavian Studies*. See also Einar Haugen, "The Living Ibsen," *Quarterly Journal of Speech* 41 (1955), 19–26, and "Ibsen in America," *Edda* (1957), 26–44; in revised form in *Norwegian-American Studies and Records* 20 (1959), 1–23. The very first English-language Ibsen performance in America, *A Doll's House* ("The Child Wife") in Milwaukee, Wisconsin, June 2–3, 1882, is documented in Einar Haugen, "Ibsen in America: A Forgotten Performance and an Unpublished Letter," *Journal of English and Germanic Philology* 33 (1934), 396–420.

Ibsen's influence on specific authors has been the subject of innumerable articles, as well as sections in their biographies; the only known book is B. J. Tysdahl, *Joyce and Ibsen: A Study in Literary Influence* (Oslo and New York: Norwegian Universities Press, 1968).

In general, the student is advised to consult the systematic bibliographies at the end of each volume of the *Oxford Ibsen*, ed. James Walter McFarlane, 8 vols. (London: Oxford University Press, 1960–77), which are now indispensable.

Epilogue

IBSEN REPEATEDLY emphasized that he was concerned only with portraying men and women and that he had no message or doctrine to proclaim (as Mencken insisted). Yet we have had the temerity to claim that his entire production was a message to the world. It is the ultimate paradox of Ibsen's drama that he wrought single-mindedly for half a century to communicate the doctrine that all doctrines, including his own, are lies. The inescapable conclusion is that communication is impossible. But Ibsen was fascinated by the "impossible": his imagination was stirred, as he put it in *Brand*, by incongruous combinations—what would happen if an owl were afraid of the dark, or a fish of water? From the noble Catiline to the artist Rubek, his characters dream of doing the impossible, specifically of being at once totally free and totally responsible. When Ibsen's characters speak of "freedom of the spirit," they mean a self-realization so far beyond the humanly possible that it can be realized only in death. When they speak of "love" they mean a love that just as totally excludes one's self-interest and that burdens one with the guilt of all humanity. Only in the light of such absolute standards can one call the truths we live by "lies."

Ibsen had learned well this lesson of Shakespeare: "The fault, dear Brutus, is not in our stars, but in ourselves . . ."[1] He lived in an age when the stars that people had long looked to for their fates were beginning to go out. He hoped for a world in which the old stars would join in new constellations that would enable men and women to live in freedom and full responsibility. But his characters were, like his Emperor Julian, victims on the altar of necessity. Like Cain and Judas, they fell before the inexorable and inscrutable decisions of the World

Will. He would not give a name to this Will, but it is not hard to see behind it the outlines of the Christian God who lived in the church steeple across the square from Ibsen's birthplace. His nurse once carried him up into this steeple and let him look down from its dizzying height on the busy little world below.

It is not surprising that some of his audiences have felt a bit uncomfortable about viewing the world from the heights of Ibsen's steeple. Except when the Italian sun is shining on it, the wind can be very chilly up there. The view is often entrancing, but in the long run most people find it impossible to see the world esthetically "through cupped hand." They would rather have human warmth around them, even if the warmth be tinged with some of the fire of hell. They would rather settle for partial goals, and short-range projects, than gamble on absolutes that are by definition impossible. But Ibsen's men and women are memorable because they are exceptional, the kind of people who are remembered by the world long after their death, the ones who have been willing to stake all on something everyone regarded as impossible.

Ibsen himself was one of these. He staked all on creating plays that would communicate, as none before or since, the duality that split his self into bohemian and bourgeois, rebel and conformist, artist and lover. He found in the drama the medium through which this conflict could be resolved most successfully. He drew from his own frustrations the life blood that he poured into his characters. They were life of his life, these "children" that he gave to the world one by one, from his earliest youth and down into old age when his mind finally failed him (though not at the time Mencken said!). One of the most tragic scenes in his plays is of Hedda burning the book she calls the "child" of Løvborg and Thea. Ibsen's plays were also his children, begotten by the trolls within the "chambers of his heart and mind," the male and female spirits that somehow cohabited in the recesses of his creativity.

Over the past century his "children" have grown up and have traveled all over the world. Some of them may seem as misbegotten as the brat the Greenclad Woman brought to Peer Gynt. But most of them are like the child that Solveig mothered "in her faith; in her hope, and in her love": the image of Peer Gynt "with his destiny clearly marked / As he first sprang from the mind of God!"[2] It is precisely because they represent the ever-present contrasts in our own selves that they have not only survived but bid fair to go on living. Wherever there are young minds, thoughtful minds, concerned minds, Ibsen's world will have something to contribute. Ibsen's plays will enable people to look beyond the little cares of the day and will give them some glimpses of eternity.

APPENDIXES

Appendix 1

Chronology of Ibsen's Life

1828   Born March 20 in Skien, Norway, to Knud and Marichen Ibsen.
1844   Arrives January 3 in Grimstad to begin apprenticeship as an apothecary.
1850   Arrives April 29 in Christiania [Oslo] to study at the university.
1851   Engaged as playwright in residence at Norwegian Theater in Bergen.
1852   Studies the theater in Copenhagen and Dresden from April to July.
1857   Becomes artistic director of the Norwegian Theater in Christiania.
1858   Marries Suzannah Thoresen, daughter of Dean H. C. Thoresen of Bergen.
1859   Birth of son Sigurd who grew up to become diplomat, politician, and writer.
1862   Given grant to collect folklore; Norwegian Theater closes.
1864   Leaves Christiania April 5 for Italy, via Copenhagen, Berlin, Vienna.
1868   Leaves Italy to settle down in Dresden in October; spends summer in Berchtesgaden.
1869   Attends the opening of the Suez Canal as Norwegian representative.
1873   Judge at International Art Exhibition in Vienna.

1874   First return visit to Norway, July to September.

1875   Moves to Munich in April for benefit of his son's education.

1877   Receives honorary doctorate from Uppsala University in Sweden.

1878   Moves to Rome for a year, then back to Munich for the winter.

1880   Returns to Italy after summering in Berchtesgaden.

1885   Second return visit to Norway, June to September; moves to Munich in October.

1889   Vacations in Gossensass in Tyrol, meets Emilie Bardach and Helene Raff.

1891   Leaves Munich to settle in Norway in July; takes tour to North Cape.

1892   Sigurd Ibsen marries Bjørnson's daughter Bergliot.

1898   Feted at seventieth-birthday celebrations.

1901   Suffers his first stroke in Christiania.

1906   Dies in Christiania on May 23.

Appendix 2

Plot Summaries of Ibsen's Plays

The summaries provide only the bare bones of the stories and are intended as no more than reminders for the forgetful. The plays appear in chronological order and are divided into six thematic groups for the reader's convenience. The English titles are those of the *Oxford Ibsen*; other translations in common use are added after a slant line. The original Norwegian titles appear in parentheses, with the date of first publication. If performance preceded publication, the date of performance is given in square brackets. Omitted from the list are plays not intended for performance (*Norma, or a Politician's Love*, 1851) or left unfinished (*The Grouse in Justedal*, 1850; *The Mountain Bird*, 1859). Information on these and other drafts can be found in the *Oxford Ibsen*.

Rebellion and Romance (1850–58):
The Apprenticeship

1. *Catiline* (*Catilina*, 1850; revised, 1875). Blank verse historical drama in three acts. Catiline, the well-known target of Cicero's denunciations, is a Roman noble, deeply troubled by the corruption of the Senate and the government of Rome in general. He is urged by his wife, Aurelia, to retire from public life, and live peacefully on his country estate. But he is challenged by a vestal virgin, Furia, who fascinates him, to fulfill his mission of reform. Unknown to him, one of her motives is to avenge his betrayal of her sister. When he accepts the

challenge and leads an army of malcontents against the forces of the Senate, she betrays him and he is defeated. In despair, he stabs his wife, while Furia stabs him in the hope of joining him in the hereafter. But he dies in his wife's arms, reconciled to her in death.

2. *The Burial Mound / The Warrior's Barrow* (*Kjæmpehøien*, [1850]; revised, 1854). Dramatic poem in one act. A young Viking chief from Norway, Gandalf, lands on the coast of Normandy (revised version: an island off Sicily). He is looking for the man who, he believes, killed his father, so that he can exact vengeance. Instead he finds Blanka, a young Christian woman who has nursed his father back to life. Convinced by her merciful act of the superiority of Christianity to paganism, he woos her and brings her back with him to transplant her faith in the still pagan Norway.

3. *St. John's Night* (*Sancthansnatten*, [1853], 1909). Prose fairy-tale comedy in three acts, with verse prologue. University students Johannes (Birk) and Julian (Poulsen) are spending Midsummer Eve with their friend Jørgen (Kvist) on a farm estate in Telemark belonging to the latter's aunt, Mrs. Berg. Juliane, Mrs. Berg's daughter, is secretly affianced to Johannes, but on closer acquaintance his enthusiasm for her cools. He is more attracted to Mrs. Berg's stepdaughter Anne, a child of nature, thought by some to be simpleminded. During the Midsummer Eve's celebrations, the farm goblin (*nisse*) drops a magic potion in the punch, causing the young people to see their partners in their true light. The events of the night lead to an exchange, so that the fatuous Juliane is matched to the spouter of romantic clichés, Julian, and the imaginative Johannes finds his true love in Anne.

4. *Lady Inger of Østråt* (*Fru Inger til Østerraad*, [1855], 1857; revised 1874 as *Fru Inger til Østråt*). Prose historical drama in five acts. Lady Inger, an early sixteenth-century Norwegian noblewoman, is involved in plans to free Norway from Danish rule, but her plans are frustrated by Sir Nils Lykke, the shrewd agent of the Danish king. In 1528 he comes to her manor and succeeds in intercepting secret messages from Count Sten Sture of Sweden. Through a series of intrigues and misunderstandings the bringer of the messages is thought to be Sten Sture's heir, Count Nils. Misled by her ambition, Lady Inger has him murdered, only to learn too late that he is her own natural son by Count Sten. In despair, she flings herself on his bier, asking only to die.

5. *The Feast at Solhoug* (*Gildet paa Solhoug*, 1856; revised 1883 as *Gildet paa Solhaug*). Ballad drama in three acts, with lyric prose dialogue and interspersed verse. A feast is to be held celebrating the third

anniversary of Lady Margit's marriage to Sir Bengt of Solhoug. She is unhappy, having married this man, who is much older than her, for his money. Her old lover, her cousin Gudmund Alfson, comes to the manor. A knight at court and a minstrel, he has incurred the king's displeasure and is taking refuge at Solhoug. He now falls in love with Margit's younger sister Signe. In the hope of winning him back, Margit tries but fails to poison her husband. Later he dies in a drunken brawl. When Sir Gudmund, her ex-lover, still rejects her, she decides to enter a convent. Gudmund is cleared of the king's charges against him and is free to marry Signe.

6. *Olaf Liljekrans* (*Olaf Liljekrans*, [1857], 1902). Lyric play in three acts. alternately verse and prose. Sir Olaf, who lives in a fourteenth-century Norwegian mountain village, is betrothed to Ingeborg, by a family compact intended to settle a long-standing feud. But when the bridal parties meet, headed by his mother, Lady Kirsten Liljekrans, and her father, Arne of Guldvik, Olaf is gone, having wandered off into the mountains. Here he meets and is entranced by Alfhild, the innocent daughter of a survivor of the Black Death, and betroths himself to her. On his return, he forgets his promise to her, and in her desperation she sets fire to the bridal house. She is condemned to death, but Olaf saves her life by offering to marry her. Ingeborg is nothing loath, since she has been in love all along with another man, her father's page.

7. *The Vikings at Helgeland/The Warriors at Helgeland* (*Hærmændene paa Helgeland*, 1858). Four-act historical drama in saga-style prose. The scene is the coast of northern Norway, where Gunnar, a peace-loving chieftain of the tenth century has his estate. Years before, he and his friend Sigurd won their wives on a raid to Iceland, with Gunnar getting the powerful and warlike Hjørdis, Sigurd the gentle and domestic Dagny. Dagny's father and Hjørdis's stepfather, Ørnulf of the Fjords, now arrives to exact vengeance for the loss of the women. Gunnar offers appropriate recompense and arranges a banquet of conciliation, which Sigurd and Dagny attend. Hjørdis deliberately stirs up trouble, eventually goading Dagny into revealing that her husband— not Gunnar, as was believed—killed the white bear that guarded Hjørdis's bower. Meanwhile Ørnulf's son is killed by Gunnar, through a misunderstanding; Ørnulf assuages his grief by composing an elegy of lament. Sigurd and Hjørdis confess their mutual but hopeless love, and she stabs first him, then herself, in the hope of being with him in Valhalla. Her hope is frustrated, since he has become a Christian; so she rides off alone to become one of Odin's valkyries.

On Being Yourself (1859–67):
Breakthrough in Verse

8. *Love's Comedy* (*Kjærlighedens Komedie*, 1862). Three-act contemporary comedy in verse. Falk, a student and budding poet, proclaims a romantic ideal of life and love, praising the joys of the moment, decrying all practical thoughts of the future. He comments satirically on the bourgeois engagements and marriages existing or being contracted about him in Mrs. Halm's house, in the suburbs of Christiania, where he is a roomer. At the celebration of his friend Lind's engagement to Anna, one of Mrs. Halm's daughters, he proclaims the doctrine that pure love can exist only if it does not lead to marriage. Svanhild, Anna's sister, is impressed by Falk's earnest idealism, and together they decide to try to realize an ideal love. But a well-to-do merchant, Guldstad, appears as Falk's rival for Svanhild's hand. He points out to them the contradiction between Falk's preaching and practice, and when Falk is unable to promise lifelong love, the lovers part so that their love may live on as an unsullied memory. Svanhild resigns herself to marrying Guldstad, while Falk heads off on his poetic career, joining a chorus of singers who are going up the mountainside.

9. *The Pretenders* (*Kongs-emnerne*, 1863; revised, 1870). Five-act historical drama in prose, with some verse. Earl Skule has been regent of Norway during the minority of King Haakon Haakonsson. In 1223 Haakon is declared king after his mother, Inga, has borne ordeal by fire to prove his right to the throne. Haakon seeks reconciliation with Skule by marrying his daughter, Margrete, by leaving him in charge of the royal seal, and by eventually naming him a duke. But the evil Bishop Nikolas of Oslo nourishes Skule's ambition and sows seeds of dissension by hinting to Skule that Haakon's title to the throne may be flawed. Lest either of them should be sure, however, Nikolas destroys the evidence while lying on his deathbed. Skule demands of Haakon that he share the throne, but Haakon refuses in the full security of his divine mission as king. He startles Skule by revealing his "kingly thought," that he will mold the feuding sections of Norway into one and make of it not only a kingdom but a people. When Skule is stripped of his offices, he raises the standard of rebellion and has some initial successes against Haakon's forces. He learns too late that he has a son, Peter, to carry on his line and is in any case tormented by self-doubts. He and Peter are killed by an incensed mob of townspeople at the monastery of Elgesæter, near Nidaros, right before Haakon arrives to pronounce the final judgment on him: "He was God's stepchild on earth."

10. *Brand* (*Brand*, 1866). Five-act contemporary verse drama. (Ibsen called it a "dramatic poem".) Brand is a fiery young pastor dedicated to the ideal of "all or nothing," which he is ambitious to impose on humanity. We meet him in the mountains, as he is about to descend and return to his native valley, a narrow fjord community in western Norway. On the way down he encounters three characters who typify for him the forces against which he must do battle: a cowardly peasant ("the faint heart"), a frivolous artist, Einar ("the light heart"), and a mad gypsy girl, Gerd ("the wild heart"). Einar's betrothed, Agnes, is awed and attracted by the power of Brand's vision and his personal courage, so that she leaves Einar to become Brand's wife. Brand is called as pastor of the local church and sets out to reform his little society. His stern demands quickly bring him into conflict with the easygoing and selfish local officials, typified by the mayor, and with his superiors in the Church, typified by the dean. His uncompromising doctrine is applied equally to his mother, whom he will not shrive unless she gives up all her property, and to his wife and child, both of whom die as a result of his refusal to leave his post for a milder climate. Thinking that it will enhance the glory of God, he uses his inheritance to build a larger church. But when the festive day of dedication arrives, he decides that this is only another form of idolatry, locks the door, and throws the key in the river. He then leads his flock into the mountains, bringing them up to the "ice church," where he thinks they will all be closer to God. However, the people find the road steep and the passage rough, and finally they refuse to follow him. They stone him and turn back to the valley. Bloody and deserted, Brand stumbles through the ice fields, where he meets Gerd, who releases an avalanche on him by shooting her enemy the hawk, which she calls "the spirit of compromise." Brand sees tempting visions of the dead Agnes, and he is moved to tears, right before he is buried by the snow. But above the roar of the avalanche a voice is heard, reminding him that "He is a God of love."

11. *Peer Gynt* (*Peer Gynt*, 1867). Five-act folktale drama in verse. (Ibsen called it a "dramatic poem".) Peer Gynt, a sturdy but irresponsible farm youth from Gudbrandsdalen, is pictured in three phases of his life: in Norway as a twenty-year old (acts I–III); in North Africa as a prosperous, middle-aged gentleman (act IV); back in Norway as an old man returning to his childhood home (act V).

In his youth Peer is a boastful, lazy, and insecure, but charming dreamer, chided by his widowed mother, Åse, for neglecting their farm and wasting his chances for a good marriage with the well-to-do farm heiress Ingrid. Peer goes uninvited to her wedding and there meets Solveig, the pure young woman who becomes his ideal love. She is charmed by him but is also repelled by his reputation as a village brawler. He then starts drinking, becomes ugly and combative, snatches the bride, and carries her into the mountains. Here he soon abandons her and turns to even grosser objects of love. In a kind of delirious dream sequence he encounters the Greenclad Woman, a supernatural creature modeled on the *huldre* of Norwegian folklore. With her he enters the underground mountain world, ruled by the Dovre King, who demands that he legitimize himself as a true *troll* if he is to become his son-in-law. The outward symbol of trolldom is the wearing of an animal tail, but the inward reality is acceptance of selfishness as a rule of life (*at være sig selv nok*). Peer is a willing enough candidate until he realizes that by accepting trolldom, he can never return to humanity. After fighting off the trolls and a mysterious creature called the Boyg, he escapes from the mountains, thanks to Solveig's abiding devotion. By having the church bells rung, she releases him from the power of evil. He is outlawed to the woods, where Solveig seeks him out in his cabin. But when the Greenclad Woman comes to join them, with Peer's and her misbegotten troll brat, Peer flees, promising to return some day. After a touching farewell with his dying mother, Peer leaves his home community for the great world.

We meet him again many years later, after he has earned a fortune in America engaging in such dubious enterprises as rum running and the slave trade. He is now in Morocco, where he has anchored his yacht off shore and is hosting an elegant dinner for four international adventurers like himself, who are English, French, German, and Swedish. They conspire to rob him of his yacht but are blown up with the yacht. Peer finds a stolen Arabian horse and gallops off into the desert, where he has various adventures, including an encounter with a tribe of Bedouins, who receive him as their "prophet." He is enchanted by the dancer Anitra, but she robs him of both horse and jewels. He then travels on foot to Cairo, where he contemplates the Pyramid of Gizeh and the Great Sphinx. A mad German named Begriffenfeldt brings him to the insane asylum that he directs, and the inmates hail Peer as one of them, crowning him "emperor of all madmen" and pressing on his head a crown of straw.

Finally we see him on a ship off the coast of Norway on his way home. The ship is wrecked, but Peer crosses the mountains to Gudbrandsdalen. On the way he encounters a series of reminders of his wasted life and is faced with the question of who he has really been and of when, if ever, he has been himself. The chief appeal to his conscience comes from the mysterious Button Moulder, who threatens to melt Peer's soul down into nothingness, just as Peer in his childhood melted worn-out tin buttons in a casting ladle. Peer cannot save his soul unless he can prove that somewhere, sometime he has been "himself" as God had destined him. But everywhere he meets a negative reply, until he finds his old sweetheart Solveig. An old woman now, she has been waiting for him through the years, and in her loving arms he finally finds the forgiveness that makes him whole.

Stocktaking (1868–74):
Experiments in Form

12. *The League of Youth* (*De unges Forbund*, 1869). Five-act political comedy in prose. Stensgaard, a young lawyer newly arrived in a small town of southern Norway, is a fluent orator ambitious for political influence. Inspired by the enthusiasm of May 17th, Norway's Constitution Day, he delivers an oration advocating liberal principles and the unseating of the establishment. This leads to the organization of a "League of Youth," which will oppose such leaders as politician Lundestad and the wealthy ironmaster, Chamberlain Bratsberg. Stensgaard's speech is misunderstood by the aging chamberlain as an attack on the opposition, led by the unscrupulous landowner Monsen and printer-journalist Aslaksen. Stensgaard confides in his old school friend Dr. Fieldbo, claiming that he is dedicated to reforming society. But when he receives an invitation to the Bratsbergs, his dedication to liberalism melts away and reveals his ambition for position, power, and wealth through marriage. He opportunistically shifts his affections from Monsen's daughter Ragna to Bratsberg's daughter Selma and finally to a tradesman's widow, Madam Rundholmen. While Lundestad shrewdly has pretended to yield to the menace of Stensgaard's political skill, he manages to inform the chamberlain of his deception and of Stensgaard's real nature. In the end none of the women are interested in marrying Stensgaard, and in a comic final scene his double-dealings are unmasked one by one. His opportunism in love underlines and typifies his lack of political principles, forcing him to retire in discomfiture and to vanish (at least temporarily) from the scene.

13. *Emperor and Galilean* (*Kejser og Galilæer*, 1873). A "world-historical" drama, consisting of two five-act plays in prose. These present and interpret successive phases in the tempestuous life of Julian, nicknamed "the Apostate" (331–63), Roman emperor and philosopher. The scene ranges from Gaul to Persia but centers on Byzantium, then the capital of the empire.

Part I: *Caesar's Apostasy* (*Cæsars Frafald*). Julian, a youthful member of the imperial family, is an ardent Christian and a learned philosopher, more interested in meditation and writing than in the perils of politics. He and his brother Gallus have alone been spared by their cousin, Emperor Constantius II. When Gallus is later murdered, Julian is selected (with the title "Cæsar") to lead the imperial troops against an uprising in Gaul. Even before this, Julian in his restless search for truth has become disillusioned by the behavior of the Christians, adherents of the new faith, and has fallen under the influence of a pagan mystic named Maximos. They participate in séances at which Maximos calls forth spirits of the past, such as Cain and Judas, in an effort to solve the riddles of history. Maximos believes that the ethics of Christianity and the beauty of classical paganism may be combined, forming the basis of a new "third empire." Julian's campaign in Gaul is successful, but when his soldiers proclaim him emperor and urge him to raise the standard of revolt, he hesitates, yielding only after definitively abandoning his Christian belief and sacrificing to the sungod Helios.

Part II. *Emperor Julian* (*Kejser Julian*). Conveniently for Julian, the emperor dies. Julian proclaims religious freedom for all, at the same time setting out to restore paganism as the state religion. Paganism and its practices are by now half forgotten, and he is unsuccessful in his attempts to institute sacrifices and bacchanalia. Gradually he comes to use force to back his decrees, dismissing and even punishing those of his old friends who come to remonstrate with him. Maximos chides him for trying to turn back history, urging him to look ahead to the time when a messiah will appear who will be at once god and emperor. Julian interprets this as literally applying to himself, and as one step toward becoming master of the world leads an expedition against the Persians who threaten the eastern border of the empire. He lets himself be misled into tactical errors that take him into the desert and cut off his means of retreat. In the heat of battle he is murdered by one of his own men, a Christian named Agathon, and falls uttering the traditional words, "Galilean, thou hast conquered." Maximos sees now that the omens were ambiguous and that Julian was just another figure like Cain and Judas, who furthered the "world will" by opposing it.

Modern Breakthrough (1875–82):
The Social Plays

14. *Pillars of Society/Pillars of the Community* (*Samfundets Støtter*, 1877). Contemporary play in four acts. Consul Karsten Bernick,

shipowner and capitalist, dominates the society in his small Norwegian seaport. He is highly respected, but it gradually becomes evident that he is guilty of a series of dishonest maneuvers. He pushed aside his real love, Lona Hessel, to marry Betty Tønnesen for money. He allowed his fiancée's brother Johan to take the blame for his own escapade with an actress. At present he is sending out inadequately repaired ships in order to collect on their insurance, and he is scheming with a small group of his fellows to monopolize the profits on a projected railroad line. He is dismayed when persons out of his past begin to appear, specifically Lona and Johan, who have been away in America for fifteen years. He fears that they will expose his past misdeeds, especially when Lona announces that she has returned in order to "let some fresh air" from the prairies into this stagnant society.

Lona and Johan do in fact exert pressure on Bernick to undo some of the harm his actions have caused. Bernick schemes to send Johan off on one of his rotten ships, only to learn that his own son Olaf is also aboard; fortunately the ship does not sail. Minor plots unfold, e.g., shipyard foreman Aune's protest at the new machinery, the orphaned Dina Dorf's escape from her engagement to the stuffy schoolmaster Rørlund and her betrothal to Johan, the sad life of Martha Bernick, the self-effacing spinster, and the comedy of the business failure Hilmar Tønnesen, who enlivens the play with inane and malicious chatter.

Eventually Bernick is goaded to reveal some of his true self and confess to the townspeople who come to honor him with a torchlight procession that he has been acting not in the public interest but for his own profit. He promises a new era in the life of the town and, in appreciation of the role played in his conversion by the women who surround him, declares that they are the true "pillars of society." But Lona sets him right: "The spirit of truth and the spirit of freedom—*those* are the pillars of society."

15. *A Doll's House/A Doll House* (*Et Dukkehjem*, 1879). Domestic drama in three acts. On Christmas Eve Nora Helmer returns in high spirits from her shopping, prepared to celebrate with her children and her indulgent husband, Torvald. He grumbles a bit at her extravagance, not knowing what she later confides to an old school friend, Mrs. Linde, that she is secretly paying off a debt incurred to save her husband's life. Women were not allowed to incur debts then, and Nora in fact had to forge her father's name on a note. She assumes that now, when her husband is about to become manager of the bank, their financial problems will be solved. But Nils Krogstad, from whom she borrowed the money, threatens to expose her unless she uses her influence to keep

him from losing his job in the bank, now promised to Mrs. Linde. Nora turns hopefully to Dr. Rank, an older friend of the family, now ill with a terminal disease, but when he counters with a declaration of love, she feels obliged to reject his proffered help.

Krogstad drops a letter in the mailbox addressed to Helmer, and Nora succeeds in delaying the exposure only by persuading her husband to postpone all business until after the Christmas celebration, which includes a ball where Nora dances the tarantella. She awaits Helmer's reaction with trepidation and is crushed to discover that instead of living up to her ideal of him, he is brutally angry and totally concerned only with himself. Her love fades, she changes to her street clothes, and sits down to reckon up with him the account of their marriage. She sees the falsity of her hope that he would assume responsibility for her fault and declares her need of finding out not only what she herself is really like but also what society and the world are like. Deaf to his pleas, she walks out of the house, leaving her children in the care of her old nurse, Anne Marie. She slams the outer door on her home, after declaring that it would take a "miracle of miracles" for them to make a new life together out of their marriage.

16. *Ghosts* (*Gengangere*, 1881). Domestic drama in three acts. Helene Alving, widow of Captain (and Chamberlain) Alving, lives on her large country estate near one of the fjords of western Norway, with her maid Regine. Mrs. Alving has used the fortune she inherited from her husband to build an orphange about to be dedicated to his memory. Her son, Osvald, has returned home after living as an artist in Paris for several years. Regine's father, the carpenter Jacob Engstrand, who has been working on the orphanage, tries to persuade her to become the chief attraction at a sailors' tavern he plans to start in town. He appeals to the family pastor, the Reverend Mr. Manders, who also has come for the dedication, to talk Regine into joining him. When Manders broaches the subject with Mrs. Alving, she reveals the fact that Regine is not Engstrand's daughter but the late chamberlain's by their maid. The shock to Manders is compounded by his discovery that Mrs. Alving has begun to question the religion she was taught and is reading "freethinking" books of which he disapproves. It also comes out that one stimulus to her independent thinking was the pastor's rejection of her love when she fled to him on discovering that her husband was dissolute. While conversing, they overhear a flirtatious scene in the next room between Osvald and Regine, neither of whom at this time knows that they are brother and sister.

It is now Mrs. Alving's turn to be shocked, since the scene repeats in ghostlike manner one that she overheard between her late husband

and Regine's mother years earlier. She sees this as an example of how the past haunts the present through dead ideas that live on beyond their time. Osvald complains to his mother about recurrent headaches and suggests that Regine could help him if she were his wife. They are interrupted by a fire that breaks out in the orphanage, which is uninsured, and so at one blow destroys Chamberlain Alving's heritage. Osvald comes back from the fire, exhausted, and Mrs. Alving tells him and Regine the truth about her parentage and about his inheritance of a venereal disease, probably from his father. Engstrand meanwhile blackmails the kindly but naive Manders into supporting his sailors' rendezvous, now to be called, appropriately, "Captain Alving's Home." When Regine learns the truth about herself and Osvald, she refuses to stay and leaves to join Engstrand. Mrs. Alving and Osvald are left alone, and he presses upon her a phial of morphine to give him when he lapses into complete paresis. The sun rises as Osvald babbles, "Mother, give me the sun," and she stands over him, hesitating over the horrible choice she has to make.

17. *An Enemy of the People/A Public Enemy* (*En Folkefiende*, 1882). Contemporary play in five acts. Thomas Stockmann is a doctor in charge of the baths in a small Norwegian seaport; he is a lively, hospitable, and self-confident man, who tends to clash with his brother Peter Stockmann, mayor of the town and chairman of the board of the baths. Peter takes the point of view that one should subordinate oneself to the welfare of the community—as he sees it. Thomas believes in the right of the individual to advocate reform. He makes the startling discovery that the baths are infected and must be closed for the season until the source of pollution can be identified and eliminated. He seeks and gets the support of the liberal press and a majority of the citizens. But when the mayor makes it clear to the people and the press what a drastic economic loss the closing of the baths will entail, they fall into line and turn against the doctor. The newspaper refuses to print his scientific report on the baths, so he calls a mass meeting to publish it. However, the meeting is taken over by the mayor and his supporters, who now include the doctor's former following, except for his family. Thomas is not allowed to present his report but seizes the floor to give a ranting speech attacking the cowardice of the people. He declares that "the minority is always right" and that what people call "truths" are in fact short-lived and quickly turn into "lies." The meeting votes to declare Doctor Stockmann "an enemy of the people" and a mob proceeds to stone his house. After considering the option of emigrating to America, the doctor decides to stay and defy public opinion. He will start a school for the town's "mon-

grel" children and bring them up in the spirit of truth and freedom. He concludes that "the strongest man in the world is the one who stands most alone."

Truth and Illusion (1883–90): The Psychological Plays

18. *The Wild Duck* (*Vildanden*, 1884). Drama in five acts. Gregers Werle is the passionately idealistic son of a wealthy industrialist, Haakon Werle. The elder Werle gives a party, ostensibly to celebrate his son's return from the outlying field station where he has been working for the family firm for several years. One of the guests is Hjalmar Ekdal. Invited as an old friend of Gregers, Hjalmar is nevertheless ineffectual and out of place in this glittering assemblage. In conversation with his father, Gregers learns that Hjalmar's wife, Gina, is their former maid, whom he suspects of having been the elder Werle's mistress, making the Ekdals' daughter, Hedvig, possibly Werle's offspring. Haakon Werle wishes to make Gregers his successor in the firm, enabling him to retire and marry his housekeeper, Mrs. Sørby. Gregers is revolted by his father's shabby treatment of his late wife, Gregers's mother, and decides to reject his father's offer.

In the meantime, Gina and Hedvig Ekdal await Hjalmar's return to their modest attic apartment. The room doubles as a photographer's studio in the daytime, and here Hjalmar practices the trade in which Mr. Werle has established him. The elder Ekdal, Hjalmar's father, who was long ago ruined in deals engineered by Mr. Werle, also lives with them. The focus of their simple but reasonably contented existence is the loft, in which they keep rabbits and fowl, most especially a wild duck given them by Mr. Werle after it had been winged, had dived to the bottom, and had been brought to the surface by a hunting dog. Hjalmar returns from the party, masking his personal defeats by high-sounding rhetoric, which is impressive but also disappointing to his family. Gregers follows, having left his home, and secures lodgings with the Ekdals. With all his inner resentments he intrudes into the idyll a set of ideal demands that constitute his life mission: to restore the Ekdals to reality. When he learns about the wild duck and its origin, he sees it as a metaphor for the morass of lies in which the Ekdals are enmeshed. He proposes to become the "good hunting dog" that brings them back up into the light of truth.

It is evident that Hjalmar Ekdal is a dreamer, out of touch with reality, and that Gina is the real breadwinner. Daughter Hedvig suffers from an eye disease strangely similar to the one that affects the elder

Werle. A counterweight to Gregers's ideals is the cynic, Dr. Relling, who makes it his business to keep the Ekdals happy in their "life lie." He does the same for Molvik, a theological candidate who thinks he is "demonic" but who in fact is drunk most of the time. In this grotesque environment Gregers manages to win Hedvig's confidence by using the poetic phrase "the depths of the sea" to describe the loft, thinking all the while that it also describes the false position of the Ekdal household. Gregers reveals the "truth" to Hjalmar in the naive expectation that he will be spiritually elevated and grateful, only to discover that Hjalmar is incapable of such elevation. He rejects his wife and daughter in a surly way, leaving Gregers master of the situation. Gregers proposes to Hedvig that to win back her father's love she should shoot the wild duck as a sacrifice. But by now Hedvig has so thoroughly identified herself with the duck that she shoots herself instead. The tragic conclusion leaves Hjalmar spouting comic platitudes, while Relling comments that people like Gregers "should stop canvassing their ideals around everybody's door."

19. *Rosmersholm* (*Rosmersholm*, 1886). Drama in four acts. The estate of Rosmersholm, home of the Rosmer family, is located near a fjord in western Norway. In conversations between the housekeeper, Mrs. Helseth, and the manager of the household, Rebecca West, it appears that the estate has a long and proud tradition, including even an authentic ghost, a white horse that appears in the local millstream to warn of an approaching death. Rebecca comes from a home in northern Norway and was employed originally as the companion of Beate, the late Mrs. Rosmer. Her husband, Johannes Rosmer, has unconsciously formed a deep, possibly platonic attachment to Rebecca, a woman of unusual charm and strength of character. Her ideas are liberated compared with those that are traditional at Rosmersholm, and she has succeeded in influencing Johannes Rosmer with some of them.

When his brother-in-law, the rigid schoolmaster Kroll, tries to involve Rosmer in the conservative politics of the community, he meets resistance which he suspects is due to Rebecca's influence. He also recalls accusations by his late sister Beate, which he then took to be mere figments of her disordered mind. The leader of the radical opposition, journalist Mortensgaard, also visits Rosmer and reports that Beate had written him some confused allusions to "goings-on" at Rosmersholm. Rosmer is deeply troubled by these suspicions allegedly held by his deceased wife, and in an effort to put all this behind him, he proposes to Rebecca. She turns him down, in great agitation. Kroll carries his attack on the new spirit at Rosmersholm into the press, making Rosmer obsessed with a sense of guilt at possibly having been the cause of Beate's suicide. Kroll openly accuses Rebecca of having engineered it, and she now confesses to her part in it but defends herself as having done it, not in cold blood, but out of love for Johannes. Rebecca now prepares to leave Rosmersholm, and when Rosmer demands an explanation, she admits that she has been broken under the spell of the Rosmer ideal. She arrived with a free, "pagan" will, but now she has found that "the Rosmer philosophy of life ennobles," "but it kills happiness."

When Rosmer questions her change of mind, she offers to prove it by following Beate into the millrace. They join themselves in an improvised wedding ceremony, and he accompanies her in suicide. Their decision is in part a result of ideas implanted by Rosmer's old tutor, Ulrik Brendel, the imaginative ne'er-do-well, whose expectations of life have ended in crushing defeat.

20. *The Lady from the Sea* (*Fruen fra Havet*, 1888). Play in five acts. Ellida Wangel, Dr. Wangel's second wife, feels dissatisfied and isolated in her marriage. She is powerfully, even mystically, attracted by the open sea and feels confined by the narrow fjord in nothern Norway where her husband has his practice. She feels doubly alienated because his two grown daughters from the first marriage, Bolette and Hilde, have not accepted her. In the open-air setting of this play there is a rich gallery of minor figures: a comic painter and dancing master, Ballested; a consumptive but romantic sculptor, Lyngstrand; and a middle-aged schoolmaster, Arnholm, who comes to pay court to his former pupil, Bolette. The girls raise the flags in memory of their mother, pretending that it is for Arnholm. Ellida admits to Arnholm, who once had proposed to her, that her heart is fixed on a young sailor, presumably drowned, to whom she had once betrothed herself. Wangel, who is troubled by his wife's condition, proposes a move to the seaside, but she is so caught up in the dream of her youth that she refuses Wangel's approaches.

Then, surprisingly, the sailor of her dreams actually appears and claims her for his own, but only if she comes of her free will. Dr. Wangel threatens him but cannot overcome his wife's fascination with the mystery of this man of the sea. When the Stranger (as he is called) appears again the next evening to get her reply, Wangel has at length learned his lesson. He, too, offers Ellida complete freedom of choice but reminds her that with freedom goes responsibility. Ellida turns back to her husband and thereby also dissolves the isolation between her and the others.

21. *Hedda Gabler* (*Hedda Gabler*, 1890). Drama in four acts. Hedda and Jørgen Tesman have just returned from a six-month honey-

moon. Tesman is a promising young scholar, whose field is the history of civilization and whose specialty is domestic arts in Brabant during the Middle Ages. It is evident from Hedda's remarks and general behavior on the morning after their return and first occupation of a new home that she is thoroughly bored not only by her husband and his scholarship but also by the general air of bourgeois domesticity which he and his loving aunts represent. Her only sophisticated friend is their lawyer, Judge Brack, to whom she admits that she married only to escape boredom and now finds herself enmeshed in an even worse state. She is also revolted at finding herself pregnant. Judge Brack offers her the entertainment of his more amusing company. Her only other amusement is practice with her two pistols, pistols inherited from her father, General Gabler, whose picture hangs in the inner salon.

An old school friend, Thea Elvsted, timidly calls on her. Thea reports that she has defied convention by leaving her husband to be with Ejlert Løvborg, the former tutor of her children. He is a brilliant scholar in the same field as Tesman but had generally been given up as lost to drink and dissipation. She has succeeded in reforming him, so that he not only has gotten a book published but has written a new manuscript which promises to be his best. Thea worries about him because she fears a relapse, and she knows there is a woman in his past whom he cannot forget. She is unaware that the woman is Hedda. When Løvborg appears, the contact is reestablished, but Hedda rejects his approaches, admitting that she is afraid of any scandal. Instead, she sees her chance to manipulate his life to undo Thea's reform work (and, incidentally, eliminate him as a rival for her husband's prospective professorship). She sends him off to a lively stag party with her husband and Judge Brack. He gets drunk, loses his new manuscript, and winds up in the boudoir of one Mlle. Diana, a red-haired singer. Jørgen picks up the manuscript and turns it over to Hedda. When Løvborg, desperate over his loss, comes to see Hedda, she keeps the manuscript concealed and encourages him to commit suicide by lending him a pistol, urging him to "do it beautifully." When he is gone, she vindictively burns the manuscript because it is "Thea's child." Løvborg returns to Mlle. Diana, accuses her of stealing the manuscript, and is shot to death in the ensuing scuffle. Brack reports the events to Hedda, making it clear that she will be protected from scandal only as long as he holds his tongue. Trapped in all directions, Hedda finds her ultimate freedom by shooting herself, while Thea and Jørgen cozily settle down to the long task of working out a new manuscript from Løvborg's notes.

Life and Art (1891–99):
The Philosophical Plays

22. *The Master Builder* (*Bygmester Solness*, 1892). Drama in three acts. Halvard Solness is a famous architect, who has reached the age when he is beginning to fear the rivalry of younger men. In his office he keeps Ragnar Brovik, his assistant, in virtual subjection, in part by maintaining an emotional hold on Ragnar's fiancée, Kaja. Solness broods on his unusual ability to master fate and thinks of it as a kind of uncanny power by which he can call on supernatural "helpers and servers" to perform his wishes. They have helped him build his career on the disaster of the fire that burned his wife's childhood home and that helped cause their twin boys to die in infancy. He subdivided the estate and built homes for people, but now it gnaws him that he willed the fire, even though he obviously did not cause it.

Youth comes knocking on his door, not as he had expected it, but in the shape of a charming and determined young woman, Hilde Wangel. She reminds him that on that very day ten years earlier he had completed the building of a church in her home village. At the dedication she saw him hang a wreath on top of the tower, and afterward he encountered her, kissed her, and promised her that in ten years he would give her a kingdom. Now she has come to claim it. Solness believes that she may provide redemption from his fear of youth and his fate: her youth against the youth of the others. He tells her that theirs was the last church tower he built; at the dedication he swore that he would no longer build temples for God but homes for people. Now he has completed a new home for his wife and himself, which combines the home with a high tower, as on a church. Hilde urges him to hang a wreath on the tower, as he did ten years ago, but he admits that he does not have the courage: he suffers from vertigo. However, she wants to see him "great" again, high up on the tower, with "harps singing in the air," as she had seen him then.

Inspired by her faith in him, he decides to try to live up to it. Everyone else tries to dissuade him from climbing the tower with the dedication wreath. He insists on attempting "the impossible," and although he does succeed in reaching the top, he is unable to sustain this position. Hilde hears her "harps in the air" and waves to him in her exultation, but he crashes to his death.

23. *Little Eyolf* (*Lille Eyolf*, 1894). Play in three acts. Alfred Allmers, proprietor, teacher, and philosopher, returns from a long hike in the mountains, prescribed by his doctor. He had been working on a big book to be called "On Human Responsibility," and he had hoped

to do some writing on his trip. Instead he reexamined his life and had a mystical experience in the mountains, which made him resolve to make a new start. Rather than *write* about responsibility, he will apply it in his life by giving more attention to his crippled child, little Eyolf. This rebirth to a higher life, a new spiritual plane, does not please his passionate wife, Rita, and in practice he almost immediately belies it by letting Eyolf, who is attracted by a strange, Pied Piper of a Rat Wife, wander off and drown in the nearby fjord. In his inconsolable and even exaggerated grief over Eyolf, he lays the blame on his wife and rejects their marriage. He flees to his half-sister Asta, with whom he grew up and whom he used to call his "big" Eyolf. But Asta has recently learned that they are not in fact brother and sister at all, and rather than risk any further emotional involvement with him, she accepts the suit of a more manly lover, an engineer and road builder named Borghejm. Even Rita pleads with her to stay as a buffer between them, but when she leaves, they turn to each other and find a project to live for. They will spend their lives educating and uplifting the poor people's children, the very ones who so callously let Eyolf drown. They will do this "under the stars" in memory of those they lost, turning their selfishness into altruism.

24. *John Gabriel Borkman* (*John Gabriel Borkman*, 1896). Drama in four acts. J. G. B. is an ex-banker, imprisoned for some years for misusing funds entrusted to him. Now he has secluded himself, pacing back and forth like a "sick wolf" on the second floor of his mansion, seeing no one but an old subordinate, Vilhelm Foldal, and Foldal's daughter, Frida. Borkman's wife, Gunhild, lives on the first floor, equally isolated. Her twin sister, Ella Rentheim, comes to visit her, partly to inform her that she, Ella, is dying of an incurable disease, partly to reassert a claim to Borkman's son, Erhart, whom she had brought up after Borkman's downfall. Gunhild hates her husband for having brought disgrace on the family and herself, which has made them financially dependent on Ella. She looks to son Erhart to perform the great "mission" of restoring the family name to its old honor. Erhart is more interested in a pretty widow, Mrs. Fanny Wilton, who comes with him to the Borkman house and eventually carries him off to a (supposed) party at a neighbor's house.

Meanwhile Frida has been playing "The Danse Macabre" for Borkman, and she is followed by her father, Vilhelm. Borkman still believes (or wishes to believe) that he will win restitution and be called back to head his old bank. He dwells on his past dreams of doing great things for humanity. When Foldal reveals some doubts, Borkman has no further use for him: their friendship was based on mutual deception. Ella then comes upstairs to see him, only to learn that her love for him had been traded for wordly success and that his downfall was due to her refusal to marry his rival Hinkel. She, in turn, accuses Borkman of the "crime for which there is no forgiveness": "To murder the love in a human being." He placed his "mission," the acquisition of power, above love. Now ensues a three-way battle over Erhart's future. Ella wants him to inherit not only her fortune but also her name. Gunhild bursts in and swears that he shall keep and restore his father's name. Borkman wants his aid in making a fresh start in life. But Erhart has no taste for being a "missionary"; he intends to live his own life and find his own happiness, which for the moment lies with Mrs. Wilton. Borkman storms out of his cage and into the winter night. He dies on a bench in the woods, after picturing to Ella once more his vision of life—the "kingdom" of which he had dreamed. When Gunhild comes to find him, the twin sisters join hands over the man they both had loved.

25. *When We Dead Awaken* (*Når vi døde vågner*, 1899). Drama in three acts (which Ibsen subtitled "A Dramatic Epilogue"). Arnold Rubek, a world-famous sculptor, returns to Norway with his young wife, Maja. They are staying at a seaside resort, clearly bored with one another's company. Rubek's fame rests primarily on a piece of statuary called "The Day of Resurrection," but in recent years he has been making busts of people, uninspired but subtly devastating portraits of the animal within. At the resort he encounters Irene, the model he used in "The Day of Resurrection," now a mental patient attended by a nun. While a supermale bear hunter, Ulfhejm, draws off Maja to look at his hunting dogs, Irene opens a conversation with Rubek, speaking as if she were dead. She still resents his exploitation of her youth and her beauty to create his masterpiece: when he had no more use for her, she vanished out of his life. She claims that she gave him her soul to put into his art, leaving her dead and empty inside. Ulfhejm suggests that the Rubeks join him at a mountain resort, where he and Maja can do some hunting. Here they meet Irene again, and Rubek begins to think that she may be able to inspire him once again to great art. He frankly tells Maja that they should part. Irene admits that she never loved either the artist in him or his art, except for "The Day of Resurrection," which she calls "their child." But she is incensed when she learns that he has greatly altered his masterpiece

since she left him, first by introducing a swarm of human faces rising out of the plinth with animal expressions on their faces, and then by introducing himself, as the figure of a man bowed down by remorse for a lost life. Irene scornfully calls him a "poet," one who justifies his rejection of her and of life by throwing a cloak of words over his treachery. While Maja and Ulfhejm go off bear hunting, Irene and Rubek make a tryst to see the sun rise on the moors. They meet on the mountain paths, Maja and Ulfhejm clambering down to the lowlands, Irene and Rubek climbing ever higher. They feel a sacred sense of wedlock as they quest for the heights, but they are surprised by an avalanche, which buries them just as the nun appears and gives them her final benediction.

NOTES

LIST OF ABBREVIATIONS

Fjelde, *Ibsen*   Rolf Fjelde, *Ibsen: A Collection of Critical Essays* (Englewood Cliffs, N.J.: Prentice-Hall, 1965).

Fjelde, *MPP*   Henrik Ibsen, *Ibsen: The Complete Major Prose Plays*, trans. Rolf Fjelde (New York: Farrar Straus and Giroux/New American Library, 1978).

HU   Henrik Ibsen, *Samlede verker [Hundreårsutgaven]*, ed. Francis Bull, Halvdan Koht, Didrik Arup Seip, 21 vols. (Oslo: Gyldendal, 1928–58).

Koht, *Life*   Halvdan Koht, *Life of Ibsen*, trans. Einar Haugen and A. E. Santaniello (New York: Blom, 1971).

McFarlane, *Ibsen*   Henrik Ibsen, *A Critical Anthology*, ed. James W. McFarlane (London: Penguin, 1970).

Meyer, *Ibsen*   Michael Meyer, *Ibsen: A Biography* (New York: Doubleday, 1971).

OI   Henrik Ibsen, *The Oxford Ibsen*, ed. James Walter McFarlane, 8 vols. (London: Oxford University Press, 1960–77).

Sprinchorn, *LS*   Henrik Ibsen, *Letters and Speeches*, ed. Evert Sprinchorn (New York: MacGibbon and Kee, 1965).

TRANSLATIONS OF QUOTATIONS

All Ibsen quotations in this book are translations from the Norwegian original, and references are given to their place of occurrence in the centennial edition (*HU*) by page and volume (e.g., 8.211 stands for volume VIII, page 211). These are followed by references to one or more English translations, usually beginning with the *Oxford Ibsen* (*OI*). The translations used in the text are by the author unless they are expressly attributed to one of the English translations cited. Quotations from other non-English authors are also by the author unless they are attributed to a specific source. "*OI* 2.150" means that one can find the passage in volume II, page 150; but "trans. from *OI* 2.150" means that it is quoted verbatim from the Oxford translation.

Notes

Introduction: A Dramatist for All Seasons

1. Quotation from *HU* 17.468; cf. *OI* 5.477.
2. Letter to Peter Hansen, 28 Oct. 1870 (*HU* 16.317; cf. Sprinchorn, *LS*, 102).
3. For detailed references see "Readings and References" for chapter 6.
4. *The Oxford Companion to American Literature*, ed. James D. Hart (London, New York, and Toronto: Oxford University Press, 1941), 839.
5. William Winter, *Shadows of the Stage* (New York: Macmillan, 1892–95), 3.330–37.
6. *The New Encyclopædia Britannica: Micropædia*, 15th ed. (Chicago: University of Chicago), 10.693.
7. *The New Republic* 45 (1926), 356–57.
8. *HU* 1.119–20; trans. from *OI* 1.109–10.
9. Koht, *Life*, 56.
10. *Ibid.*, 112.
11. Letter to Peter Hansen, 28 Oct. 1870 (cf. *OI* 2.360).
12. Trans. from Meyer, *Ibsen*, 207. The letter is in *HU* 16.96–98; Sprinchorn, *LS*, 34.
13. Koht, *Life*, 147.
14. *HU* 15.339–40; English trans. in McFarlane, *Ibsen*, 74–75; also *OI* 2.359, Sprinchorn, *LS*, 29–30.
15. For a detailed account of the reception of *Brand* see Koht, *Life*, 206–11; Meyer, *Ibsen*, 247–52; *OI* 3.445–50.
16. Koht, *Life*, 208. The article appeared anonymously in *Morgenbladet*, 1 and 4 Dec. 1866. See also Meyer, *Ibsen*, 251–52.
17. Koht, *Life*, 208. Bjørnson's first impression is in a letter to Clemens Petersen, printed in Bjørnstjerne Bjørnson, *Gro-tid* (Christiania and Copenhagen: Gyldendal, 1912), 2.189–92 (written 30 Mar. 1866).
18. Koht, *Life*, 208.
19. Gustaf af Geijerstam, "Två minnen om Ibsen," *Ord och Bild* 7 (1898), 116–17.
20. Letter to F. Hegel, 14 Dec. 1869 (*HU* 16.260; *OI* 4.553).

21. Robert Buchanan, "The Modern Drama and Its Minor Critics," *Contemporary Review* 56 (1889), 908–25; see *OI* 5.434.

22. Trans. from Fjelde, *MPP*, 117–18; *OI* 5.126; *HU* 8.148.

23. Meyer, *Ibsen*, 459; Koht, *Life*, 321.

24. *HU* 9.92; Fjelde, *MPP*, 238; *OI* 5.384.

25. *Pall Mall Gazette*, 8 Apr. 1891; extracts in George Bernard Shaw, *The Quintessence of Ibsenism: Now Completed to the Death of Ibsen* (London: Constable, 1913), 91–93, reprinted in Michael Egan, *Ibsen: The Critical Heritage* (London: Routledge, 1972), 209–14.

26. Shaw, *Quintessence*, 93 (footnote).

27. Anon. in *Athenæum*, 12 May 1894; cit. in *OI* 6.441.

28. Letter to F. Hegel, 2 Sept. 1884 (*HU* 18.32–33; *OI* 6.439; Sprinchorn, *LS*, 236–37).

29. Review in *Aftenposten* (Oslo); cit. in Koht, *Life*, 359.

30. Review in *Morgenbladet* (Oslo); cit. in Koht, *Life*, 359.

31. W. L. Courtney, *Studies at Leisure* (London, 1892); cit. in *OI* 6.441.

32. Shaw, *Quintessence*, 97.

33. *Saturday Review*, reprinted in Shaw, *Our Theatres in the Nineties* (London: Constable, 1931), 3.136–44; *OI* 6.442.

34. Letter to Georg Brandes, 12 June 1883 (*HU* 17.515; Sprinchorn, *LS*, 219–20; *OI* 6.425).

35. Robert Brustein, *The Theatre of Revolt* (Boston: Little Brown, 1964), 48.

36. David E. R. George, *Henrik Ibsen in Deutschland* (Göttingen: Vandenhoeck and Ruprecht, 1968), *Palaestra* 251, 86–90.

37. On Ibsen in Russia, see Martin Nag, *Ibsen i russisk åndsliv* (Oslo: Gyldendal, 1967), and Nils Åke Nilsson, *Ibsen in Russland* (Stockholm: Almqvist, 1958).

38. On Miller's adaptation see chapter 3 of this book, p. 67. See also Eric Bentley, "A Personal Statement," reprinted in *Ibsen: A Collection of Critical Essays*, ed. Rolf Fjelde (Englewood Cliffs, N.J.: Prentice-Hall, 1965), 15–16; Brustein, *The Theatre*, 72, footnote 19; note 26 to chapter 3 of this book.

1. Who Was Henrik Ibsen?

1. Letter to Ludwig Passarge, German translator (*HU* 17.402; Sprinchorn, *LS*, 187).

2. Speech in Christiania, 23 Mar. 1898 (*HU* 15.412; trans. from Sprinchorn, *LS*, 331).

3. Conversation with William Archer, 2 Jan. 1882, in *Monthly Review* (London), June 1906; cit. in McFarlane, *Ibsen*, 93.

4. Lorentz Dietrichson, *Svundne Tider*, 4 vols. (Christiania: Cappelen, 1899–1917), 1.351; cf. Meyer, *Ibsen*, 288–89.

5. Letter of 28 May 1869 (*HU* 16.238; Sprinchorn, *LS*, 80–81; Meyer, *Ibsen*, 288).

6. *HU* 14.404–5.

7. *HU* 14.461.

8. The Swedish theater director Ludvig Josephson charmingly describes how Ibsen met him at the dock near Dresden in full formal regalia on a visit in 1873: "The guise he had assumed was more suitable for a wealthy merchant or a banking magnate than for the meditative philosopher and poet." (*Ett och annat om Henrik Ibsen och Kristiania Teater* [Stockholm: Bonnier, 1898], p. 43.)

9. Herman Bang, "Personlige Erindringer om Henrik Ibsen," in *Det ny Aarhundrede* (Copenhagen), vol. 3, part 2 (1906), 239–40.

10. Letter of 18 Nov. 1877 (*HU* 17.290–92; Sprinchorn, *LS*, 171–72; cf. Koht, *Life*, 53).

11. Letter of 21 Sept. 1882 (*HU* 17.484; Sprinchorn, *LS*, 212–13).

12. See Hans I. Kleven, *Klassestrukturen i det norske samfunn* (Oslo: Ny Dag, 1965) for a Marxistic view of Norwegian class structure.

13. Edmund Gosse, "Ibsen the Norwegian Satirist," *Fortnightly Review* (London), vol. 73, n.s. (1 Jan. 1873), 74–88.

14. On Norwegian history see T. K. Derry, *A History of Modern Norway, 1814–1972* (Oxford: Clarendon, 1973); for a survey of its modern culture see Ronald G. Popperwell, *Norway* (London: Benn, 1972).

15. Ibsen's genealogy is traced in some detail in Koht, *Life*, 20–25, and in Meyer, *Ibsen*, 3–4.

16. Oskar Mosfjeld, *Henrik Ibsen og Skien* (Oslo: Gyldendal, 1949).

17. Interview with Daniel Grini, *Nationen* (Oslo), 4 Aug. 1920; cit. in Koht, *Life*, 30, 468.

18. Ibsen, "Om Vigtigheden af Selvkundskab," dated 3 Feb. 1848 (*HU* 15.23; trans. from Meyer, *Ibsen*, 36).

19. Christopher Due, *Erindringer fra Henrik Ibsens ungdomsaar* (Copenhagen: Akademisk, 1909), 38–39; trans. from Meyer, *Ibsen*, 39.

20. *HU* 1.43; trans. from *OI* 1.39.

21. *HU* 1.112; trans. from *OI* 1.106.

22. Meyer, *Ibsen*, 60.

23. Interview with Henrikke Holst-Tresselt by Herman Bang, *Af Dagens Krønike* (Copenhagen, 1889), 340–44; trans. from Meyer, *Ibsen*, 109.

24. Letter to Peter Hansen, 28 Oct. 1870 (*HU* 16.317; Sprinchorn, *LS*, 101).

25. "Tak," *HU* 14.401, originally in *Digte* (1871), including following passages of this poem.

26. *HU* 14.387–400, from *Digte* (1871).

27. *HU* 4.162; *OI* 2.117.

28. *HU* 4.243; *OI* 2.196.

29. *HU* 4.249; *OI* 2.202.

30. *HU* 14.400.

31. Gustave Flaubert, letter to his mother, 15 Dec. [1850], in Gustave Flaubert, *Correspondence*, ed. R. Descharmes (Paris: Librairie de France, 1922), 1.373.

32. Shaw, *Man and Superman* (London: Constable, 1903), act I, p. 22.

33. Tennessee Williams, review of Paul Bowles, *The Delicate Prey and Other Stories, Saturday Review of Literature*, 23 Dec. 1950, 19.

34. Laurie Johnson, *New York Times*, 30 Jan. 1928.

35. John Paulsen. *Mine erindringer* (Copenhagen: Gyldendal, 1900), 15.

36. Speech in Copenhagen, 1 Apr. 1898 (*HU* 15.414–15; Sprinchorn, *LS*, 334).

37. Dietrichson, *Svundne Tider* 1.338.

38. Letter of 16 Sept. 1864 to Bjørnson (*HU* 16.102; Sprinchorn, *LS*, 37).

39. Carl Snoilsky, "Till Henrik Ibsen." In *Henrik Ibsen: Festskrift i anledning af hans 70de fødselsdag* (issue of *Samtiden*, ed. Gerhard Gran, 1898), 6.

40. Examples are Ingjald Nissen, *Sjelelige kriser i menneskets liv: Henrik Ibsen og den moderne psykologi* (Oslo: Aschehoug, 1931); Arne Duve, *Symbolikken i Henrik Ibsens skuespill* (Oslo: Gyldendal, 1945); Arne Duve, *Ibsen—bak kulissene* (Oslo: Gyldendal, 1971).

41. Meyer, *Ibsen*, 621; Charles R. Lyons, *Henrik Ibsen: The Divided Consciousness* (Carbondale, Ill.: Southern Illinois University Press, 1972).

42. Letter to Bjørnson, 16 Sept. 1864 (*HU* 16.101; Sprinchorn, *LS*, 36).

43. Bergliot Ibsen, *De tre: Erindringer om Henrik Ibsen, Suzannah Ibsen, Sigurd Ibsen* (Oslo: Gyldendal, 1948); trans. as *The Three Ibsens* by G. Schjelderup (London: Hutchinson, 1951).

44. Martin Schneekloth, *En Ungdom*, ed. Peter Schindler (Copenhagen: Nyt nordisk forlag, 1942), 120–22; trans. from Meyer, *Ibsen*, 275–76.

45. Koht, *Life*, 391; Meyer, *Ibsen*, 613–15.

46. Koht, *Life*, 432; Meyer, *Ibsen*, 731.

47. Erik Werenskiold's official painting is reproduced (in black and white) in *HU* 20.245, his drawing in *HU* 20.247 (with the quotation from Ibsen).

48. The verse is in *HU* 14.461.

2. Topics of the Times

1. Letter to F. Hegel, 10 Oct. 1868 (*HU* 16.218).

2. One example of many: George Saintsbury (1845–1933) wrote, "He is not for all time. He is parochial, and not of a very large or a very distinguished parish," in his *The Later Nineteenth Century* (New York: Scribner's, 1907), 326. William Archer, "The Mausoleum of Ibsen," *Fortnightly Review* (July 1883), reprinted in part in Michael Egan, *Ibsen: The Critical Heritage* (London: Routledge, 1972), 304–12, has more examples.

3. Henry James is extensively cited in Egan, *Ibsen*, e.g., on page 150 (see index).

4. Cit. from Einar Østvedt, *Henrik Ibsen som student og blant studenter* (Skien: Rasmussen, 1971), 37; the Garborg quotation is from *Bondestudentar* (1883), see Arne Garborg, *Skriftir i samling* (Christiania: Aschehoug, 1908), 1.56.

5. Letter to Bjørnson, 28 Jan. 1865 (*HU* 16.106; Sprinchorn, *LS*, 40).

6. "Ballonbrev til en svensk dame" (dated Dresden, December, 1870), in *HU* 14.409–23; cit. in Koht, *Life*, 266.

7. Review of P. A. Jensen, *Huldrens Hjem*, first printed in *Andhrimner* 1851, col. 182–86, dated 22 June (*HU* 15.81; cf. Meyer, *Ibsen*, 77).

8. Act III (*HU* 5.249), trans. from Henrik Ibsen, *Brand*, trans. G. M. Gathorne-Hardy (Seattle: University of Washington Press, 1966), 101; cf. *OI* 3.142.

9. *HU* 5.139; trans. from *OI* 2.331.

10. *HU* 5.89; trans. from *OI* 2.283.

11. Francis Bull, *Henrik Ibsens Peer Gynt* (Oslo: Gyldendal, 1937), 183.

12. Line from his bittersweet poem of greeting to the Norwegian millennial celebration on 18 July 1872 (*HU* 14.455).

13. *HU* 14.433.

14. *HU* 5.193; trans. from Gathorne-Hardy's *Brand*, 46–47.

15. E.g., in Finn Thorn's book on *Peer Gynt* as a drama of Christian identity: *Henrik Ibsens "Peer Gynt"* (Oslo: Aschehoug, 1971). Theodore Jorgenson in *Henrik Ibsen: A Study in Art and Personality* (Northfield, Minn.: St. Olaf College Press, 1945), 252–54, compares Peer's return to that of the Prodigal Son.

16. *HU* 17.85; trans. from Sprinchorn, *LS*, 137. On Hegel's influence see the brief discussions in *OI* 4.10–11, 4.601; McFarlane tends to think that Ibsen got his Hegelianism indirectly through J. L. Heiberg, and emphasizes the similarity of his ideas to those of Friedrich Hebbel (*Mein Wort über das Drama*, 1843). On the Neoplatonic tradition behind Ibsen's philosophy see Halvdan Koht, "Skapinga, menneska og det tredje rike," in his *På leit etter liner i historia* (Oslo: Aschehoug, 1953), 124–35 (originally printed in 1916).

17. Critics of *Emperor and Galilean* have generally been less interested in its philosophy than in its historicity; on the latter see McFarlane's admirable summary in *OI* 4.597–603.

18. Letter to J. P. Andresen, 10 Feb. 1870 (*HU* 16.274–76; Sprinchorn, *LS*, 90–92; *OI* 4.554); to F. Hegel, 22 Dec. 1868 (*HU* 16.224); to Magdalene Thoresen, 29 May 1870 (*HU* 16.297; *OI* 4.554).

19. See Francis Bull, "Indledning" in *Georg og Edv. Brandes: Brevveksling med nordiske forfattere og videnskabsmænd*, ed. Morten Borup (Copenhagen: Gyldendal, 1939), vol. 4, part 1, p. xxvi. Concerning Brandes's first review of *Brand*, he writes that "Brandes was still bound by the dogmas of his teachers in esthetics." Henning Fenger shows this in detail in "Ibsen og Georg Brandes indtil 1872," in *Edda* 64 (1964), 81–116.

20. Interview in *Verdens Gang* (Christiania), 12 Dec. 1899 (*HU* 19.226). On the term "cycle" see Brian Johnston, *The Ibsen Cycle* (Boston: Twayne, 1975), p. 2 and *passim*.

21. Koht, *Life*, 305–6.

22. Koht, *Life*, 318–19, minimizes Mrs. Kieler's role as the model for Nora, but Meyer, *Ibsen*, 457, accepts it.

23. Georg Pauli, *Mina romerska år* (Stockholm: Bonnier, 1924), 111–20.

24. *HU* 9.206; trans. from *OI* 6.28.

25. Letter to H. Brækstad, 18 Aug. 1890 (*HU* 18.251–52); Sprinchorn, *LS*, 292; trans. from Meyer, *Ibsen*, 637.

26. Act. V (*HU* 5.352; trans. from Gathorne-Hardy's *Brand*, 199).

27. *HU* 14.421.

3. The Play's the Thing

1. *HU* 15.219.

2. Speech given 10 Sept. 1874 (*HU* 15.393; trans. from Sprinchorn, *LS*, 150).

3. In a letter to Bjørnson of 28 Dec. 1867, he wrote: "For a poet, working in a theater is equivalent to repeated, daily abortions." (*HU* 16.203; trans. from Sprinchorn, *LS*, 71). For a list of his productions see *OI* 1.647–48, 669–72.

4. On Ibsen's work as stage manager see Meyer, *Ibsen*, pp. 104–8, and the sources he cites there. *OI*, vol. 2, is especially valuable in listing plays performed in Christiania 1850–51 (Appendix II) and plays produced at the Bergen Theater 1851–57 (Appendix IV).

5. Otto Lous Mohr, *Henrik Ibsen som maler* (Oslo: Gyldendal, 1953), 14.

6. Bergliot Ibsen, *De tre* (Oslo: Gyldendal, 1948), 41–42. The Koht reference is in *Life*, 219.

7. Letter to H. Schrøder, 14 Nov. 1884 (*HU* 18.48; Sprinchorn, *LS*, 242–43; *OI* 6.440).

8. John Northam, *Ibsen's Dramatic Method* (London: Faber, 1952; 2d. ed., Oslo: Universitetsforlaget, 1971), 12.

9. Einar Østvedt, *Med Henrik Ibsen i fjellheimen* (Skien: Rasmussen, 1967).

10. *HU* vol. 2; *OI* 1.263–366.

11. *HU* 2.121–336; *OI* 2.27–93.

12. *HU* 5.19–154; *OI* 2.217–341.

13. *HU* 4.143; trans. from *OI* 2.99.

14. *HU* 5.179; trans. from *OI* 3.77.

15. *HU* 6.131; *OI* 3.325.

16. Meyer, *Ibsen*, 377.

17. *HU* 7.328; *OI* 4.452.

18. *HU* 7.81; trans. from *OI* 4.245.

19. *HU* 6.357; *OI* 4.23.

20. William Archer to Charles Archer, 13 June 1889, here cited from Michael Meyer's translation of *A Doll's House* (London: Rupert Hart-Davis, 1965), 112.

21. Letter to F. Hegel, 9 Sept. 1882 (*HU* 17.480; Sprinchorn, *LS*, 210).

22. Arthur Miller, adaptation of *An Enemy of the People* (New York: Viking, 1951), 7–12.

23. For more details see Einar Haugen, "Ibsen as a Fellow Traveler" (forthcoming). For a contemporary criticism see Alan Thomas, "Professor's Debauch," *Theatre Arts* 35 (March

1951), 27. The adaptation is discussed in Dennis Welland, *Arthur Miller* (New York: Grove, 1961), 41–49; Leonard Moss, *Arthur Miller* (New York: Twayne, 1967), 11. See also note 36 to the Introduction in this book.

24. I was present at a performance of the production. I am grateful to director and adapter for kindly permitting me to have a copy of the script. See my forthcoming article "Rebecca in Repertory."

25. Richard Eder, theater page, *New York Times*, 13 Jan. 1978.

26. For a collection of his instructions see Berit Erbe, "Actors' Problems at the Ibsen Premières," in *Contemporary Approaches to Ibsen 3*, ed. Daniel Haakonsen et al. (Oslo: Universitetsforlaget, 1977), 179–88.

27. Letter of 14 Dec. 1882, in Henrik Ibsen, *Brevveksling med Christiania Theater, 1878–1899*, ed. Øyvind Anker (Oslo: Teaterhistorisk Selskap, 1965), *Skrifter* no. 6, 17.

28. Per Lindberg, *August Lindberg* (Stockholm: Natur och Kultur, 1943), 145–48.

29. Letter from Munich, 16 Jan. 1887, in Ibsen *Brevveksling*, 54.

30. Letter to Sofie Reimers, 25 Mar. 1887 (*HU* 18.130–31; Sprinchorn, 265–66).

31. Erbe, "Actor's Problems," 187.

32. Report by Bergliot Ibsen in *De tre* (Oslo: Gyldendal, 1948), 98.

33. Constantin Stanislavsky, *My Life in Art* (Boston: Little Brown, 1924), 404; see pp. 458–67 for his story of "the beginnings of my system."

34. Philip Hamburger, "Hedda Get Your Gun!" *New Yorker*, 23 Jan. 1954, 73.

35. Elizabeth Robins, *Ibsen and the Actress* (London: Woolf, 1928); see also her *Theatre and Friendship* (London: Cape, 1932).

36. Robins, *Ibsen and the Actress*, 46.

37. *About Hedda Gabler* (New York: The Opposites Co., 1970), containing Rebecca Thompson, "On Playing *Hedda Gabler*," and Alice Bernstein, "A Short History of *Hedda Gabler* Criticism, 1890–1970."

38. Koht, *Life*, 396.

39. Frederick J. and Lise-Lone Marker, *The Scandinavian Theatre: A Short History* (Totowa, N.J.: Rowman and Littlefield, 1975), 167. Bloch's direction of *The Wild Duck* two years later is studied in great detail by Carla Waal in "William Bloch's *The Wild Duck*," *Educational Theatre Journal* 30 (Dec. 1978), 495–512.

40. See references in Meyer, *Ibsen*, on these directors; on Lindberg see the biography by Per Lindberg (note 28 above); on Josephson see his memoirs: *Ett och annat om Henrik Ibsen och Kristiania Teater* (Stockholm: Bonnier, 1898).

41. For full information on all films based on Ibsen's writing see Karin S. Hansen, *Henrik Ibsen, 1828–1978: A Filmography* (Oslo: Norsk Filminstitutt, 1978).

4. Under the Surface

1. *HU* 10.87; trans. from Fjelde, *MPP*, 429.

2. *Theatre*, April 1893.

3. *Athenæum*, 25 Feb. 1892.

4. *Pall Mall Gazette*, 17 Feb. 1893; here from McFarlane, *Ibsen*, 149–50. On James see also Michael Egan, *Henry James: The Ibsen Years* (London: Vision Press, 1972).

5. Max Nordau, *Degeneration* (New York: Appleton, 1895), 392; trans. from 2d. ed. of *Entartung* (Berlin: Duncker, 1893), 2.263.

6. Act V, scene 1, lines 7–17.

7. Maurice Maeterlinck, *Le trésor des humbles* (Paris, 1896), 200; trans. as *The Treasure of the Humble* by Alfred Sutro (New York: Dodd, Mead, 1899).

8. R. Ellis Roberts, *Henrik Ibsen: A Critical Study* (London: Secker, 1912), 136.

9. Henrik Ibsen, *Brand*, trans. C. H. Herford (London, 1898), iii.

10. Jennette Lee, *The Ibsen Secret: A Key to the Prose Dramas of Henrik Ibsen* (New York: Putnam's, 1907), 13–14.

11. See p. 101 of Inga-Stina Ewbank, "Ibsen's Dramatic Language as a Link between His 'Realism' and His 'Symbolism,'" *Contemporary Approaches to Ibsen*, ed. Daniel Haakonsen (Oslo: Universitetsforlaget, 1966), 96–123.

12. Rainer Maria Rilke, *The Notebook of Malte Laurids Brigge* (London: Woolf, 1930), 78; trans. by John Linton from *Aufzeichnungen des Malte Laurids Brigge* (Leipzig: Im Insel, 1910).

13. Henry James, "On the Occasion of The Master Builder," *Pall Mall Gazette*, 17 Feb. 1893; reprinted in Michael Egan, *Ibsen: The Critical Heritage* (London: Routledge, 1972), 268, and McFarlane, *Ibsen*, 149.

14. *HU* 8.148; *OI* 5.126; trans. from Fjelde, *MPP*, 118 (by misprint Bernick's and Aune's speeches were placed at the end; they belong on the preceding page).

15. Letter to Count Prozor, 23 Jan. 1891 (*HU* 18.282; trans. from Sprinchorn, *LS*, 300).

16. Letter to Sophie Adlersparre, 24 June 1882 (*HU* 19.310; Sprinchorn, *LS*, 208; *OI* 5.477).

17. *HU* 8.334; *OI* 5.259.

18. Preface to the second edition of *Catiline* (1875); *HU* 1.123; *OI* 1.112; trans. from Sprinchorn, *LS*, 12.

19. Interview in *HU* 10.38; trans. from *OI* 6.440.

20. Bernard Shaw, "Tolstoy: Tragedian or Comedian?" in *The London Mercury* 4 (May 1921), 31–34.

21. Karl S. Guthke, *Modern Tragicomedy: An Investigation into the Nature of the Genre* (New York: Random House, 1966), esp. 144–65.

22. Letter to F. Hegel, 2 Sept. 1884 (*HU* 18.32; trans. from *OI* 6.439).

23. *HU* 10.65; *OI* 6.150; Fjelde, *MPP*, 409.

24. *HU* 9.220; trans. from *OI* 6.41.

25. *HU* 10.114; cf. *OI* 6.197; trans. from Fjelde, *MPP*, 450.

26. *HU* 10.84; trans. from *OI* 6.169.

27. *HU* 10.86; trans. from Fjelde, *MPP*, 429.

28. "Picasso Speaks," *The Arts* (New York), May 1923; here cit. from Dore Ashton, *Picasso on Art: A Selection of Views* (New York: Viking, 1972), 3.

29. Francis Fergusson, "*The Lady from the Sea*," in *Contemporary Approaches* (1966), 51.

30. *HU* 13.220; trans. from *OI* 8.243–44; Fjelde, *MPP*, 1036.

31. *Peer Gynt*, act V (*HU* 6.229; *OI* 3.411).

32. *HU* 12.117; trans. from *OI* 7.439; Fjelde, *MPP*, 854.

33. *HU* 12.267; *OI* 8.106; Fjelde, *MPP*, 936.

34. *HU* 13.126; trans. from *OI* 8.233; Fjelde, *MPP* 1024.

35. *HU* 13.261; trans. from *OI* 8.278; Fjelde, *MPP*, 1072.

36. *HU* 13.263; *OI* 8.278–79; trans. from Fjelde, *MPP*, 1073.

37. *HU* 13.263; trans. from *OI* 8.279; Fjelde, *MPP*, 1073.

38. *HU* 13.259; trans. from *OI* 8.276; Fjelde, *MPP*, 1070.

39. *HU* 13.283; *OI* 8.297; trans. from Fjelde, *MPP*, 1092.

40. Ibsen wrote to Ludvig Daae on 23 Feb. 1873 about *Emperor and Galilean*, "The play deals with the struggle between two irreconcilable forces in the history of the world, a struggle that will be repeated in all ages, and because of this universality I call the book 'a world-historic drama.'" (*HU* 17.73; Sprinchorn, *LS*, 135; *OI* 4.604).

41. *HU* 13.238; trans. from *OI* 8.259; Fjelde, *MPP*, 1052.

5. Poetry in the Round

1. *HU* 5.367; trans. based on *OI* 3.38. See discussion of the epic *Brand* by McFarlane in *OI* 3.4–12; this was the incomplete draft of a narrative poem, which Ibsen abandoned in favor of the drama.

2. Letter to Bjørnson, 9 Dec. 1867 (*HU* 16.198; Sprinchorn, *LS*, 67; *OI* 3.488).

3. Speech to Norsk Kvindesagsforening (Norwegian League for Women's Rights), 26 May 1898 (*HU* 15.417; Sprinchorn, *LS*, 337; *OI* 5.456).

4. Francis Fergusson, *The Idea of a Theater* (Garden City, N.Y.: Doubleday, 1953; orig. pub. 1949), 160.

5. William Empson, *Seven Types of Ambiguity* (New York: New Directions, n.d.; orig. pub. London: Chatto and Windus, 1930).

6. *HU* 14.243.

7. Leif Mæhle, *Ibsens rimteknikk*, *Småskrifter* no. 27, ed. F. Bull (Oslo: Malling, 1955), 42.

8. *HU* 5.277–78; *OI* 3.169.

9. Åse Hiorth Lervik, *Ibsens verskunst i Brand* (Oslo: Universitetsforlaget, 1969), 41.

10. Koht, *Life*, 132.

11. Opus 25, "Six Songs," is all by Ibsen; information from Arvid Vollsnes (personal communication).

12. Letter, 25 May 1883 (*HU* 17.511; Sprinchorn, *LS*, 218).

13. *HU* 14.425; cf. Meyer, *Ibsen*, 340.

14. Letter to Clemens Petersen, 4 Dec. 1865 (*HU* 16.122).

15. Letter to Edmund Gosse, 15 Jan. 1874 (*HU* 17.123; Sprinchorn, *LS*, 145).

16. On the Norwegian language problem see Einar Haugen, *Language Conflict and Language Planning: The Case of Modern Norwegian* (Cambridge, Mass.: Harvard University Press, 1966), esp. 54–61.

17. For details see Trygve Knudsen, "Phases of Style and Language in the Works of Henrik Ibsen," *Scandinavica* 2 (1963), 1–20.

18. *HU* 15.434 (statement made in 1899).

19. *HU* 6.370; *OI* 4.35.

20. In *Scandinavica* 2 (1963), 52–56.

21. Meyer, *Ibsen*, 433.

22. Letter to Schröder, 14 Dec. 1882 (in Ibsen, *Brevveksling med Christiania Theater, 1878-1899*, ed. Øyvind Anker (Oslo: Theaterhistorisk Selskap, 1965), *Skrifter* no. 6, 25–31.

23. E.g., Billing in *OI* 6.64, Stockmann in *OI* 6.119, 121; Fjelde, *MPP*, 325, 379,381.

24. Kristian Gløersen, "Henrik Ibsen: minder fra mit samvær med ham i utlandet." *Kringsjaa* (Christiania) 1906, 343–44.

25. Alf Sommerfelt, *Sproget som samfundsorgan* (Oslo: Stenersen, 1935), 21.

26. John Paulsen, *Samliv med Ibsen* (Copenhagen and Christiania: Gyldendal, 1906), 168.

27. Letter to Victor Barrucand, 6 Mar. 1891 (*HU* 18.288; Sprinchorn, *LS*, 301).

28. *HU* 11.62, 66; trans. from *OI* 7.38; Fjelde, *MPP*, 602, 605.

29. Edmund Gosse, *Fortnightly Review*, 1 Jan. 1891.

30. *HU* 8.34; *OI* 5.24; Fjelde, *MPP*, 16.

31. Erik Vullum, review of *Et Dukkehjem* in *Dagbladet*, 6 and 13 Dec. 1879; here from Meyer, *Ibsen*, 455.

32. Letter from William to Charles Archer, printed in "Ibseniana," *Edda* 31 (1931), 455–56; *OI* 5.457.

33. Letter, Repertory Theater Recording of Miller's adaptation of *An Enemy of the People*, 1971.

34. Max Nordau, *Degeneration* (New York: Appleton, 1895), 358.

35. *HU* 10.426; trans. from *OI* 6.369; Fjelde, *MPP*, 573.

36. *HU* 10.363; *OI* 6.310; trans. from Fjelde, *MPP*, 514.
37. *HU* 10.438; *OI* 6.380; Fjelde, *MPP*, 584.
38. *HU* 11.153; *OI* 7.120; trans. from Fjelde, *MPP*, 685.
39. *HU* 14.463; *OI* 7.521.
40. *HU* 12.51-52; *OI* 7.375; Fjelde, *MPP*, 800.
41. *Manden*, 23 Mar. 1851 (*HU* 15.45).
42. *HU* 12.203; trans. from *OI* 8.50; Fjelde, *MPP*, 879.
43. *HU* 13.86; trans. from *OI* 8.197.
44. *HU* 13.124; *OI* 8.231; trans. from Fjelde, *MPP*, 1021.
45. *HU* 13.251; *OI* 8.270; trans. from Fjelde, *MPP*, 1063.
46. *HU* 13.271; *OI* 8.285; Fjelde, *MPP*, 1080.
47. Georg Brandes, review of Ibsen's poems, *Illustreret Tidende* (Copenhagen), 22 Oct. 1871; here from Meyer, *Ibsen*, 348-49.
48. Kristian Gløersen, *Kringsjaa*, 347; cit. in Meyer, *Ibsen*, 517.
49. E. M. Forster, "Ibsen the Romantic," in *Abinger Harvest* (London: Arnold, 1936), 82; reprinted in Fjelde, *Ibsen*, 174-78, and in McFarlane, *Ibsen* 231-36.

6. Ibsenites and Ibsenism

1. *HU* 15.417; Sprinchorn, *LS*, 337.
2. Arnljot Strømme Svendsen, "Ibsen på scenen og Ibsens teaterpublikum. En sosiologisk og statistisk studie." In *Contemporary Approaches to Ibsen 3*, ed. Daniel Haakonsen et al. (Oslo: Universitetsforlaget, 1977), 189-209.
3. Various authors in *Contemporary Approaches 3* (1977), 11-47.
4. For further comment on the *Oxford Ibsen* see Readings and References to the Introduction of this book.
5. Letter to Bernhard Dunker, 4 Mar. 1866 (*HU* 16.123; *OI* 3.440).
6. Letter to Sophie Adlersparre, 24 June 1882 (*HU* 19.251; trans. from *OI* 5.477; Sprinchorn, *LS*, 207-8).
7. Speech, Rome, 27 Feb. 1879 (*HU* 15.403).
8. Cit. in Miriam A. Franc, *Ibsen in England* (Boston: Four Seas, 1919), 60-61.
9. Roxane Witke, *Comrade Chian Ch'ing* (Boston and Toronto: Little Brown, 1977), 97-99, 101-2.
10. Somerset Maugham, *Of Human Bondage* (New York: Doran, 1915), 117.
11. *HU* 15.417, Sprinchorn, *LS*, 338.
12. Speech, Christiania, 10 Sept. 1874 (*HU* 15.394-95; Sprinchorn, *LS*, 151).
13. Speech, Copenhagen, 3 Oct. 1885 (*HU* 15.408).
14. *Dagbladet* (Christiania), 11 June 1885 (*HU* 15.422); note that Bjørn was Bjørnstjerne's oldest son, later a theater director.
15. Speech, Christiania, 22 Mar. 1898 (*HU* 19.154; trans. from *OI* 8.359).
16. Paul Schlenther, *Ibsens sämtliche Werke in deutscher Sprache*, vol. 6 (Berlin: Fischer, 1900), p. XVIII.
17. Gurli Linder, *Sällskapsliv i Stockholm under 1880- och 1890-talen* (Stockholm: Norstedt, 1918), 160; cit. in Meyer, *Ibsen*, 511.
18. Meyer, *Ibsen*, 718.
19. Vivienne K. Macleod, "The Influence of Ibsen on Joyce: Addendum," *Publications of the Modern Language Association 62* (June 1947), 573-80.
20. James Joyce, "Ibsen's New Drama," *Fortnightly Review* (London), n.s. 67 (1 April 1900), 575-90; extracts in McFarlane, *Ibsen*, 172-80, and in Michael Egan, *Ibsen: The Critical Heritage* (London: Routledge, 1972), 385-91.

21. Richard Ellmann, *James Joyce* (New York: Oxford, 1959), 90–91; a Norwegian version of this, prepared by Joyce himself, was sent to Ibsen, but happily the original is preserved.

22. Ellmann, *James Joyce*, 78.

23. B. J. Tysdahl, *Joyce and Ibsen: A Study in Literary Influence* (Oslo and New York: Norwegian Universities Press, 1968), 157.

24. Sigmund Freud, "Some Character-Types Met with in Psychoanalytic Work" (1916), in his *Psychological Works*, ed. James Strachey (London: Hogarth Press, 1957), 14.324–31; reprinted in McFarlane, *Ibsen*, 392–99.

25. Koht, *Life*, 388–89.

26. Meyer, *Ibsen*, 457.

27. Wilhelm Stekel, "Analytic Notes on *Peer Gynt*," in *Compulsion and Doubt* (New York: Liveright, 1949), 2.509–600; here from Meyer, *Ibsen*, 273.

28. Smith Jelliffe and Louise Brink, "The Wild Duck," *The Psychoanalytic Review* 6 (1919), 357–78.

29. Ingjald Nissen, *Sjelelige Kriser i menneskets liv: Henrik Ibsen og den moderne psykologi* (Oslo: Aschehoug, 1931); Arne Duve, *Symbolikken i Henrik Ibsens skuespill* (Oslo: Gyldendal, 1945); Arne Duve, *Ibsen—bak kulissene* (Oslo: Gyldendal, 1971).

30. Archibald Henderson, *Bernard Shaw: Playboy and Prophet* (New York: Appleton, 1932), 312.

31. Henderson, *Shaw*, 314. For a more sober view of Shaw's role see Egan, *Ibsen*, 21–22.

32. George Bernard Shaw, *Plays Pleasant and Unpleasant* (New York: Brentano's, 1910), 1.98.

33. See Engels's letter, 5 June 1890, to Paul Ernst, in Marx-Engels, *Werke* (Berlin: Dietz, 1967), 37.411–13.

34. Plekhanov's essay, "Henrik Ibsen," appeared originally in St. Petersburg in 1906, in eight chapters, to which a ninth was added in the German version in *Die neue Zeit*, 10 July 1908; reprinted in G. W. Plechanow, *Kunst und Literatur* (Berlin: Dietz, 1955), 875–928. An English version in Angel Flores, ed., *Henrik Ibsen, a Marxist Analysis* (New York: The Critics Group, 1937), 35–92, is entitled "Ibsen, Petty Bourgeois Revolutionist."

35. *Encyclopædia Britannica: Macropædia*, 15th ed., 14.570.

36. Rainer Maria Rilke, *The Notebook of Malte Laurids Brigge* (London: Woolf, 1930), 76; trans. by John Linton from *Aufzeichnungen des Malte Laurids Brigge* (Leipzig: Im Insel, 1910).

37. Johanna Kröner, *Die Technik des realistischen Dramas bei Ibsen und Galsworthy* (Leipzig: Tauchnitz, 1935), 3.

38. For a survey of Strindberg's shifting views on Ibsen see Göran Lindström, "Strindberg contra Ibsen," in *Ibsenårbok, 1955-56* (Skien: Ibsenforbundet, 1956), 77–98. Meyer, *Ibsen*, dwells on it, e.g., 454–55, 591–92, 648–49.

39. R. A. Cordell, *Henry Arthur Jones and the Modern Drama* (New York: Long and Smith, 1932), 207–8.

40. Ibsen, *A Doll's House*, trans. H. L. Mencken (Boston and London: Luce, 1909), ii.

41. H. L. Mencken, "Journeyman Dramatist," *Dial* 63 (1917), 323–25; reprinted as introduction to *Eleven Plays of Henrik Ibsen* (New York: Modern Library, 1935); now in McFarlane, *Ibsen*, 236–42.

42. McFarlane, *Ibsen*, 238, 239.

43. Eric Bentley, *The Playwright as Thinker* (New York: Reynal and Hitchcock, 1946), 125–126.

44. *Ibid.*, 93.

45. Joseph Wood Krutch, "The Tragic Fallacy," *Atlantic* 142 (1928), 606–7.

46. Bentley, *Playwright*, 93.

47. Maurice Maeterlinck, *Treasure of the Humble*, trans. Alfred Sutro (New York: Dodd, Mead, 1899), 115–19 (in original, 196–200).

48. Frederic Fleisher, "Livsløgnen hos O'Neill—og 'Vildanden,'" *Vinduet* (Oslo) 10 (1956), 154–59; Sverre Arestad, "*The Iceman Cometh* and *The Wild Duck*," *Scandinavian Studies* 20 (1948), 1–11.

49. Rilke, *Notebook*, 75–79.

50. Cited by Otto Oberholzer, "Henrik Ibsen auf dem Theater und in der Forschung," *Contemporary Approaches to Ibsen 3* (1977), 30. Apropos of the term "Ibsenite," William Archer in his "Mausoleum of Ibsen," *Fortnightly Review* (London), July 1893, attributed its first use in print to Clement Scott and described it as an "exceedingly astute" method of slurring Ibsen's admirers as "adepts of some esoteric doctrine."

Epilogue

1. *Julius Caesar*, act I, scene 2, line 9.

2. *HU* 6.240; trans. from *OI* 3.420–21.

BIBLIOGRAPHY

Bibliography

Norwegian Collections of Ibsen's Work

Brevveksling med Christiania Theater, 1878-1899. Ed. Øyvind Anker. *Skrifter* no. 6. Oslo: Teaterhistorisk Selskap, 1965.

Samlede verker [*Hundreårsutgaven*] . Ed. Francis Bull, Halvdan Koht, Didrik Arup Seip. 21 vols. Oslo: Gyldendal, 1928-58.

Samlede verker. Ed. Didrik Arup Seip. 3 vols. Oslo: Gyldendal, 1960.

German Collection of Ibsen's Work

Sämtliche Werke in deutscher Sprache. Ed. Paul Schlenther et al. 10 vols. Berlin: Fischer, 1900-1904.

French Collection of Ibsen's Work

Œuvres complètes. Trans. P. G. la Chesnais. 16 vols. Paris: Plon, 1930-45.

Selected English Translations of Ibsen's Work

Ibsen's works are presented in chronological order. For each work, the major references (*The Oxford Ibsen* and William Archer's *The Collected Works of Henrik Ibsen*) appear first, followed by a chronological listing of other translations. Abbreviations are used for the most frequently cited collections (see Key to Abbreviations), full references for the others. Early translations (prior to Archer's *Collected Works*) are not included. Reprints are usually not listed, especially such collections as *Works* (New York: Black, 1928) and *Eleven Plays* (New York: Modern Library, 1935), in which Archer and Sharp translations have been pirated without credit.

Key to Abbreviations

Collections

Archer	*The Collected Works of Henrik Ibsen*. Ed. William Archer, 12 vols. London: Heinemann, 1906–12.
Everyman	Everyman's Library. Volumes mostly translated by R. Farquharson Sharp. New York: Dutton, 1910, 1911, 1913, 1915, 1921, 1966.
Fjelde, *FMP*	*Four Major Plays*. Trans. Rolf Fjelde. 2 vols. New York: New American Library, Signet Classics, 1965, 1970. (Each volume includes four plays.)
Fjelde, *MPP*	*Ibsen: The Complete Major Prose Plays*. Trans. Rolf Fjelde. New York: Farrar Straus and Giroux/New American Library, 1978. (Collects the plays in *FMP* and four others in one volume.)
Meyer	Volumes translated by Michael Meyer. London: Rupert Hart-Davis, 1960ff; New York: Doubleday, Anchor Books, 1960ff.
Modern Library	*Six Plays by Henrik Ibsen*. Trans. Eva Le Gallienne. New York: Modern Library, 1957.
OI	*The Oxford Ibsen*. Ed. James Walter McFarlane. 8 vols. London: Oxford University Press, 1960–77.
Orbeck	*Early Plays*. Trans. Anders Orbeck. New York: American-Scandinavian Foundation, 1921.
Penguin	Volumes translated by Una Ellis-Fermor, London: Penguin Books, 1950, 1958; and by Peter Watts, London: Penguin Books, 1964, 1965, 1966.

Translators

AGC	A. G. Chater	JA	Jens Arup
CA	Charles Archer	JF	Johan Fillinger
CF	Christopher Fry	JK	James Kirkup
CHH	C. H. Herford	JM	James McFarlane
EG	Edmund Gosse	KM	Kathleen McFarlane
ELG	Eva Le Gallienne	MM	Mary Morison
EM-A	Eleanor Marx-Aveling	PW	Peter Watts
ER	Evelyn Ramsden	RFS	R. Farquharson Sharp
FEA	Frances E. Archer	UE-F	Una Ellis-Fermor
GO	Graham Orton	WA	William Archer
GW	Glynne Wickham		

TRANSLATIONS OF PLAYS

1. *Catiline*: OI 1.35–125 (GO); Orbeck 1921.
2. *The Burial Mound*: OI 1.127–83 (JM); Orbeck 1921 (*The Warrior's Barrow*).
3. *St. John's Night*: OI 1.201–61 (JM, KM).
4. *Lady Inger*: OI 1.263–366 (GO); Archer 1 (CA); Everyman 1915 (RFS: *Lady Inger of Ostraat*).
5. *The Feast at Solhoug*: OI 1.367–426 (GO); Archer 1 (WA, MM).
6. *Olaf Liljekrans*: OI 1.459–554 (JM); Orbeck 1921.
7. *The Vikings at Helgeland*: OI 2.27–93 (JM); Archer 2 (WA); Everyman 1911 (RFS: *The Warriors at Helgeland*).
8. *Love's Comedy*: OI 2.95–202 (JA); Archer 1 (CHH); Everyman 1915 (RFS).
9. *The Pretenders*: OI 2.217–341 (ER, GW); Archer 2 (WA); Everyman 1913 (RFS).

10. *Brand*: *OI* 3.73–250 (JK, JM); Archer 3 (CHH); F. E. Garrett, London, 1894 (reprinted in his *Lyrics and Poems*, London: Dent, 1912, also in Everyman 1915); James Forsyth, A New Stage Version, with introd. by Tyrone Guthrie, New York: Theatre Arts Books, 1960 [free verse]; Meyer 1960 (with introd. by W. H. Auden); G. M. Gathorne-Hardy, Seattle, Wash.: University of Washington Press, 1966 (also London: Allen and Unwin, 1966; Oslo: Universitetsforlaget).

11. *Peer Gynt*: *OI* 3.251–421 (CF, JF); Archer 4 (WA, CA); R. Ellis Roberts, London: Secker, 1912; Everyman 1921 (RFS); Gotfried Hult, New York: Putnam's, 1933; Norman Ginsbury, London: Hammond, [1945]; Paul Green, An American version, New York: French, 1951 [adaptation] ; Meyer 1963; Rolf Fjelde, New York: New American Library, 1964; Kai Jurgensen and Robert Schenkkan, with introd. by John Simon, New York: Appleton-Century-Crofts, 1966; Penguin 1966 (PW).

12. *The League of Youth*: *OI* 4.19–146 (JM); Archer 6 (WA); Everyman 1915 (RFS); Penguin 1965 (PW).

13. *Emperor and Galilean*: *OI* 4.195–459 (GO); Archer 5 (WA).

14. *Pillars of Society*: *OI* 5.19–126 (JM); Archer 6 (WA); Everyman 1913 (RFS); Penguin 1950 (UE-F: *The Pillars of the Community*); Meyer 1961; Fjelde, *MPP*, 1978, 9–118.

15. *A Doll's House*: *OI* 5.197–286 (JM); Archer 7 (WA); H. L. Mencken, Boston: Luce, 1909; Everyman 1910 (RFS); Norman Ginsbury, London: French, 1950; Modern Library 1957 (ELG); Fjelde, *FMP*, 1965 (*MPP*, 1978, 119–96: *A Doll House*); Penguin 1965 (PW); Meyer 1965.

16. *Ghosts*: *OI* 5.345–422 (JM); Archer 7 (WA); Everyman 1911 (RFS); Norman Ginsbury, London: French, 1938; Bjørn Koefoed, New York: French, 1952; Modern Library 1957 (ELG); Penguin 1964 (PW); Kai Jurgensen and Robert Schenkkan, An Authoritative Text Edition, New York: Avon, 1965; Meyer 1966; Fjelde, *FMP*, 1970 (*MPP*, 1978, 197–276).

17. *An Enemy of the People*: *OI* 6.19–126 (JM); Archer 8 (EM-A); Everyman 1911 (RFS); Norman Ginsbury, London: French, 1938; Arthur Miller, An Adaptation, New York: Viking, 1951; Modern Library 1957 (ELG); Penguin 1964 (PW: *A Public Enemy*); Meyer 1966; Fjelde, *FMP*, 1970 (*MPP*, 1978, 277–386).

18. *The Wild Duck*: *OI* 6.127–242 (JM; also in An Authoritative Text Edition, ed. Henry Popkin, New York: Avon, 1965); Archer 8 (FEA); Everyman 1910 (RFS); Penguin 1950 (UE-F); Max Faber, Adaptation, with introd. by T. C. Worsley, London: Heinemann, 1958; Meyer 1961; Otto Reinert, in *Modern Drama*, ed. by the same, Boston: Little Brown, 1961–62, 1–86; Fjelde, *FMP*, 1965 (*MPP*, 1978, 387–490); Kai Jurgensen and Robert Schenkkan, with introd. by John Simon, New York: Appleton-Century-Crofts, 1966; Dounia B. Christiani, *A New Translation; The Writing of the Play; Criticism*, New York: Norton, 1968; R. V. Forslund, *Four Plays*, Philadelphia: Chilton, 1968.

19. *Rosmersholm*: *OI* 6.289–381 (JM); Archer 9 (CA); Everyman 1913 (RFS); Modern Library 1957 (ELG); Penguin 1958 (UE-F); Brian J. Burton, *The House of Rosmer*, Birmingham: Cambridge, 1959; Arvid Paulson, *Last Plays*, New York: Bantam, 1962; Meyer 1966; Fjelde, *MPP*, 1978, 491–586.

20. *The Lady from the Sea*: *OI* 7.25–124 (JM); Archer 9 (FEA); Everyman 1910 (RFS, EM-A); Meyer 1960; Penguin 1965 (PW); Fjelde, *FMP*, 1970 (*MPP*, 1978, 587–688).

21. *Hedda Gabler*: *OI* 7.167–268 (JA); Archer 10 (EG, WA); Eva Le Gallienne, *Preface to Ibsen's Hedda Gabler*, with a new trans., London: Faber, 1948 (also in Modern Library 1957 and Everyman 1966); Penguin 1950 (UE-F); Norman Ginsbury, London: French, n.d.; Alan S. Downer, New York: Appleton-Century-Crofts, 1961; Meyer 1961; Arvid Paulson, *Last Plays*, New York: Barton, 1962; Otto Reinert, San Franc.: Chandler, 1962;

Fjelde, *FMP*, 1965 (*MPP*, 1978, 689–778); Max Faber, London: Heinemann, 1966; John Osborne, *An Adaptation*, London: Faber, 1972; Kai Jurgensen and Robert Schenkkan, An Authoritative Text Edition, ed. Henry Popkin, New York: Avon, 1975.

22. *The Master Builder*: OI 7.353–445 (JM); Archer 10 (EG, WA); Eva Le Gallienne, New York: New York University Press, 1955 (also in Modern Library 1957 and Everyman, 1966); Penguin 1958 (UE-F); Meyer 1960; Arvid Paulson, *Last Plays*, New York: Bantam, 1962; Fjelde, *FMP*, 1965 (*MPP*, 1978, 779–860); R. V. Forslund, *Four Plays*, Phila.: Chilton, 1968.

23. *Little Eyolf*: OI 8.35–106 (JM); Archer 11 (WA); H. L. Mencken, Boston: Luce, 1909; Penguin 1958 (UE-F); Meyer 1961; R. V. Forslund, *Four Plays*, Phila.: Chilton, 1968; Fjelde, *MPP*, 1978, 861–936.

24. *John Gabriel Borkman*: OI 8.151–233 (JM); Archer 11 (WA); Penguin 1958 (UE-F); Norman Ginsbury, London: French, 1960 and Everyman 1966; Meyer 1960; Arvid Paulson, *Last Plays*, New York: Bantam, 1962; Fjelde, *FMP*, 1970 (*MPP*, 1978, 937–1024).

25. *When We Dead Awaken*: OI 8.235–297 (JM); Archer 11 (WA); Meyer 1960; Arvid Paulson, *Last Plays*, New York: Bantam, 1962; Penguin, 1964 (PW: *When We Dead Wake*); R. V. Forslund, *Four Plays*, Phila.: Chilton, 1968; Fjelde, *MPP*, 1978, 1025–92.

TRANSLATIONS OF OTHER MATERIAL

Poems: R. F. Garrett, *Lyrics and Poems*, London and New York: Dent, 1912; Theodore Jorgenson, *In the Mountain Wilderness and Other Works*, Northfield, Minn.: St. Olaf College, 1957.

Letters and Speeches: OI (includes relevant quotations under each play); J. N. Laurvik and Mary Morison, *Letters*, New York: Duffield, 1905; Arne Kildal, *Speeches and New Letters*, Boston: Badger, 1910; Evert Sprinchorn, *Letters and Speeches*, London: MacGibbon and Kee, 1965.

Drafts and Notes: In OI included with each play; Archer 12: *From Ibsen's Workshop* (AGC).

Selected Works about Ibsen

About Hedda Gabler: Rebecca Thompson, "On Playing *Hedda Gabler*"; Alice Bernstein, "A Short History of *Hedda Gabler* Criticism, 1890–1970." New York: The Opposites Co., 1970.

Andersen, Annette. "Ibsen in America." *Scandinavian Studies* 14 (1937), 65–109, 115–46.

Anderson, Andrew R. "Ibsen and the Classical World." *Classical Journal* 11 (1916), 216–25.

Archer, William. *Playmaking*. London: Chapman, 1913.

Arestad, Sverre. "*The Iceman Cometh* and *The Wild Duck*." *Scandinavian Studies* 20 (1948), 1–11.

Bang, Herman. "Lidt om Henrik Ibsen som ung." *Af Dagens Krønike* 1 (1889), 340–44.

——— . "Personlige Erindringer om Henrik Ibsen." *Det ny Aarhundrede* 3, 2 (1906), 237–42, 325–30.

Bardach, Emilie. "Meine Freundschaft mit Ibsen." *Neue Freie Presse* (Vienna), 31 Mar. 1907; also in *Verdens Gang* (Christiania), 3 Apr. 1907.

Bentley, Eric. *The Playwright as Thinker*. New York: Reynal and Hitchcock, 1946.

Bernstein, Alice. See *About Hedda Gabler*.

Bien, Horst, *Henrik Ibsens realisme: Det klassisk kritisk-realistiske dramas opprinnelse og utvikling*. Trans. from German ms. by Frode Rimstad. Oslo: Universitetsforlaget, 1973.

Bjørnson, Bjørnstjerne. *Gro-tid: Brev fra årene 1857–1870*. Ed. Halvdan Koht. 2 vols. Christiania and Copenhagen: Gyldendal, 1912.

Brustein, Robert. *The Theatre of Revolt*. Boston: Little Brown, 1964.

Buchanan, Robert. "The Modern Drama and Its Minor Critics." *Contemporary Review* 56 (1889), 908–25.

Bull, Francis. Introduction (*Indledning*) to *Georg og Edvard Brandes: Brevveksling med nordiske Forfattere og Videnskabsmænd*, ed. Morten Borup, vol. 4, part 1. Copenhagen: Gyldendal, 1939.

————. *Henrik Ibsens Peer Gynt*. Oslo: Gyldendal, 1937.

Clurman, Harold. *Ibsen*. New York: Macmillan, 1977.

Contemporary Approaches to Ibsen. Proceedings of the First International Ibsen Seminary, Oslo, August 1965. Ed. Daniel Haakonsen. Oslo: Universitetsforlaget, 1966 (also vol. 8 of *Ibsenårboken*).

Contemporary Approaches to Ibsen 2. Proceedings of the Second International Ibsen Seminary, Cambridge, August 1970. Ed. Daniel Haakonsen. Oslo: Universitetsforlaget, 1971 (also vol. 11 of *Ibsenårboken*).

Contemporary Approaches to Ibsen 3. Reports from the Third International Ibsen Seminar, Bergen, 1975. Ed. Daniel Haakonsen et al. Oslo: Universitetsforlaget, 1977 (also *Ibsenårboken* 1975/76).

Cordell, R. A. *Henry Arthur Jones and the Modern Drama*. New York: Long and Smith, 1932.

Courtney, W. L. *Studies at Leisure*. London, 1892.

Derry, T. K. *A History of Modern Norway, 1814–1972*. Oxford: Clarendon, 1973.

Dietrichson, Lorentz. *Svundne Tider*. 4 vols. Christiania: Cappelen, 1899–1917.

Downs, Brian W. *Ibsen: The Intellectual Background*. Cambridge: University Press, 1948.

Due, Christopher. *Erindringer fra Henrik Ibsens ungdomsaar*. Copenhagen: Akademisk, 1909.

Duve, Arne. *Ibsen—bak kulissene*. Oslo: Gyldendal, 1971.

————. *Symbolikken i Henrik Ibsens skuespill*. Oslo: Gyldendal, 1945.

Egan, Michael. *Henry James: The Ibsen Years*. London: Vision Press, 1972.

————. *Ibsen: The Critical Heritage*. London: Routledge, 1972.

Eller, William Henri. *Ibsen in Germany, 1870–1900*. Boston: Badger, 1918.

Ellmann, Richard. *James Joyce*. New York: Oxford, 1959.

Empson, William. *Seven Types of Ambiguity*. New York: New Directions, n.d. (orig. pub. London: Chatto and Windus, 1930).

Encyclopædia Britannica, The New: Micropædia. 15th ed. Chicago: University of Chicago, 1974.

Erbe, Berit. "Actors' Problems at the Ibsen Premières." In *Contemporary Approaches to Ibsen 3*, ed. Daniel Haakonsen et al., 179–88. Oslo: Universitetsforlaget, 1977.

Ewbank, Inga-Stina. "Ibsen and 'the far more difficult art' of prose." In *Contemporary Approaches to Ibsen 2*, ed. Daniel Haakonsen, 60–83. Oslo: Universitetsforlaget, 1971.

————. "Ibsen's Dramatic Language as a Link between His 'Realism' and His 'Symbolism.'" In *Contemporary Approaches to Ibsen*, ed. Daniel Haakonsen, 96–123. Oslo: Universitetsforlaget, 1966.

Faaland, Josef. *Henrik Ibsen og antikken*. Oslo: Tanum, 1943.

Fenger, Henning. "Ibsen og Georg Brandes indtil 1872." *Edda* 64 (1964), 169–208.

Fergusson, Francis. *The Idea of a Theater*. Garden City, N.Y.: Doubleday, 1953 (orig. pub. 1949).

————. "*The Lady from the Sea*." In *Contemporary Approaches to Ibsen*, ed. Daniel Haakonsen, 51–59. Oslo: Universitetsforlaget, 1966.

Fjelde, Rolf. *Ibsen: A Collection of Critical Essays*. Englewood Cliffs, N.J.: Prentice-Hall, 1965.

Flaubert, Gustav. *Correspondence*. Ed. R. Descharmes. Paris: Librairie de France, 1922.

Fleisher, Frederic. "Livsløgnen hos O'Neill—og 'Vildanden.'" *Vinduet* 10 (1956), 154–59.

Flores, Angel, ed. *Henrik Ibsen, a Marxist Analysis*. New York: The Critics Group, 1937. (See also Plechanow.)

Forster, E. M. "Ibsen the Romantic." In his *Abinger Harvest*, 81–86. London: Arnold, 1936. (Reprinted in Fjelde, *Ibsen*, 174–78, and in McFarlane, *Ibsen*, 231–36.)

Franc, Miriam A. *Ibsen in England*. Boston: Four Seas, 1919.

Freud, Sigmund. "Some Character-Types Met with in Psychoanalytic Work." In his *Psychological Works*, ed. J. Strachey, vol. 14, 324–31. London: Hogarth Press, 1957.

Garborg, Arne. *Skriftir i samling*. Christiania: Aschehoug, 1908.

Geijerstam, Gustaf af. "Två minnen om Ibsen." *Ord och Bild* 7 (1898), 116–17.

George, David E. R. *Henrik Ibsen in Deutschland: Rezeption und Revision. Palaestra* 251. Göttingen: Vandenhoeck and Ruprecht, 1968.

Gløersen, Kristian. "Henrik Ibsen: minder fra mit samvær med ham i utlandet." *Kringsjaa* (1906), 343–44.

Gosse, Edmund. "Ibsen the Norwegian Satirist." *Fortnightly Review* (London), vol. 73 n.s. (1 Jan. 1873), 74–88.

Gran, Gerhard, ed. *Henrik Ibsen: Festskrift i anledning af hans 70de fødselsdag*. Bergen, 1898 (also an issue of *Samtiden*).

Gray, Ronald. *Ibsen—a Dissenting View: A Study of the Last Twelve Plays*. Cambridge: University Press, 1977.

Gregersen, Halfdan. *Ibsen and Spain*. Cambridge, Mass.: Harvard University Press, 1936.

Guthke, Karl S. *Modern Tragicomedy: An Investigation into the Nature of the Genre*. New York: Random House, 1966.

Haakonsèn, Daniel. *Henrik Ibsen realisme*. Oslo: Aschehoug, 1957.

———. "'The Play-within-the-play' in Ibsen's Realistic Drama." In *Contemporary Approaches to Ibsen 3*, ed. Daniel Haakonsen, 101–17. Oslo: Universitetsforlaget, 1977.

Hamburger, Philip. "Hedda Get Your Gun!" *The New Yorker*, 23 Jan. 1954, 73.

Hansen, Karin S. *Henrik Ibsen, 1828–1978: A Filmography*. Oslo: Norsk Filminstitutt, 1978.

Hart, James D. *The Oxford Companion to American Literature*. London, New York and Toronto: Oxford University Press, 1941.

Haugan, Jørgen. *Henrik Ibsens metode: Den indre utvikling gjennom Ibsens dramatikk*. Oslo: Gyldendal, 1977.

Haugen, Einar, "Ibsen as a Fellow Traveler" (forthcoming).

———. "Ibsen in America." *Edda* 57 (1957), 26–44. (In revised form also in *Norwegian-American Studies and Records* 20 [1959], 1–23.

———. "Ibsen in America: A Forgotten Performance and an Unpublished Letter." *Journal of English and Germanic Philology* 33 (1934), 396–420.

———. *Language Conflict and Language Planning: The Case of Modern Norwegian*. Cambridge, Mass.: Harvard University Press, 1966.

———. "The Living Ibsen." *Quarterly Journal of Speech* 41 (1955), 19–26.

———. "Rebecca in Repertory" (forthcoming).

Heiberg, Hans. *Ibsen: A Portrait of the Artist*. Trans. Joan Tate. Coral Gables, Fla.: University of Miami Press, 1969.

Henderson, Archibald. *Bernard Shaw: Playboy and Prophet*. New York: Appleton, 1932.

Holtan, Orley I. *Mythic Patterns in Ibsen's Last Plays*. Minneapolis: University of Minnesota Press, 1970.

Hurt, James. *Catiline's Dream: An Essay on Ibsen's Plays*. Urbana: University of Illinois Press, 1972.

Ibsen, Bergliot. *De tre: Erindringer om Henrik Ibsen, Suzannah Ibsen, Sigurd Ibsen*. Oslo: Gyldendal, 1948. (Trans. as *The Three Ibsens* by G. Schjelderup, London: Hutchinson, 1951.)

Ibsen Yearbook (*Ibsenårbok*), Published as *Årbok* of Ibsenforbundet 1952–62, ed. Einar Østvedt, 6 vols. Skien: Rasmussen. Since 1963, ed. Daniel Haakonsen et al. 9 vols. to 1976 (three of which are identical with *Contemporary Approaches to Ibsen*). Oslo: Universitetsforlaget.

"Ibseniana." *Edda* 31 (1931), 455-56.

Jakobson, Roman. "Linguistics and Poetics." In *Style in Language*, ed. Thomas A. Sebeok, 350-77. Cambridge, Mass.: MIT Press.

James, Henry. "On the Occasion of the Master Builder." *Pall Mall Gazette*, 17 Feb. 1893.

Jelliffe, Smith and Louise Brink. "The Wild Duck." *The Psychoanalytic Review*, 6 (1919), 357-78.

Johnston, Brian. *The Ibsen Cycle: The Design of the Plays from Pillars of Society to When We Dead Awaken*. Boston: Twayne, 1975.

Jorgenson, Theodore. *Henrik Ibsen: A Study in Art and Personality*. Northfield, Minn.: St. Olaf College Press, 1945.

Josephson, Ludvig. *Ett och annat om Henrik Ibsen och Kristiania Teater*. Stockholm: Bonnier, 1898.

Joyce, James. "Ibsen's New Drama." *Fortnightly Review*, n.s. 67 (1 Apr. 1900), 575-90.

Klein, Leonard S. See Hans G. Meyer, *Henrik Ibsen*.

Kleven, Hans I. *Klassestrukturen i det norske samfunn*. Oslo: Ny Dag, 1965.

Knudsen, Trygve. "Phases of Style and Language in the Works of Henrik Ibsen." *Scandinavica* 2 (1963), 1-20.

Koht, Halvdan. *Life of Ibsen*. Trans. Einar Haugen and A. E. Santaniello. New York: Blom, 1971.

———. "Skapinga, menneska og det tredje rike." In his *På leit etter liner i historia*, 124-35. Oslo: Aschehoug, 1953.

Kröner, Johanna. *Die Technik des realistischen Dramas bei Ibsen und Galsworthy*. Leipzig: Tauchnitz, 1935.

Krutch, Joseph Wood. "The Tragic Fallacy." *Atlantic* 142 (1928), 601-11.

Lee, Jennette. *The Ibsen Secret: A Key to the Prose Dramas of Henrik Ibsen*. New York: Putnam's, 1907.

Lervik, Åse Hiorth. *Ibsens verskunst i Brand*. Oslo: Universitetsforlaget, 1969.

Lindberg, Per. *August Lindberg: Skådespelaren och människan; interiörer från 80- och 90-talens teaterliv*. Stockholm: Natur och Kultur, 1943.

Linder, Gurli. *Sällskapsliv i Stockholm under 1880- och 1890-talen*. Stockholm: Norstedt, 1918.

Lindström, Göran. "Strindberg contra Ibsen." In *Ibsenårbok, 1955-56*, ed. Einar Østvedt, 77-98. Skien: Ibsenforbundet, 1956.

Lyons, Charles R. *Henrik Ibsen: The Divided Consciousness*. With a Preface by Harry T. Moore. Carbondale, Ill.: Southern Illinois University Press, 1972.

McFarlane, James W., ed. *Henrik Ibsen: A Critical Anthology*. London: Penguin, 1970.

Macleod, Vivienne K. "The Influence of Ibsen on Joyce: Addendum." *Publications of the Modern Language Association* 62 (1947), 573-80.

Mæhle, Leif. *Ibsens rimteknikk. Småskrifter* 27, ed. F. Bull. Oslo: Malling, 1955.

Maeterlinck, Maurice. *Le trésor des humbles*. Paris, 1896. (Trans. as *The Treasure of the Humble* by Alfred Sutro. New York: Dodd, Mead, 1899.)

Marker, Frederick J. and Lise-Lone. *The Scandinavian Theatre: A Short History*. Totowa, N.J.: Rowman and Littlefield, 1975.

Maugham, Somerset. *Of Human Bondage*. New York: Doran, 1915.

Mencken, Henry Louis. "Journeyman Dramatist." *Dial* 63 (1917), 323-25.

Meyer, Hans G. *Henrik Ibsen* (with Appendix on American productions by Leonard S. Klein, pp. 185-90). New York: Ungar, 1972.

Meyer, Michael. *Ibsen: A Biography*. New York: Doubleday, 1971.

Mohr, Otto Lous. *Henrik Ibsen som maler*. Oslo: Gyldendal, 1953.

Môri, Mitsuya. "Ibsen's Dramatic Irony." In *Contemporary Approaches to Ibsen 3*, ed. Daniel Haakonsen et al., 118–39. Oslo: Universitetsforlaget, 1977.

Mosfjeld, Oskar. *Henrik Ibsen og Skien*. Oslo: Gyldendal, 1949.

Moss, Leonard. *Arthur Miller*. New York: Twayne, 1967.

Nag, Martin. *Ibsen i russisk åndsliv*. Oslo: Gyldendal, 1967.

Nilsson, Nils Åke. *Ibsen in Russland*. Stockholm: Almqvist, 1958.

Nissen, Ingjald. *Sjelelige kriser i menneskets liv: Henrik Ibsen og den moderne psykologi*. Oslo: Aschehoug, 1931.

Nordau, Max. *Entartung*. 2d ed. Berlin: Duncker, 1893. (Trans. as *Degeneration*, New York: Appleton, 1895.)

Northam, John. *Ibsen: A Critical Study*. Cambridge: University Press, 1973.

———. *Ibsen's Dramatic Method*. London: Faber, 1952.

Oberholzer, Otto. "Henrik Ibsen auf dem Theater und in der Forschung." In *Contemporary Approaches to Ibsen 3*, ed. Daniel Haakonsen et al., 27–32. Oslo: Universitetsforlaget, 1977.

Østvedt, Einar. *Henrik Ibsen: Barndom og ungdom*. Skien: Rasmussen, 1973.

———. *Henrik Ibsen som student og blant studenter*. Skien: Rasmussen, 1971.

———. *Ibsenforbundet gjennom 25 år: 1948–1973*. Skien: Rasmussen, 1973.

———. *Med Henrik Ibsen i fjellheimen*. Skien: Rasmussen, 1967.

Pauli, Georg. *Mina romerska år*. Stockholm: Bonnier, 1924.

Paulsen, John. *Mine erindringer*. Copenhagen: Gyldendal, 1900.

———. *Samliv med Ibsen*. Copenhagen and Christiania: Gyldendal, 1906.

Pearce, John C. "Hegelian Ideas in Three Tragedies by Ibsen." *Scandinavian Studies* 34 (1962), 245–57.

Pettersen, Hjalmar. *Henrik Ibsen bedømt af samtid og eftertid*. Oslo: Published by the author, 1928.

Plechanow, G. W. [Plekhanov, Georgij]. "Henrik Ibsen." In his *Kunst und Literatur*, 875–928. Berlin: Dietz, 1955 (orig. pub. in German in 1908). (Trans. as "Ibsen, Petty Bourgeois Revolutionist," in Angel Flores, ed., *Henrik Ibsen, a Marxist Analysis*, 35–92. New York: The Critics Group, 1937.)

Popperwell, Ronald G. *Norway*. London: Benn, 1972.

———. Review of *The Oxford Ibsen*. *Scandinavica* 2 (1963), 52–56.

Pound, Ezra. "Mr. James Joyce and the Modern Stage." *Drama* vol. 6, no. 2 (Feb. 1916).

Reque, Dikka A. *Trois auteurs dramatiques Scandinaves Ibsen, Bjørnson, Strindberg devant la critique Française, 1889–1901*. Paris: Champion, 1930.

Rilke, Rainer Maria. *Aufzeichnungen des Malte Laurids Brigge*. Leipzig: Im Insel, 1910. (Trans. as *The Notebook of Malte Laurids Brigge* by John Linton. London: Woolf, 1930.)

Roberts, R. Ellis. *Henrik Ibsen: A Critical Study*. London: Secker, 1912.

Robins, Elizabeth. *Ibsen and the Actress*. London: Woolf, 1928.

———. *Theatre and Friendship*. London: Cape, 1932.

Saintsbury, George. *The Later Nineteenth Century*. (Ibsen, pp. 307–26.) New York: Scribner's, 1907.

Sato, Toshihiko. "Henrik Ibsen in Japan." *Edda* (1962), 3–20.

Schneekloth, Martin. *En Ungdom: Efterladte Papirer 1844–1871*. Ed. Peter Schindler. Copenhagen: Nyt nordisk forlag, 1942.

Seip, Didrik Arup. "Henrik Ibsen og språket." In his *Studier i norsk språkhistorie*, 228–36. Oslo: Aschehoug, 1934 (orig. pub. in 1928).

————. "Ibsens retskrivning og sprogform." In Ibsen, *Samlede verker* [*Hundreårsutgaven*], ed. Francis Bull, Halvdan Koht, and Didrik Arup Seip, vol. 1, 16–24. Oslo: Gyldendal, 1928.

Sethi, S. S. *The Theatre of Ibsenites in Punjab: A Critical Study*. Patiala: Madaan, 1976.

Shaw, George Bernard. *Man and Superman*. London: Constable, 1903.

————. *Our Theatres in the Nineties*. London: Constable, 1931.

————. *Plays Pleasant and Unpleasant*. New York: Brentano's, 1910.

————. *The Quintessence of Ibsenism: Now Completed to the Death of Ibsen*. London: Constable, 1913.

————. "Tolstoy: Tragedian or Comedian?" *The London Mercury* 4 (1921), 31–34.

Sommerfelt, Alf. *Sproget som samfundsorgan*. Oslo: Stenersen, 1935.

Stanislavsky, Constantin. *My Life in Art*. Boston: Little Brown, 1924.

Stekel, Wilhelm. "Analytic Notes on *Peer Gynt*." In his *Compulsion and Doubt*, vol. 2, 509–600. New York: Liveright, 1949.

Storm, Johan. "Ibsen og det norske Sprog." In *Henrik Ibsen: Festskrift*, ed. Gerhard Gran, 147–205. Bergen, 1898.

Svendsen, Arnljot Strømme. "Ibsen på scenen og Ibsens teaterpublikum. En sosiologisk og statistisk studie." In *Contemporary Approaches to Ibsen 3*, ed. Daniel Haakonsen et al., 189–209. Oslo: Universitetsforlaget, 1977.

Tedford, Ingrid. *Ibsen Bibliography, 1928–57. Norsk bibliografisk bibliotek*, vol. 20. Oslo and Bergen: Universitetsbiblioteket, 1961.

Tennant, P. F. D. *Ibsen's Dramatic Technique*. Cambridge: University Press, 1948.

Thomas, Alan. "Professor's Debauch." *Theatre Arts* 35 (Mar. 1951), 27.

Thompson, Rebecca. See *About Hedda Gabler*.

Thorn, Finn. *Henrik Ibsens "Peer Gynt": Et drama om kristen identitet*. Oslo: Aschehoug, 1971.

Tysdahl, B. J. *Joyce and Ibsen: A Study in Literary Influence*. Oslo and New York: Norwegian Universities Press, 1968.

Waal, Carla. "William Bloch's *The Wild Duck*." *Educational Theatre Journal* 30 (Dec. 1978), 495–512.

Weigand, Hermann J. *The Modern Ibsen: A Reconsideration*. New York: Holt, 1925.

Welland, Dennis. *Arthur Miller*. New York: Grove, 1961.

Williams, Tennessee. Review of Paul Bowles, *The Delicate Prey and Other Stories*. *Saturday Review of Literature*, 23 Dec. 1950, 19.

Winter, William. *Shadows of the Stage*. 3 vols. New York: Macmillan, 1892–95.

Witke, Roxane. *Comrade Chian Ch'ing*. Boston and Toronto: Little Brown, 1977.

INDEX

Index

Stanislavsky, Konstantin, 69, 88
Stekel, Wilhelm, 116
Stensgaard, in *The League of Youth*, 64
Stockmann, Dr. Thomas, in *An Enemy of
the People*, 65: parallel to Gregers, 12,
83; anarchistic views, 50; comparison
between Ibsen and, 67, 80; played by
Stanislavsky, 69; analysis, 79; profanity
used by, 101
Stockmann house, Skien, 25
Strawman, the Reverend, in *Love's Comedy*,
44, 59
Strindberg, August, 14, 118
"Student Factory," 38. *See also* Heltberg,
Henrik
Students, 114
Suez Canal, opening, 22
Svanhild, in *Love's Comedy*, 31, 59
"Swan, A," poem, 98
Sweden, 24, 40
Switzerland, 111
Symbolism, in Ibsen's plays, 17, 58, 73-94,
108

Tempest, The, 19
"Terje Vigen," poem, 97, 98
Theater, *see* Actors and Actresses; Directors;
Staging of Ibsen's plays
Théâtre libre, Paris, 11
"Third Empire," in *Emperor and Galilean*,
46, 62-64, 65
Thompson, Rebecca, 70
Thoresen, Magdalene, 29
"Torpedo under the Ark," 21
"Tragic Muse," in Vatican, 39
Tragicomedy, 81
Translation problems: in verse dramas, 58,
97; in prose, 96, 100
Translators, 67, 165-68
Tysdahl, B.J., 116

Ullmann, Liv, 112
Ulysses, 116
Unexpected visitor, device of, 76
United States, 60, 112

Valhalla, 57
Verse, *see* Poetry; Rhyme; Verse drama
Verse drama, 58-62, 97
Victorian era, 23

Viking Age, 57
Vikings at Helgeland, The, play: first ap-
pearance, 28; characters, 42; theme, 42;
on stage, 57; prose form, 99; plot, 131
"Vine leaves in the hair," 38, 88, 104
Vinje, Aasmund, 8
Virgil, 19
Volsunga Saga, 57
Von der Lippe family, 23
Vullum, Erik, 102

Wagner, Richard, 57, 73, 102
Wangel, Ellida, in *The Lady from the Sea*,
29, 88
Wangel, Hilde, in *The Master Builder* (also in
The Lady from the Sea), 35, 50, 70,
101, 105
War with Germany (*1864*), 40
Warrior's Barrow, The, play: plot, 130
*Warriors at Helgeland, The, see Vikings at
Helgeland, The*
Watts, Peter, 112
Weigand, Hermann, 77
Welhaven, J.S., 97
Well-made play, 66, 81
Werenskiold, Erik, 35
Wergeland, Henrik, 40, 97
Werle, Gregers, in *The Wild Duck*, 12, 85,
101
Werle, Haakon, in *The Wild Duck*, 24
West, Rebecca, in *Rosmersholm*, 45, 56,
68, 69
When We Dead Awaken, play, 48: sexual
symbolism, 13; blessing in Latin from,
39; interpretation, 92-93; poetry, 107;
review by Joyce, 115; plot, 146-47
Wild Duck, The, play: first appearance, 12;
reception, 12; innovations in, 12, 82;
lighting, 56; on stage, 69, 83-84; filmed,
71; quotation from, 73; interpretation,
81-87; Ibsen comments on performance
of, 82; translation, 101; poetic style,
103; performed in England, 111; Bentley's views on, 119-20; plot, 140-41
Williams, Tennessee, 32
Wilson, Edmund, 4
Winter, William, 4
"With a Water Lily," poem, 98
Witke, Roxane, 114
Wolf, Lucie, 98

Women: problems of, 9; roles for, 69, 113;
    Ibsen's admiration for, 113. *See also*
    Feminism
Women's Rights League, 95, 114

Yiddish theater, 14
Youth, 110, 113, 114-16

Zola, Émile, 48